Dynamics of Regional Integration

Contributions to Economics

Christoph M. Schneider
Research and Development Management: From the Soviet Union to Russia
1994. ISBN 3-7908-0757-5

Bernhard Böhm/Lionello F. Punzo (Eds.)
Economic Performance
1994. ISBN 3-7908-0811-3

Lars Olof Persson/Ulf Wiberg
Microregional Fragmentation
1995. ISBN 3-7908-0855-5

Ernesto Felli/Furio C. Rosati/Giovanni Tria (Eds.)
The Service Sector: Productivity and Growth
1995. ISBN 3-7908-0875-X

Giuseppe Munda
Multicriteria Evaluation in Fuzzy Environment
1995. ISBN 3-7908-0892-X

Giovanni Galizzi/Luciano Venturini (Eds.)
Economics of Innovation: The Case of Food Industry
1996. ISBN 3-7908-0911-X

David T. Johnson
Poverty, Inequality and Social Welfare in Australia
1996. ISBN 3-7908-0942-X

Rongxing Guo
Border-Regional Economics
1996. ISBN 3-7908-0943-8

Oliver Fratzscher
The Political Economy of Trade Integration
1996. ISBN 3-7908-0945-4

Ulrich Landwehr
Industrial Mobility and Public Policy
1996. ISBN 3-7908-0949-7

Arnold Picot/Ekkehard Schlicht (Eds.)
Firms, Markets, and Contracts
1996. Corr. 2nd printing 1997.
ISBN 3-7908-0947-0

Thorsten Wichmann
Agricultural Technical Progress and the Development of a Dual Economy
1997. ISBN 3-7908-0960-8

Ulrich Woitek
Business Cycles
1997. ISBN 3-7908-0997-7

Michael Carlberg
International Economic Growth
1997. ISBN 3-7908-0995-0

Massimo Filippini
Elements of the Swiss Market for Electricity
1997. ISBN 3-7908-0996-9

Giuseppe Gaburro (Ed.)
Ethics and Economics
1997. ISBN 3-7908-0986-1

Frank Hoster/Heinz Welsch/Christoph Böhringer
CO_2 Abatement and Economic Structural Change in the European Internal Market
1997. ISBN 3-7908-1020-7

Christian M. Hafner
Nonlinear Time Series Analysis with Applications to Foreign Exchange Rate Volatility
1997. ISBN 3-7908-1041-X

Sardar M.N. Islam
Mathematical Economics of Multi-Level Optimisation
1998. ISBN 3-7908-1050-9

Sven-Morten Mentzel
Real Exchange Rate Movements
1998. ISBN 3-7908-1081-9

Lei Delsen/Eelke de Jong (Eds.)
The German and Dutch Economies
1998. ISBN 3-7908-1064-9

Mark Weder
Business Cycle Models with Indeterminacy
1998. ISBN 3-7908-1078-9

Tor Rødseth (Ed.)
Models for Multispecies Management
1998. ISBN 3-7908-1001-0

Michael Carlberg
Intertemporal Macroeconomics
1998. ISBN 3-7908-1096-7

Sabine Spangenberg
The Institutionalised Transformation of the East German Economy
1998. ISBN 3-7908-1103-3

continued on page 210

Uwe Walz

Dynamics of Regional Integration

With 7 Figures
and 11 Tables

Physica-Verlag
A Springer-Verlag Company

Series Editors
Werner A. Müller
Martina Bihn

Author
Prof. Dr. Uwe Walz
Department of Economics
University of Tübingen
Mohlstr. 36
D-72074 Tübingen
Germany

This is a revised version of my "Habilitationsschrift" which has been accepted by the Department of Economics of the University of Mannheim. This study is printed with the financial support of the Deutsche Forschungsgemeinschaft.

Cataloging-in-Publication Data applied for
Die Deutsche Bibliothek – CIP-Einheitsaufnahme
Walz, Uwe: Dynamics of regional integration; with 11 tables / Uwe Walz. – Heidelberg: Physica-Verl., 1999
(Contributions to economics)
ISBN-13: 978-3-7908-1185-8 e-ISBN-13: 978-3-642-99807-2
DOI: 10.1007/978-3-642-99807-2

Softcover Design: Erich Kirchner, Heidelberg

SPIN 10702905 88/2202-5 4 3 2 1 0 – Printed on acid-free and non-ageing paper

Preface

Deepening and enlarging regional integration blocs is high on the political agenda, as can be seen most notably in the last decade of the European integration process. The effects of this process have been studied extensively. But, until recently, these studies have been limited to the theoretical analysis of static effects of regional integration. The revival of growth theory has, however, in principle provided a set of models and tools which allow to investigate the dynamic effects of regional integration. At the same time, the "new regional economics" (or economic geography) literature allowing to focus on the special features of regional integration and integration blocs has emerged.

The aim of this study is to merge endogenous growth approaches with "new regional economics" models in order to investigate various aspects of the long-run effects of regional integration in a dynamic general equilibrium framework. It is needless to say that such an analysis can cover only selected issues and leaves others aside. It is the purpose of the present study, however, to look at both types of regional integration: the dynamic effects of a deepening of the integration process as well as of an enlargement of the integration bloc. This is done on the basis of an investigation of empirical regularities of regional developments in an integration bloc (mainly in the European Union).

We develop a coherent regional endogenous growth model which serves as the starting point of the entire analysis. This basic model enables us to contrast and complement the analysis of level effects with that of dynamic (rate) effects of regional integration. It allows us to look into cases in which the dynamic effects reinforce the static ones and to investigate situations in which these effects stand in sharp contrast to each other. With the help of our regional economics approach, the long-run impact of regional integration on the economic geography inside and outside the integration bloc can also be looked upon.

This study is a revised version of my "Habilitationsschrift" which has been accepted at the Department of Economics of the University of Mannheim. I am very grateful to Juergen von Hagen for supervising my work during this period of time. His support and constant encouragement have been crucial for my work. I also owe many thanks to Konrad Stahl with whom it was always a pleasure discussing matters, especially in the area of regional economics. I also have to thank them as well as H.-J. Hoitsch for giving their written opinion on my "Habilitationsschrift".

During the entire time of my "Habilitation" project I was supported by the German Science Foundation with a grant (grant no. Wa 825/2-1/2) which gave me the chance to pursue my project as fast as possible. Moreover, the German Science Foundation enabled the print of this book via grant no. Wa 825/4-1.

Parts of the material of this study have been presented at seminars at the University of Dresden, Dortmund, Konstanz, Mannheim, Munich, and Rostock, the ADRE conference on "Recent Developments in International Economics" in Aix-en-Provence, at CEPR workshops in Heidelberg, the London School of Economics as well as the annual conferences of the Verein fuer Socialpolitik in Linz, Kassel and Bern and at the annual conferences of the European Economic Association in Prague and Helsinki. I would like to thank seminar participants and my discussants at various occasions, especially Joshua Aizenmann, Christopher Bliss, Stefan Lutz, Wolfram Richter, and Jacques Thisse, as well as my colleagues in Mannheim who were always willing to listen to my often disordered problems, questions and ideas. I am also indebted to my friend and collegue Dietmar Wellisch with whom I could always discuss problems at any time and place.

All this would have been impossible without the understanding and patience of my wife, Elke, who overlooked many spells of absent-mindedness.

Contents

Chapter 1

Introduction

1.1 The Issues

Globalization and regionalization are the two major developments of the post-war world economy. Globalization refers to trade liberalization (e.g. through the General Agreement of Tariffs and Trade (GATT)) and increasing capital mobility on a worldwide scale. Regionalization characterizes the formation of regional groups of countries with liberalized internal trade and factor mobility, i.e., regional integration. The past three decades have seen a growing number of regional integration blocs[1] including more and more countries with an increasing degree of integration. The most prominent examples are the European Union (EU) and the North American Free Trade Association (NAFTA). There are a large number of regional integration blocs in the developing world with a wide variety of integration levels, including the Association of South-East Asian Nations (ASEAN), the Carribean Community (CARICOM) and the Economic Community of West African States (ECOWAS), to name just a few.[2]

The growing importance of regional integration has been accompanied by a substantial body of literature dealing with the various steps of the integration process. The most outstanding representative is the literature on customs unions (cf. Viner (1950), Lipsey (1960)). Only few authors focus

---

[1] With regional integration blocs, we describe in the following the whole array of regional integration formations: free trade zones, customs unions, common markets, as well as economic unions.

[2] For a more extensive list, see El-Agraa (1994).

on the transition to a common market (cf. e.g. Wooton (1988)). The common feature of this branch of the literature is the static nature of the analysis. Early writers stressed the importance of dynamic (growth) effects of regional integration (cf. Allais (1960), Bhagwati (1961), Scitovsky (1956)) but, in the absence of an appropriate theoretical framework, the dynamic analysis of regional integration in a rigorous theoretical framework was abandoned. With the development of endogenous growth models, which provide the basic tool for such an analysis, this obstacle has been overcome.

The negligence of growth effects of regional integration is one of the major reasons why traditional estimates of the impact of regional integration policies on welfare and income are rather small (cf. Baldwin (1989)). For example, given the large scale of policy changes and the degree of public as well as political attention, common estimates of income gains associated with the completion of the Common Market (Europe 1992) – between one and six per cent of GDP (cf. Ohly (1992)) – are surprisingly small. It is less astonishing when one realizes that only static level effects are taken into account. This is in stark contrast to popular expectations that regional integration contributes to stronger economic growth. Growth effects would change the picture: a change in the long-run growth rate caused by regional integration would imply much larger effects in the long-run. An analysis of the link between regional integration and growth is, therefore, essential in order to evaluate the overall impact of such policies.[3]

Observing the static nature of the existing literature represents the starting point of our analysis of the long-run effects of regional integration. We argue that regional integration affects the incentive to accumulate physical capital, human capital and especially knowledge capital, i.e. the incentive to undertake research and development to generate technological change. Trade liberalization, for example, alters the size of the market and, hence, the rate of profit of firms operating with economies of scale. This induces a higher incentive to invest in R&D in order to develop new products and improve the quality of existing goods and production processes. More generally, regional integration policy changes resource allocation, inducing resources to flow into or away from the fast-growing sectors of the economy.

Regional integration not only alters the overall performance of the integration bloc, but also affects the relative performance among the participating

[3] A similar argument in the course of global trade liberalization is put forward by Romer (1994).

countries. Liberalizing migration, for example, influences production and specialization patterns of the participating countries. This calls for an analysis of the impact of regional integration not only on the performance of the group as a whole, but also on the relative dynamic performance of its members and their production and specialization patterns. Besides emphasizing the dynamic effects of regional integration we focus on two further neglected aspects of regional integration in which the above issues will be very important: the discussion of the transition from a free trade zone or a customs union to a common market and an economic union, respectively, and the enlargement of an integration bloc. In the course of the enlargement process, new member states are integrated into an integration bloc. The degree of integration between the "old" countries of the integration bloc remains the same.

The standard paradigm of international trade theory characterizes countries by their fixed factor endowments. With regional integration beyond the level of a customs union, this paradigm is no longer suitable: "One need only mention 1992 in Europe: as Europe becomes a unified market, with free movement of capital and labor, it will make less and less sense to think of the relations between its component nations in terms of the standard paradigm of international economics." (Krugman, 1991a, p.8). With the possibility of international factor movements, it is inappropriate to determine the specialization and production patterns of countries by their given relative factor endowments. Instead, it is necessary to introduce elements of regional economics or economic geography. A suitable model must bring out the interaction between agglomeration advantages and agglomeration disadvantages. In recent years, starting with Fujita (1988, 1990), Rivera-Batiz (1988) and Krugman (1991a,c), a new branch of the literature emerged, analyzing issues of regional economics in general equilibrium models. In these models spatial aspects, e.g. in the form of transport costs or the regional distribution of land, are explicitly taken into account. Furthermore, these studies incorporate international trade into models of regional economics.

In this study we take up these basic ideas and building blocs and incorporate them in a framework of endogenous growth. This enables us to analyze regional integration policies in a dynamic general equilibrium model of economic geography. In addition, it becomes feasible to assess for the impact of integration measures on location and migration decisions of private agents.

A further important difference between global liberalization and regional integration is the discriminatory character of the regional integration against non-member countries. Regional integration limits liberalization to a subset of countries, while existing impediments to trade and factor flows with the rest of the world remain unaffected. Global integration and regional integration, therefore, are different issues. This of course, was already pointed out in the traditional literature which distinguished between trade creation and trade diversion effects of regional integration. In this study, we show that the discriminatory nature of regional integration matters for the dynamic effects, as well. Inferring long-run effects of regional integration from an analysis of global liberalization is misleading and in many instances results in wrong policy advice.

1.2 Objectives and Methods of the Study

With the present analysis, we aim to overcome the two major shortcomings of the literature outlined above. First, we want to extend the study of regional integration to include an explicit dynamic setting that enables us to look at the growth effects of regional integration measures in a rigorous manner. Second, by incorporating aspects of economic geography and regional economics into our general equilibrium framework with two or more countries, we stress the fact that, in the course of regional integration, concentration on nation states with a given factor endowment is no longer suitable. At the same time, however, we are able to investigate the role of international trade for the determination of specialization and production patterns. Furthermore, we concentrate on two important aspects of the integration process which have been largely excluded from the analysis of regional integration: the impact of the formation of common markets or economic unions and the implications of enlargement of an existing integration bloc. In doing so, we want to sharply distinguish between the two forms of regional integration: deepening of an existing integration bloc and enlarging the integration area.

Our analysis aims at improving the understanding of the adjustments associated with the integration process and providing a theoretical basis for empirical estimates of these effects. Due to the wide array of different regional integration policies we do not intend to cover the subject completely. We concentrate on the changes in the "real" sector of the economy (reduction in obstacles to trade, migration flows etc.) and largely exclude changes in the financial sector such as financial liberalization. Our framework, however, can form the basis for investigating further issues. Incorporating, for example, a financial sector in the model, would allow for the analysis of financial liberalization in a common market.

In order to develop a basic framework, we introduce concepts of regional economics into a model of endogenous growth. The growth process is driven by continuous product development initiated through investment in research and development (R&D) by profit-maximizing, forward-looking firms. We make use of the growth approach with endogenous technological change of Grossman/Helpman (1991a) and Romer (1990).

This endogenous growth approach has three basic advantages. First, it follows the notion that technological change is *the* driving force of the growth process (cf. Solow (1994)). The accumulation of other factors (physical capital, human capital) is regarded as being ultimately limited by the speed of technological change. Only the continuous accumulation of knowledge via product and process innovations is not limited by any resource constraint (cf. Romer (1994)). Thus, the adoption of a growth model with endogenous technological change is not an arbitrary choice, but rather portrays the conviction that technological change is the most important dynamic force which is influenced in the course of regional integration.

Second, this approach lends itself to the incorporation of a detailed microeconomic structure which is needed in order to build a meaningful dynamic model of economic geography. Aspects of economic geography can be introduced without making the analysis intractable. Regional specialization patterns are determined by the interaction of agglomeration advantages and disadvantages. The former (e.g. local knowledge spillovers or the combination of economies of scale and transport costs) call for a regional concentration of industrial activity. The existence of agglomeration disadvantages leads to regionally dispersed industrial production and innovative activities, given that they are not overcompensated by agglomeration advantages.

Third, our approach allows us to explain aspects of circular and cumulative causation stressed in the older regional economics literature in a rigorous model (cf. Myrdal (1957), Perroux (1955)). In contrast to traditional (neoclassical) growth theory (cf. Borts/Stein (1964), Siebert (1969), Richardson (1978)), we do not assume exogenous growth rates of countries (or regions), but rather determine their dynamic performance through their basic characteristics. Different interregional rates of growth are not exogenously imposed (via different rates of exogenous technological change), but are caused by the underlying fundamentals or by historical accidents. With increasing returns to scale and spatial externalities, multiple long-run equilibria can emerge.

1.3 Organization of the Study

This study is divided into seven chapters. In the next chapter, we discuss stylized facts of the interregional structure of an integration bloc and its evolution over time. This is mainly done against the background of the European case.

In chapter 3, we briefly summarize the relevant literature. We discuss static models analyzing the impact of regional integration on specialization and trade patterns, reviewing both traditional approaches with perfectly competitive markets as well as studies of imperfect markets. While the former can be translated into a general equilibrium framework, the latter are carried out in partial equilibrium frameworks. Furthermore, we take a look at recent studies investigating the possible link between growth and global integration. We argue that the latter approaches give a useful first insight into the dynamics of regional integration as well. But this literature does not capture the specific elements of economic geography which are gaining increasing prominence in the analysis of regional integration. Furthermore, the discriminatory element of regional integration as well as the enlargement process are missing in these studies.

The basic model serving as the basic tool for our discussion of the regional integration process is developed in chapter 4. The basic ideas can be sketched as follows. Successful research and development (R&D) efforts enable innovators to earn pure (monopolistic) profits. New blueprints constitute an entrance fee, limiting market entry and allowing for the existence of pure profits in imperfectly organized markets. Potential innovators undertake R&D efforts if they expect discounted profits to cover or exceed R&D costs. The latter are sunk costs. In this way, we get dynamic economies of scale. The notion of the local availability of inputs (differentiated producer goods and services) is depicted through transport costs in the intermediate goods sector. Economies of scale, together with transport costs, create an agglomeration advantage which is confronted with an agglomeration disadvantage (a given endowment with an immobile factor of production in each country). One factor of production is mobile between the countries. In this set-up, either a core-periphery pattern emerges with innovation and production of differentiated products being completely concentrated in only one country, or an interior solution with dispersed innovative activities results. With an interior solution, production of differentiated goods produced under dynamic economies of scale takes place in two countries. Which of the two settings occurs depends on the relative strength of the agglomerative and deglomerative forces. The other industries are footless.

The *general* mechanism of regional integration policies (e.g. trade liberalization with respect to existing or new partners in the integration bloc, migration liberalization etc) with respect to specialization and growth patterns is common to our entire analysis. By influencing either the agglomeration disadvantage or the agglomeration advantage in the participating countries, regional integration policies alter the incentive to locate production and innovative activities in the two countries. The relative specialization and production patterns change, implying either more or less industrial concentration. The relative productivity of the immobile factor of production is altered. Regional integration also influences the incentive to undertake R&D and, consequently, the rate of economic growth. Regional integration changes the profit rate of innovators and hence their willingness to invest in R&D by one of the following major channels: changes in the extent of the market, changes in resource costs and/or a higher degree of competition.

Chapters 5 and 6 contain our main analysis of the long-run implications of regional integration. Chapter 5 deals with various aspects of deeper regional integration. Chapter 6 is devoted to the study of the enlargment of an existing integration bloc. By using our basic two-country framework, the analysis of deeper regional integration starts in the first part of section 5.1 with gradual trade liberalization (tariff reductions). By strengthening the agglomerative forces, trade liberalization leads to a shift of production in the country with an already higher concentration of industrial production. The effect on the growth rate taking place via a shift of resources is non-monotone. Starting with high barriers to trade, resources are shifted away from the dynamic sector, implying a decline in the steady state growth rate. With initially low barriers to trade, however, the incentive to innovate rises and resources are shifted to the dynamic sector, i.e. the sector in which, due to permanent innovation, ongoing productivity enhancements take place. The growth rate increases.

This basic procedure is prominent in the entire analysis. That is, we look at the effects of policies associated with regional integration on agglomeration disadvantages and agglomeration advantages and on the overall rate of knowledge accumulation and hence, growth. Looking at the effects of regional integration on the interplay of agglomeration advantages and disadvantages asks requires investigating the impact of integration on interregional production and specialization patterns. The effect of regional integration on knowledge accumulation influences the growth process in the countries and the integration bloc as a whole. We concentrate on two different classes of regional integration effects. The first type of effects, i.e. the effects of regional integration on specialization and trade patterns, do not necessarily require a dynamic setting. In contrast, the second class of effects, the growth rate effects, call by definition for a dynamic framework. Our approach enables us to address both types of effects in a single framework. Furthermore, we are able to investigate the relationship between the two different types of effects. For instance, it can be shown how a policy-induced shift in interregional specialization patterns affects the country specific growth process and the integration bloc as a whole.

The second part of section 5.1 deals with the implications of migration between the countries of the integration bloc. Liberalization of barriers to migration depicts the transition from a customs union to a common market (as for example the creation of "Europe 1992"). The induced migration flows affect the regions' endowments and their specialization patterns, as well as the incentive to accumulate knowledge.

In section 5.2 we take the partial liberization character of regional integration with respect to trade liberalization and a relaxation of migration barriers into account. For this purpose, we extend our basic framework to a three-country setting.

In section 5.3 we address the consequences of regional policy conducted in the course of regional integration in order to overcome regional disparities. In the course of deeper regional integration, the objective of reducing regional disparities with respect to income and production structure comes more and more to the fore (cf. Commission (1991) and CEPR (1992)). Hence, (redistribution-oriented) regional policy is closely related to regional integration and is the most prominent policy area associated with deeper regional integration. We examine the long-run implications of different regional policy measures on regional specialization patterns and growth rates. The underlying questions to be addressed are: do regional policy instruments achieve their target of reducing regional disparities? Is there a potential trade-off between "spatial equality" (the objective of reducing regional income disparities) and dynamic efficiency?

In contrast to chapter 5 with a given number of countries in the integration bloc, in chapter 6 we allow for an increase in the number of countries participating in the integration bloc. Such enlargement has been and will most probably remain a very prominent topic.[4] Chapter 6 is divided into three parts. In the first two, we look at cases in which the enlargement process leaves the countries' general specialization and production patterns unchanged. A country which is initially specialized in traditional goods production will remain so after integration. The degree of specialization, however, might change. In section 6.1, we address the integration of a technologically backward country (e.g. the integration of the Eastern European countries in the EU or Mexico via NAFTA). In the course of the enlargement process various integration steps are considered (trade liberalization, liberalization of factor flows). Integrating a technologically advanced country (e.g. Austria in the EU) is the subject in section 6.2. In section 6.3 we allow for a change in the general specialization patterns and look for conditions, under which leapfrogging of one country by another country can occur. We investigate the possibility of the newly integrated country becoming relatively more attractive as a location of dynamic industries compared to countries which are already part of the integration bloc. We show that it might very well be the case that a "newcomer", initially completely specialized in the traditional sector, can surpass the technologically lagging country in the integration bloc. After integration, innovation takes place in the newcoming country and ceases in the "old" country. That is, we stress the possibility that after integration, innovation ceases, for example, in Portugal, whereas it is profitable to locate dynamic industries in Hungary.

In the last chapter we briefly review our most important findings.

[4]Most recent examples are the integration of Austria, Sweden and Finland in the EU and Mexico's integration in the NAFTA, consisting initially of Canada and the US. In the near future, it is most likely that some Eastern European countries will become members of the EU. Concrete plans to enlarge NAFTA by integrating Chile exist as well (see Financial Times (1994b)).

Chapter 2

Some Empirical Observations

In this chapter we discuss some stylized facts relevant to our topic. We focus on three areas central to my theoretical analysis: the growth performance of countries and regions in an integration bloc, the evolution of regional specialization patterns, as well as the dispersion of innovative activities in space in an integration bloc. We concentrate mainly on the experience of the countries and regions in the European Union (EU).[1] The EU represents the largest and most advanced regional integration bloc, including after the fourth enlargement step (integration of Austria, Sweden and Finland) about 30% of the world's GDP. In some instances, we compare European with North American data, the second main integration bloc.

We concentrate on the absolute and relative performance of countries and regions over time and the changes in their interregional specialization and trade patterns. We address the "convergence issue" by first discussing different concepts of income convergence among countries and regions. Then, we turn to the experience of the European countries and regions. We find that income development paths among European countries and regions since 1975 converged to a much lesser extent than in the decades before. In a period of increased regional integration in which the integration bloc was substantially enlarged and deepened, regional convergence did take place at a quite low rate

[1] We mainly use the term European Union, but in cases where we deal with the pre-1992 period we also use the term European Community (EC).

(about 1%), implying that it takes almost 70 years until income differences are halved. It turns out that the speed of convergence is lower between the countries in the integration bloc than between other European countries outside of the EU. Furthermore, we find increasing disparities of industrial employment among the regions, in the EU as well as in the US.

We look at technological change as a determinant of economic growth. We argue that technological change can be seen as the driving force behind economic growth processes. The empirical observations together with theoretical arguments justify concentrating on technological change as the main source of economic development in our theoretical work. Regional integration processes alter the long-run dynamics of participating countries by affecting the incentives to accumulate knowledge.

We observe that innovative activities are much more concentrated than other economic activities. This stylized fact is at the center of our theoretical approach.

2.1 The Development of European Regions

One of the prominent issues related to the long-run implications of regional integration is whether – given the degree of regional integration – convergence in the integration bloc takes place over time. An even further reaching question is the relationship between regional integration and convergence among participating regions or countries. Does increasing regional integration foster convergence?

Before we look at convergence or divergence among countries and regions, we have to be more specific about the variables we focus on. In a detailed analysis of regional disparities in the EC until 1970, Molle (1980) used a wide array of variables, including population density, unemployment, sectoral composition of production and employment, remuneration per worker in different sectors, and GDP per capita. Since we are interested in the long-run economic performance of regions with respect to growth and specialization patterns, we concentrate mainly on two measures: income per capita and the sectoral composition of regional employment. The former also has the advantage that it lends itself to direct comparison with existing studies.

Convergence with respect to per capita income and sectoral compositions of regions can, but need not be related issues. It might very well be that convergence with respect to per capita income takes place in the presence of strong disparities in the sectoral specialization patterns of regions.

Convergence or non-convergence of regions in integration blocs with respect to income is especially important with respect to regional policy. Given the political objective of reducing regional disparities (what could be called a "spatial equity" target), non-convergence and even more so divergence of regions with regard to per capita income calls for active regional policy. The Treaty of Rome explicitly considers the reduction of regional disparities as a goal of European integration. The convergence of regions is also a prominent topic with regard to the enlargement of an integration bloc. For example, if Eastern European countries are admitted into the EU and do not catch up with the older members soon, substantial income transfers via regional policy would be necessary to achieve some stability in the EU (cf. CEPR (1992)). The question of convergence and the influence of the integration process on the convergence process is, therefore, a decisive issue for incumbent as well as new member states with respect to accepting further integration steps.

The second variable, interregional disparities of specialization patterns, matters for different reasons. Suppose, for example, that the European regions display strong and growing disparities in specialization patterns. Sectoral shocks then affect regions more and more unequally. In the absence of a sufficient degree of labor mobility this would aggravate asymmetric fluctuations of regional employment. If policy makers are not willing to accept these different fluctuations of regional employment, regional stabilization measures are required. Given a single currency, this calls for a more pronounced role of fiscal policy and/or interregional transfer which aim at the stabilization of regional shocks.

It is therefore important to analyze the impact of regional integration on regional disparities with respect to per capita income (or related measures), as well as with regard to regional specialization patterns. In this section we undertake a step in investigating the issues raised above. We consider the past experience of European countries and regions in this context.

In recent years, the convergence debate (with respect to per capita income) has been fueled by the development of "new" growth theory approaches. In contrast to traditional neoclassical growth theory, endogenous growth models do not necessarily predict the convergence of geographical entities to a common steady-state level or growth rate of per capita income.

According to traditional growth theory, poor regions grow faster than rich ones and all converge to a common steady state if countries or regions are similar with respect to preferences and technology. The main reason for convergence to a common steady-state (cf. Solow (1956) and Cass (1965)) are the diminishing returns to physical capital. Countries with low capital-to-labor ratios (i.e. the low-income countries) have a higher marginal product of capital. It is more profitable to invest in these countries. International capital mobility accelerates the speed of convergence. In the presence of perfect capital mobility, investment should take place exclusively in low-income countries (cf. Lucas (1989)). In contrast, endogenous growth theory predicts convergence of each country to its own steady-state, and different countries can have different steady-states (see e.g. Romer (1986) and Grossman/Helpman (1990)). But nevertheless, these models exhibit transitional dynamics. Countries grow slower (faster) when they are above (below) their steady state. An exception is Rebelo (1990) where no transitional dynamics take place.

Starting with Baumol (1986), a number of authors have addressed the convergence of countries (cf. DeLong (1988), Romer (1990a), Barro (1991), and Mankiw et al. (1992)). Robert Barro and Xavier Sala-i-Martin (1990, 1991) have directed this debate to the analysis of regional convergence, especially with respect to the US, Japan, and the EC.[2]

2.1.1 Different Concepts of Convergence

There are two widely used interpretations of income convergence which describe, in general terms, the following economic patterns:

1. Convergence takes place if poor countries or regions grow faster than rich ones and thereby tend to catch up with the country or region having an average level of per-capita income.

2. Convergence takes place if disparities with respect to per capita GDP decline.

Barro and Sala-i-Martin (1990) refer to the first type of convergence as β-convergence. It involves a test for mean reversion. The larger the β-convergence measure, the faster a sample of regions converges to its mean. We can distinguish two forms of β-convergence: conditional and unconditional β-convergence. Unconditional β-convergence takes place if countries or regions approach a common steady-state income level or steady-state growth

[2] An extensive discussion of the issues can also be found in Sala-i-Martin (1996).

path. The observation of unconditional β-convergence indicates that the data may be better described with a traditional neoclassical growth model than with an endogenous growth model.[3] The opposite is true if the hypothesis of unconditional β-convergence is rejected by the data. This can be regarded as evidence against the traditional Solow growth approach.

The second form of β-convergence, conditional β-convergence, allows for different steady-state income levels or steady-state growth rates which the regions or countries approach. The basic idea is that countries approaching their steady-state from below (i.e. from an income level which is smaller than the long-run equilibrium level) tend to grow faster than countries approaching their long-run equilibrium path from above (having initially a higher income relative to the steady-state one). If conditional β-convergence is observed, this simply implies that the economies under consideration experience a phase of transitional dynamics towards the steady-state. Transitional dynamics towards the steady-state are predicted in extended Solow-models (e.g. human-capital augmented models, see e.g. Mankiw et al. (1992)) as well as in more elaborate endogenous growth models (cf. e.g. Lucas (1988) and Grossman/Helpman (1990)). In particular, endogenous growth models with multiple equilibria are perfectly compatible with conditional β-convergence (cf. Bernard/Durlauf (1991)). Endogenous growth theories have the advantage that they are able to come up with more explanations of the different steady-state paths of different economies than Solow-models with an exogenous rate of growth.

The second convergence concept is referred to as σ-convergence. σ-convergence is usually measured by the change of the standard deviation of the respective variable over time (e.g. the standard deviation of interregional income over time). $\sigma-$convergence requires a significant drop of the respective standard deviation over time. Other disparity measures for σ-convergence are the Gini and the Theil coefficients.

To understand why these two concepts do not necessarily describe the same dynamic pattern, let us look at the example of the ordinal ranking of a given number of universities at different points in time. By definition, σ-convergence cannot take place in this example. Disparities among the different universities as a whole is always the same. The standard deviation

[3]But even in this case, there is an important merit from applying an endogenous growth framework. Only with such a model, we can look at the growth rate effect of different policies.

remains the same when a change in the rankings takes place. However, β-convergence can take place if the initial champions tend to mediocrity and the worse universities tend to be ranked closer to the average.

Most of the convergence-literature, including the papers cited above, employ the β-convergence concept. Since β-convergence does not allow for any inferences on the reduction of income disparities, Danny Quah (1993) and Milton Friedman (1992) argued that the β-convergence test (i.e. testing the hypothesis of a negative relation between initial levels and subsequent growth rates) are afflicted with Galton's regression fallacy.[4] These authors seem to suggest that β-convergence is essentially a misleading concept.[5] Quah (1993, 1996) and Hall et al. (1992) proposed alternative measures for convergence which are directed towards σ-convergence.

In our following analysis of European regions, we will stick to an investigation of β and σ-convergence. This is done for two reasons. First, it enables us to compare our results with the ones in the existing literature. Second, these two concepts allow for an investigation of two different issues which are both important. The reduction in disparities among regions implies the need for less interregional transfers and less compensation in the case of asymmetric shocks. If unconditional β-convergence takes place, it is possible for poor regions to catch up with the initially rich ones. Income differences do not persist. Conditional β-convergence on the other hand allows for an evaluation of the relative importance and length of the transition period. Furthermore, one of the main reasons for β-convergence not leading to reduced disparities (σ-convergence) is the possibility of overshooting (i.e. a poor country becoming a rich country and vice versa). In view of most existing growth models (including our own in this study), we suspect that overshooting is the exception rather than the rule. It is, however, important to keep in mind the shortcomings of the tests of reversion to the mean as a measure for convergence in a narrower sense.

Let us now turn to an estimation procedure for β-convergence. Estimates of β-convergence are usually carried out on the basis of the following equa-

[4] Francis Galton observed that sons of tall fathers, tended to be shorter than their fathers whereas the fathers of tall sons tended to be smaller than the sons. From this observation he inferred a reduction in height disparities over time.

[5] See, however, Sala-i-Martin (1996) who is arguing against this view.

tion:[6]

$$\frac{1}{T}\ln(y_{iT}/y_{i0}) = x_i^* + \frac{1}{T}\ln(y_i^*/\hat{y}_{i0})(1 - e^{-\beta T}), \tag{2.1}$$

where T describes the total time horizon, x_i^* denotes the steady-state growth rate and $\hat{y}_{i0}$ the output per employed person, adjusted for technological progress in the initial period 0. $\hat{y}_i^*$ stands for the the steady-state level of output per person adjusted for technological progress in region i. The β-coefficient is the rate of convergence indicating the rate at which adjusted output per employed person approaches its steady-state level. With convergence, the β-coefficient has to be positive.

In a test for unconditional β-convergence, we implicitly assume the same steady-state output and growth levels for all economies under consideration. By allowing for different steady-state levels, a positive β-coefficient in (2.1) indicates conditional convergence. Even if (conditional) β-convergence can be observed this can very well imply that different regions approach different long-run levels of per capita income.

In practice it is very difficult to measure $\hat{y}_i^*$, which depends on the technology and preference parameters in the neoclassical growth model and in endogenous growth models on variables sometimes even more difficult to observe. Hence, the following estimation equation is used in practical empirical work:

$$\frac{1}{T}\ln(y_{iT}/y_{i0}) = \alpha - \frac{1}{T}\ln(y_{i0})(1 - e^{-\beta T}) + Proxies_i + u_{it}, \tag{2.2}$$

with y_{i0} being the income measure at time 0. The error term, u_{it} is a distributed lag of disturbances between 0 and T. The proxies describe structural variables such as the sectoral composition of economies, human capital endowment or country dummies. They are employed to control for the steady-state variables of the different economies. But they can also be used to allow for other influences on the speed of convergence besides the income gap to the steady-state. By leaving these proxy-variables aside, equation (2.2) becomes a test for unconditional convergence.

Rather than using the non-linear estimation, other authors employ a simple log-linear estimation equation of the form (cf. Grahl/Sims (1993)):

$$\frac{1}{T}\ln(y_{iT}/y_{i0}) = \alpha + \beta\ln(y_{i0}) + u_{it}. \tag{2.3}$$

[6]The equation can also be interpreted as the approximation of a region i as described by a generalized neoclassical growth model (see Barro/Sala-i-Martin (1990)).

In the following, we employ the non-linear form (2.2). But it turns out that the linear estimates are rather similar with respect to the β-coefficient and the fit of the regression.

2.1.2 Convergence among Countries in the European Community

We start with a first look at the growth experience of the EC 12 countries. This sample contains the member states of the EC before the fourth enlargement: Belgium (B), Denmark (D), France (F), West-Germany (G) (excluding the Eastern part of Germany), Greece (Gr), Ireland (Ir), Italy (It), Luxembourg (L), Netherlands (NL), Spain (E), Portugal (P), and the United Kingdom (UK).

To provide a first insight on the development of GDP per capita among the different parts in the EC 12, table 2.1 summarizes the result of a(n) (unconditional) convergence estimation for these 12 European countries in the period 1950-1990.

The growth rates of the countries are plotted against logarithmic income of the respective base year in Figure 2.1. Income is measured as GDP per capita in constant prices of a common currency (US-dollars).

The country data in this subsection are extracted from the Summers and Heston (1991) data set. The 1988-1990 data are extracted from the German Statistical Year Book (1993).

Table 2.1: (Uncond.) Convergence among the EC12-countries, 1950-1990

Period	β	R^2	Prob(F-statistics)
1950-1990	1.65 (3.69)	0.70	0.0004
1950-1975	2.55 (4.49)	0.78	0.00009
1960-1990	1.50 (4.47)	0.74	0.0002
1970-1990	0.77 (1.59)	0.15	0.11
1975-1990	-0.03 (-0.07)	0.001	0.95

The t-statistics are in parentheses. $\bar{R}^2$ is the adjusted coefficient of determination.

Figure 2.1:

Figure 2.1a: Period 1950-1975

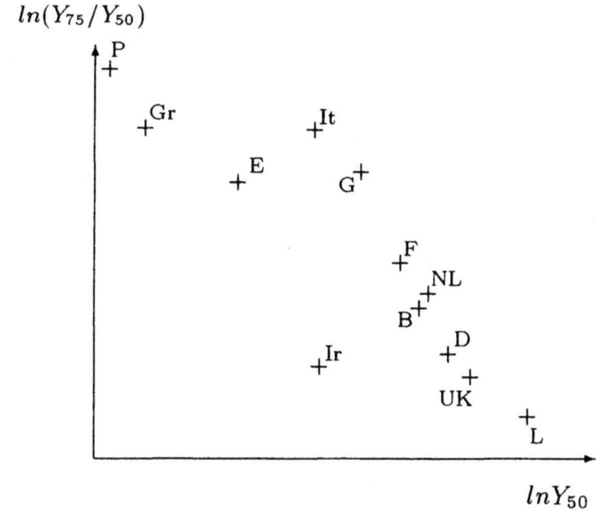

lnY_i: log of GDP per capita in year i

Figure 2.1b: Period 1975-1990

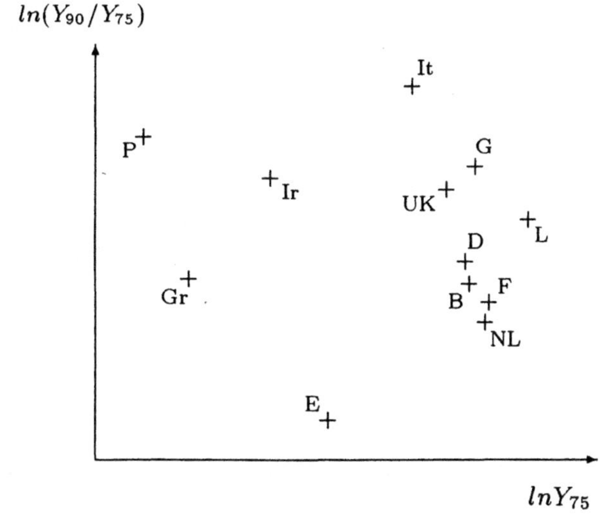

As the results in table 2.1 indicate and figure 2.1 illustrates, strong conditional convergence took place from 1950 to the mid 1970's. Starting from relatively high income levels, the Benelux countries and the UK experienced modest growth rates. In contrast, the Southern European countries, including Italy as well as Germany, starting from low levels, grew at high rates.

The regression results show that β-convergence became less and less significant over time. The absolute value of the β-coefficient as well as its significance level decreased. Constraining the β-coefficient to be the same for all four decades (from 1950-1990) indicates significant β-convergence in the post-war period with a β-coefficient of 1.65. However, using a likelihood-ratio statistic we can strongly reject the hypothesis of a stable β-coefficient across the four decades.[7] After the early 1970's, the data do not show any sign of (unconditional) convergence between the countries of the EC-12. If anything, the β-coefficient suggests divergence between EC-countries. The negative β-coefficient for the 1975-1990 period is, however, not significant. In contrast to the hypothesis that regional integration leads to faster convergence, we observe less convergence in periods of deeper and enlarged regional integration than in the earlier decades.[8]

In order to address the relation between integration and convergence more closely, I added Austria, Finland, Norway, Sweden, and Switzerland to the above sample, thereby looking at all European OECD countries. We find very much the same patterns as with our smaller sample (see table 2.2). The speed of (unconditional) convergence declines over time. Strong convergence in the initial phase (1950-1970/75) is followed by the disappearence of observed convergence in later periods (1970/75-1990). After 1970, the convergence parameter becomes insignificant. For the 1975-1990 period, the β-coefficient has a negative sign. Once again the hypothesis of the stability of the β-coefficient across the four decades can be rejected.[9]

The potential impact of integration on the speed of convergence is tested in a simple manner. We introduce a slope or interactive dummy variable in the regression equation. This interactive dummy measures the difference in

[7] The likelihood ratio statistic is 53.8, the p-value is 0.000.

[8] We will stress here and in the rest of the study the decisive difference between regional and international integration (see chapter 3 for details). For empirical evidence on the link between growth, convergence and international integration see Ben-David (1994, 1995) and Harris (1996).

[9] The resulting likelihood ratio statistic amounts to 71.5 with a corresponding p-value of 0.000.

Table 2.2: Convergence and integration, 1950-1990

Period	coefficients in %	$\bar{R}^2$
	All Countries	
1950-1990	$\beta = 1.4(7.56)$	0.63
1950-1970	$\beta = 2.06(5.42)$	0.65
1970-1990	$\beta = 0.71(1.66)$	0.10
1980-1990	$\beta = -0.38(-0.57)$	0.001
1950-1970	$\beta = 2.18(4.45)$ EC-Dummy: 0.04(1.00)	0.65
1970-1980	$\beta = 1.78(2.80)$ EC-Dummy: $-0.05(-1.15)$	0.32
1975-1990	$\beta = -0.022(-0.04)$ EC-Dummy: $-0.02(-0.55)$	0.01

The t-statistics are in parentheses. $\bar{R}^2$ is the adjusted coefficient of determination.

convergence between the EC- and the non EC-sample. We define a dummy variable D which is equal to 1 for the countries inside and 0 for the countries outside the integration bloc. The interactive dummy variable is constructed by multiplying D with the logarithmic income of the respective initial period. For example, in the initial period of the existence of the EC we attribute a 1 to all six founding members of the EC and a 0 to the remaining countries. Then, we multiply this dummy variable with the logarithmic income of the countries in 1950. The regression coefficient of this interactive dummy variable indicates the difference in convergence among the two subsamples (EC and non-EC). A negative (positive) coefficient shows a higher (lower) rate of convergence among the countries outside the integration bloc than among those in the integration bloc.

We look at three different time periods. In the first time period, from 1950-1970, the EC sample contains the six founding members of the EC. In the second period, from 1970-1980, we include the EC-10 countries in the EC sample. For the last period (1975-1990) we take the third enlargement of the

EC into account and include Spain and Portugal in the EC-sample.[10]

For the two latter periods, the coefficient of the interactive dummy is negative (see table 2.2). The rate of convergence is smaller in the EC than outside the integration bloc. In the first period the coefficient is positive but insignificant. In other words, we can reject the hypothesis that regional integration fosters convergence for all periods. For the latter periods we even find the wrong sign of the decisive coefficient. This hypothesis is in the center of static trade theory. Eliminating barriers to trade and reducing barriers to migration points in the direction of factor price equalization (cf. e.g. Razin/Sadka (1992)). Factor price differentials which can be sustained with restricted trade and barriers to migration are reduced in the course of integration. The same prediction results from neoclassical growth approaches. Increasing factor mobility leads to an increase in the rate of convergence (cf. Barro et al. (1992)).

One could argue that stochastic influences, especially the oil shocks, contributed to the non-convergence result in the EC. Countries are affected asymmetrically by these shocks. If the poor countries are affected more adversely, this could disturb the underlying convergence process and lead to the empirical observation of non-convergence. Explaining non-convergence with stochastic influences implies, however, that we should not observe any kind of convergence among any other country sample. Our analysis provides, however, a counterargument to an explanation of the non-convergence result on the ground of stochastic influences. For example, in the period between 1970 and 1980 we observe a β-coefficient of 1.37% for the countries outside the EC, which is significant at the ten per cent level.

Our observation of a non-positive relationship between integration and convergence has important policy consequences. It indicates that income disparities might even increase in the course of integration, calling for more regional assistance and transfers. One of the major objectives of policy makers, namely to reduce income disparities with the liberalization of goods and factor flow does not seem to work. This is in contrast to the existing (static) integration literature and calls for an alternative theoretical approach. Admittedly, our analysis has been only a first step to investigate the relation between regional integration and convergence and calls for more detailed re-

[10] One could argue that Spain and Portugal did not join the EC before 1986 and cannot, therefore, be attributed to the member states to the EC before that period of time. But excluding these two countries as member states strengthens our argument. In addition, these countries have been linked to the EC via association treaties well before 1986.

Table 2.3: The distribution of regions across nations

Country	NUTS-1-sample	NUTS-2-sample
Belgium	Régions (3)	Provinces (9)
Denmark	(1)	(1)
France	Zeat(8)	Régions (21)
Germany (West)	Laender (11)	Regierungsbezirke (31)
Greece	Groups of dev. reg. (4)	Development regions (13)
Ireland	(1)	(1)
Italy	Gruppi di regioni (11)	Regioni (20)
Luxembourg	(1)	(1)
Netherlands	Landsdelen (3)	Provinces (9)
Portugal	(1)	Comm. de coord. reg. (5)
Spain	Agrup. de com. aut. (7)	Com. autonomas (18)
United Kingdom	Standard Regions (11)	Standard Regions (11)

search on this important topic. We will move in this direction by looking in the following on the development paths of the European regions.

2.1.3 Regional Disparities in the EU

We explore in this subsection the income development paths for the regions in the EU for the 1980-1995 period. The analysis of regional data provides a clearer picture of regional disparities within the EU and their development over time. Here, we use data from the EU before the fourth enlargement.

The statistical office of the EU, Eurostat, distinguishes between three layers of regions. The NUTS-1 level includes 71 regions, whereas the NUTS-2 level consists of 183 regions (after German unification). For most purposes, the NUTS-3 division is, due to the lack of much of the required data, not suitable for interregional comparisons. We use two different samples of regions based on the NUTS-1 and the NUTS-2 definition. As a consequence of missing observations in the second sample and the exclusion of the Eastern German regions, we perform the estimation on the basis of 140 NUTS-2 regions. The NUTS-1 sample contains 62 regions after exclusion of the new Laender in East Germany. In both samples we exclude East Germany. Table 2.3 gives an overview of the distribution of regions across countries.

In the following, data for the European regions are, if not mentioned otherwise, taken from Eurostat's REGIO database. We use the GDP figures of this data base in purchasing power parities. These purchasing power parities adjust for the national price levels and, therefore, correct for fluctuating exchange rates deviating from relative international prices. Unfortunately, this data base deflates the income of regions in one country by the same national price level. Data with strictly regional purchasing power parities are not available.

In both samples we exclude the region of Groningen (NUTS-2) and the corresponding region of Noord-Nederland at the NUTS-1 level. A major part of GDP per capita of this region stems from gas and oil extraction in the North Sea, artificially attributed to this region. As a consequence of the drop in oil and gas prices in the early 1980's the relative income position of Groningen (Noord-Nederland) dropped drastically. From being by far the richest region in the EU in 1980, it dropped to just above the European average in 1995. Since the income level of Groningen was artificially inflated (the gas and oil production do not reflect the economic activities in the region itself), we choose to eliminate this data point from our regression analysis.

There are considerable differences in per capita income levels among European regions. For 1995 we find the following picture. The regions with the highest per capita income are concentrated in the Benelux countries, Germany, Northern Italy, and France, whereas the low-income regions are mostly in Southern European countries. With the exception of Ireland, the so-called "objective one" regions, the main recipients of regional policy funds provided by the Community are located in Southern Europe.

In 1995, at the NUTS-2 level, the ratio between per capita GDP in purchasing power parities of the richest region (Hamburg) and the poorest region (Iperios, Greece) was at 4.52. Even if one excludes the German "city-states" because of their specific situation (consisting exclusively of an urban center), we still observe a ratio of 4.04, with Darmstadt/Germany having the highest GDP per capita. Despite all the problems with such an interregional comparison of income levels (e.g. adequate local prices, especially of nontraded goods), we can state that regional disparities between the regions of the EU 12 are quite pronounced. The critical question is how these disparities evolve over time.

Barro and Sala–i-Martin (1991) were the first to address this question in an econometric study. Their results can be summarized as follows. Using data for 73 European regions in the period between 1950 to 1985 they find (conditional) β convergence of about 2% per year. Thus, the European regions converged to their respective steady-state levels. Due to data limitations, especially for earlier periods Barro and Sala-i-Martin (1991) used non-deflated GDP data and concentrated mostly on Northern European regions (from Belgium, Denmark, France, Italy, (West) Germany, Netherlands, and the UK).

Especially with respect to the latter point, Armstrong (1995) challenged and modified their analysis by including data for Southern European regions as well and extending the data set to the 1985-1990 period. He shows that the inclusion of Southern European regions significantly alters the convergence rates. Roughly speaking, the values of β are still significant but halved in value. Furthermore, he finds that the regional convergence rates have fallen in the 1970s and 1980s, when compared to the 1960s. Grahl/Sims (1993) who use Northern European regional data for the 1960-1990 period reach a similar conclusion. They split their sample into two subperiods (1960-1975 and 1976-1990). Whereas they find convergence in the first subperiod, they detect very small and insignificant β-coefficients for the second period.

Furthermore, Armstrong (1995) argues on the basis of his empirical findings that the analysis of the convergence process depends in an important manner on the selected sample of regions. Similarly, Neven and Gouyette (1994) find convergence rates differing sharply when splitting the European regional sample in different subsamples.

We will extend in the following these studies by looking at a more recent data set and by using a potentially deeper level of regional disaggregation. The period of investigation is 1980-1995 in order to focus on more recent developments. We restrict our analysis to this period for two reasons. First, and most importantly, in contrast to the above studies, we use GDP data on the basis of purchasing power parity estimates issued by Eurostat. These data are unavailable for a sufficiently broad regional basis for earlier periods. Using purchasing power parities enables us to exclude the effects of different regional inflation paths as well as to exclude the impact of exchange rate movements which are not in line with purchasing power parity. The second reason for the choice of the time period under investigation is, that earlier periods seem to produce rather clear-cut results whereas the more recent period in which the integration process was pushed forward significantly seems to be still open to discussion. By using different regional aggregation levels we can analyze the effects of different regional definition and ask whether they matter for the convergence results.

Figure 2.2: Relative Growth Performance of European Regions

Figure 2.2.a: NUTS-1 regions

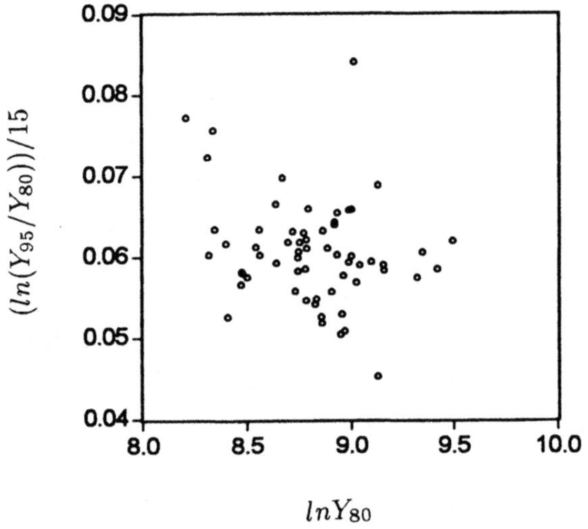

Figure 2.2.b: The NUTS-2 regions

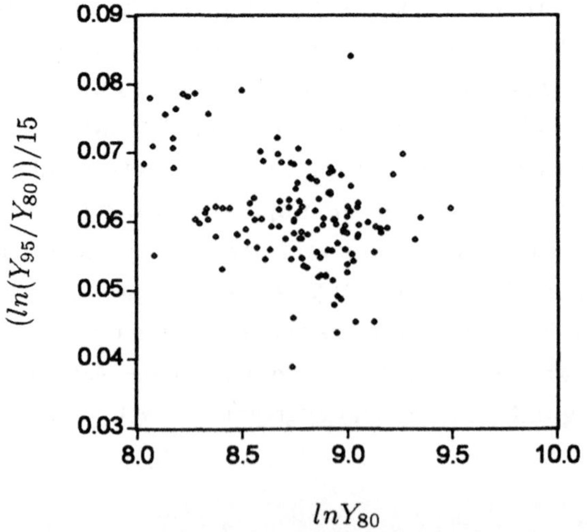

We proceed in three steps. First, we estimate equation (2.2) for our two samples (NUTS-1 and NUTS-2 sample). In a second step we introduce country dummies and other structural variables. In the third step, we split the respective sample into a Southern and a Northern European sub-sample and repeat the estimation procedure for each subset of regions. We use heteroskedasticity-corrected t-statistics (see White (1980)) in order to allow for different error variances for observations from different countries.

In figure 2.2 the average growth rates of the regions of our NUTS-1- and NUTS-2-samples over the period 1980-1991 are plotted against GDP per capita in 1980. Our unconditional estimate for the 1980-1995 period reveals a quite different picture for our two regional samples. Whereas the β-convergence estimate is positive and significant at the 5% level for the broader NUTS2-sample, the β-coefficient is smaller and only significant at the 10% level for the NUTS1-sample (see table 2.4). For the NUTS2-sample we find a β of about one per cent, implying that almost 70 years ($=ln2/\beta$) are required to reduce an existing income gap by one half.

Adding country dummies to the basic equation leaves the overall picture almost unchanged. With country dummies the β-coefficient is still not significant for the NUTS1-sample and remains so for the NUTS2-sample. The β-coefficients are slightly lower with added country dummies compared to the unconditional estimate. The country dummies are used as proxies which aim to capture differences in steady-state income levels and growth of GDP per capita levels among countries as well as grasping fixed regional effects in the disturbance term. With country dummies, the β coefficient measures the degree of convergence within countries whereas in the first row of table 2.4 β represents a mixture of within-country convergence and between-country convergence. A comparision of rows 1 and 2 in table 2.4 shows that at least for the NUTS2-sample the convergence process is more due to between-country convergence.

Undertaking now our third step, we add more sectoral share variables which are used to capture industry structure differences between the regions. For the NUTS1-sample we used the sectoral composition of employment (i.e. the share of employment in agriculture and manufacturing in total employment) in 1980. Due to non-availability of corresponding date for the NUTS2-sample we had to refer to the sectoral employment composition in 1988 for the NUTS2-sample. Against the background, however, that these employment share variables do change rather slowly in such a relatively short period of

Table 2.4: A test of β-convergence for EU12-regions

	NUTS 1 sample	NUTS 2 sample
unconditional estimate	$\beta = 0.0059$ (1.84) $\bar{R}^2 = 0.04$	$\beta = 0.0105$ (4.46) $\bar{R}^2 = 0.14$
including country dummies	$\beta = 0.0022$ (0.55) $\bar{R}^2 = 0.19$	$\beta = 0.0086$ (2.75) $\bar{R}^2 = 0.36$
including country dummies and sectoral share variables	$\beta = 0.003$ (0.59) $\bar{R}^2 = 0.18$	$\beta = 0.009$ (2.72) $\bar{R}^2 = 0.40$

The heteroskedasticity-corrected t-statistics are in parentheses. We estimated eq. (2.2).

time, this should not make much of a difference. Adding structural variables does not change, however, our results much (see table (2.4)).

Up to now our analysis of the regional convergence process in the EU has shown that in the 1980-1995 period, the convergence process was at best slow and substantially slower than the one in earlier periods. The slow convergence process also leaves doubts with respect to the hypothesis that regional integration leads to regional convergence. In the period associated with deeper regional integration and the integration of further countries into the EU, [11] the convergence process became less and less important. Our analysis based on regional data supports the doubts which arose already in the previous subsection.

Our results are also somewhat in contrast to the ones of Barro and Sala-i-Martin (1991) for earlier periods and the early 1980's. Besides our more

[11] Enlargement took place in four steps. In 1973, the UK, Ireland and Denmark joined the six founding states. In 1981, Greece entered the EC. In 1986, the EC was enlarged by integrating Spain and Portugal. With the fourth enlargement step, the former EFTA countries, Austria, Sweden and Finland, joined the EU.

recent data set and time period, there are two potential explanations for these differences. First and most important, we used GDP data based on purchasing power parities which exclude the effects of different regional or national inflation rates. In order to investigate this issue, we reestimated our model by using the GDP data of the REGIO database expressed in current prices. In this exercise, we find much larger and more significant β coefficients for the NUTS1-sample as well as the NUTS2-sample. A second potential source of our slow or even non-existing convergence process is that we use a broader regional sample rather than relying mainly on Northern European regions as Barro and Sala-i-Martin (1991) did.

In order to follow this latter route of argument we split our samples in two respective subsamples: a Northern European and a Southern European subsample. Thereby, we also follow the line of argument of convergence tests in an international setting in which the division of the entire data sample into more homogenous subsamples is proposed (cf. Durlauf/Johnson (1992)). According to this argument, the assumption of identical preferences and technology are more likely met in these subsamples. We divide our two samples into two subsamples consisting of Northern and Southern European regions, respectively. The latter subsample includes all Greek, Portuguese and Spanish regions as well as the Southern Italian regions (South of Rome). For the NUTS-2 (NUTS-1) sample we get 96 (44) Northern European and 44 (18) Southern European regions.

We then carry out the same analysis as before. The results of this procedure is given in tables 2.5 and 2.6. As in the preceding analysis with the entire samples an important pattern emerges: the results with respect to the β-coefficients and their statistical significance depend very much on the level of regional disaggregation. In both subsamples, the Northern as well as the Southern European sample, the rate of convergence is very small and insignificant for the NUTS1-sample whereas it is in most cases significant and substantially larger for the NUTS2-sample compared to the NUTS1-sample. A second finding is that the convergence process is more pronounced in the Southern European regions compared to the Northern European regions. This difference is most obvious for the NUTS2 data set. That is, there is more of a catch-up process going on between the Southern European regions and between Southern and Northern European regions than between the Northern European regions themselves.

In a nutshell, our analysis on the recent convergence process in Europe

Table 2.5: Northern European regions and β-convergence

	NUTS 1 sample	NUTS 2 sample
unconditional estimate	$\beta = 0.0015$ (0.31) $\bar{R}^2 = 0.001$	$\beta = 0.0083$ (1.97) $\bar{R}^2 = 0.04$
including country dummies	$\beta = 0.0040$ (0.76) $\bar{R}^2 = 0.17$	$\beta = 0.0082$ (1.96) $\bar{R}^2 = 0.35$
including country dummies and sectoral share variables	$\beta = -0.0016$ (0.24) $\bar{R}^2 = 0.16$	$\beta = 0.0065$ (1.52) $\bar{R}^2 = 0.37$

The heteroskedasticity-corrected t-statistics are in parentheses. We estimated eq. (2.2).

leads us to three conclusions. First, the estimates of the convergence process depend very much on the level of regional disaggregation. If, for example, a catching-up area is split into more parts, the overall convergence rate emerging from our regression analysis increases. Second, using GDP per capita data based on purchasing power parities lead to substantially different results compared to GDP data in current prices. Eliminating the (misleading) effects of interregional inflation and exchange rate differences substantially lowers the β-coefficient in the period under investigation. For our purposes, the third results proves to be the most crucial one. Our analysis based on purchasing power parities, reveals that the regional convergence process in the European Community has – at a statistically significant level – vanished altogether or took place at less than one per cent being less than half of the often proposed two per cent per years. This low convergence coefficient implies quite long time periods which are required in order to reduce existing income disparities. Together with our previous analysis based on national data, we can conclude that our analysis is in contrast to the hypothesis that

Table 2.6: Southern European regions and β-convergence

	NUTS 1 sample	NUTS 2 sample
unconditional estimate	$\beta = 0.008$ (0.80) $\bar{R}^2 = 0.01$	$\beta = 0.018$ (2.87) $\bar{R}^2 = 0.185$
including country dummies	$\beta = 0.001$ (0.09) $\bar{R}^2 = 0.01$	$\beta = 0.0168$ (2.34) $\bar{R}^2 = 0.28$
including country dummies and sectoral share variables	$\beta = 0.003$ (0.23) $\bar{R}^2 = 0.08$	$\beta = 0.022$ (2.46) $\bar{R}^2 = 0.44$

The heteroskedasticity-corrected t-statistics are in parentheses. We estimated eq. (2.2).

regional integration leads to faster regional convergence.

These results should, however, be interpreted cautiously due to data limitations and the rather short period. One major shortcoming of the data is that regions are defined according to institutional and political criteria. In many cases, this definition is not a good matching with a suitable economic definition. One obvious example is the artificial division of an economic area like the Rhein-Main area into two German states. Nevertheless, it seems fair to state that our analysis sheds severe doubts on the hypothesis that integration spurs regional convergence among participating countries. Our theoretical analysis will provide explanations of why this might not have occured.

Let us now take a closer look on σ-convergence for the NUTS-2 regions of the EC 10 (excluding Spain and Portugal) and of the EC 12 in figure 2.2. σ-convergence is measured by the population-weighted standard deviation of GDP per capita (in purchasing power parities) among the respective regions. Since data for Spain and Portugal are available only since 1977, the series for

Figure 2.3: σ-convergence of European regions

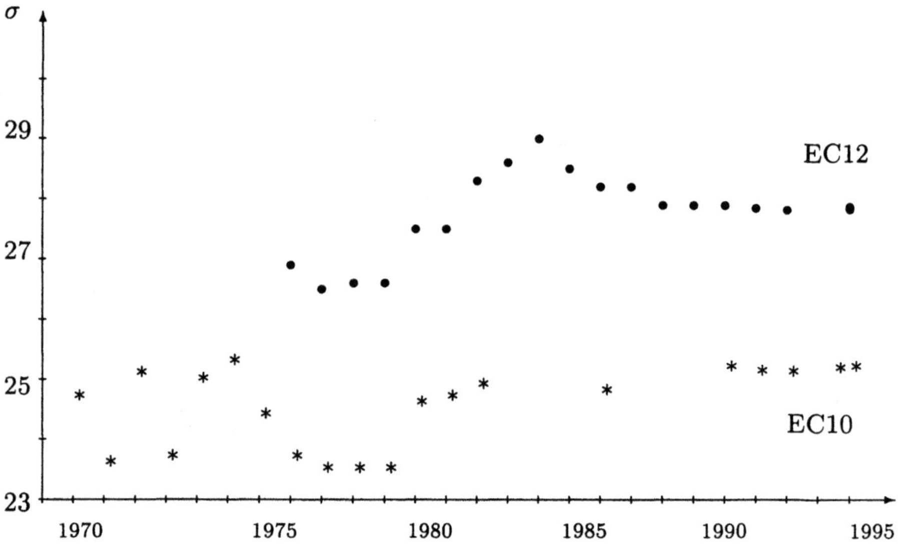

$\sigma \equiv$ population-weigthed standard deviation of per capita GDP in purchasing power parity units. *Source:* Commission (1987, 1991, 1994) and own calculations on the basis of the REGIO-database.

EC 12 countries does not start before that year.

The dispersion in GDP per capita between the regions of the EC 10 countries remained virtually unchanged in the 1970's. In the first half of the 1980's this measure indicates divergence among European regions. There are no profound differences between the EC 10 and the EC 12 regions. Figure 2.3 reveals increasing disparities among the regions of the European Community with respect to per capita income in the first half of the 1980's. In the second part of this decade, the disparities decreased slightly. In 1995, however, the weighted standard deviation of per capita income in the EC10 was slightly higher than in 1970. If anything, the σ-convergence measure suggests for the entire period under investigation an increase in income disparities among the regions of EC 12 countries.

2.1.4 The Evolution of Interregional Specialization Patterns

In this subsection we briefly look at the interregional sectoral disparities in the EU and their evolution over time. Furthermore, we contrast the European experience with data on the US system of states. The common characteristic of the development of sectoral employment patterns in the post world war II period is the increasing dominance of the service sector and the diminishing share of agricultural employment in total employment. The manufacturing sector's share, at least in Europe, grew more important until 1970 and declined thereafter. In the US, the manufacturing share fell continuously from 46% in 1950 to 24.8% in 1970 and 18.1% in 1990.[12] The importance of the service sector is much greater in the US compared to Europe.

Interregional disparities are roughly of equal size among the European regions and among the US states (see the details of measurement below). The evolution of dispersion of industrial employment in European regions is similar to the patterns among the US states. The level of dispersion is, however, more pronounced in the latter. In 1991, the most highly industrialized European region at the NUTS-1 level, Baden-Wuerttemberg, had an employment share of 47% in the manufacturing sector (as a percentage of total employment), the least industrialized, Calabria, a share of 14.3%. The corresponding numbers are 31% for North Carolina and 3.8% for Washington DC.

Using industry data at the SITC-2 level, Krugman (1991a) argues that the spatial distribution of industries is considerably more dispersed in the US than in the EU. That is, particular industries are more heavily concentrated in space in the US compared to Europe. Accepting the notion that the US is a more integrated area than the EU and hence a model for the EU, this suggests that deeper integration in Europe could lead to more dispersed locations of industries.

We will corrobate this hypothesis by looking at the development of interregional, sectoral disparities over time rather than across integration blocs. Unfortunately, there are no industry specific regional data available for the European regions. Hence, we limit ourselves to the analysis of the evolution of sectoral disparities across regions. We analyze sectoral disparities in the EU and the US. For this purpose we constructed a Gini coefficient for man-

[12] The data for the US states are collected from various editions of the Annual Survey of Manufactures published by the Bureau of Census, Washington.

Table 2.7: The evolution of disparities of industrial employment

	Gini coefficient			
	1950	1960	1970	1990
US states	0.11	-	0.113	0.130
European regions	0.167	0.123	0.098	0.132

Source: Molle (1980, p.406), various issues of the Annual Survey of Manufactures, and own calculation using REGIO.

ufacturing employment share in the EU and the US at different moments in time. The Gini coefficient for the EU measures the degree of dispersion of industrial employment between the European regions. The Gini coefficient for the US measures sectoral dispersion among the fifty US states. The larger the coefficient, the more unequal the industrial employment pattern in the respective sample. In order to get a longer time series for Europe, we look at a sample of the 73 regions forming the founding states of the EU. For the US we calculated the Gini coefficient with the help of the Annual Survey of the Manufactures. With respect to the Gini coefficient of industrial location in Europe in 1990, we applied the sectoral employment shares published in the REGIO data base. The Gini coefficients for 1950, 1960, and 1970 for Europe are taken from Molle (1980).

Our results in table 2.7 indicate an increased variance of industrial employment among the EU regions after 1970. The Gini coefficient for the US indicates a slow increase in sectoral disparities among the US states for the entire period. This suggests divergence rather than convergence of specialization patterns among the European regions and the US states for the last two decades.

2.2 Technology, Geography, and Growth

Technological change is often regarded as the main driving force of economic growth of nations and regions (cf. e.g. Malecki/Varaiya (1986)). In this section we will provide some recent evidence for this view. In addition, we address the geographical concentration of technological activities in the EU.

2.2.1 Technology and Growth

The growth-accounting literature investigates the contribution of different factors of production to macroeconomic growth by starting from the following macroeconomic production function:

$$Y_t = f(A_t, K_t, L_t), \tag{2.4}$$

where A_t, K_t, and L_t are the stocks of knowledge, capital, and the amount of employed labor at time t, respectively. Since the measurement of the stock of knowledge is problematic (see Griliches (1973)), its contribution is calculated as the residual of the growth rate, remaining after the impact of capital and labor accumulation has been taken into account. Based on assumptions about the form of the macroeconomic production function, one can estimate the contribution of capital and labor to aggregate growth. The remaining fraction of growth is then attributed to technological change (Solow-residual). Almost all studies use the following underlying assumption with respect to the macroeconomic production function: constant returns-to-scale, neutrality of technological change, and profit-maximization in perfectly competitive markets. The measured impact of technological change varies considerably between these studies.[13]

In a more recent study Boskin/Lau (1990, 1993) question and reject these underlying assumptions with data for France, Germany, Japan, UK and the US. Using an alternative approach allowing for increasing returns-to-scale and non-neutral technical progress, they conducted an alternative growth accounting exercise. Their results are displayed in table 2.8.

With the exception of the US, more than half of the contribution to growth seems to stem from technological change. The stocks of capital and knowledge together account almost entirely for the observed growth in the post-war period. Boskin and Lau's estimates of the contribution of technological change are higher than traditional ones. This is because the contribution of the stock of knowledge is underestimated in traditional studies assuming constant returns-to-scale when the factors are in fact not paid their marginal product and the macroeconomic production function exhibits increasing returns-to-scale.

Results of growth accounting exercises give a first impression, but do not allow for any direct inferences on the sources of growth. For example, we can-

[13] See for an overview, Boskin/Lau (1993).

Table 2.8: Percentage contribution of factors to growth in GDP

	contribution of (in%)		
Country	K	L	A
France (1957-1985)	28	-4	76
West Germany (1960-1985)	32	-10	78
Japan (1957-1985)	40	5	55
UK (1957-1985)	32	-5	73
US (1948-1985)	24	27	49

Source: Boskin/Lau (1993, p.47)

not conclude that capital accumulation explains 28% of the French growth rate between 1957 and 1985. Capital accumulation and R&D efforts are not unrelated. By exploring the dynamic interaction among R&D and capital investment in science-based industries, Lach and Schankerman (1989) found an asymmetric relationship between the two variables: the interaction between R&D and capital accumulation is unidirectional. R&D Granger-causes capital investment but investment in capital does not Granger-cause R&D. This strengthens the role of R&D and productive knowledge in the growth process. Technological change contributes directly to the growth process, but also does so indirectly by inducing investment in capital. Firms would be much less inclined to invest in additional machinery if their new machinery would have the same productive impact as already existing ones. Given diminishing returns of capital at the firm level, the marginal product of new machinery would even decline.

Recent empirical studies support the hypothesis of the central role of technological progress in the growth process. Lichtenberg (1992), for example, detects that the number of scientists and engineers enters significantly into the determination of per capita income levels. Coe and Helpman (1995) show that a country's accumulated spending in R&D has significant exploratory power for total factor productivity in the OECD countries.

Another important issue in the empirical investigation of R&D is that the social returns to investment in R&D often exceed the corresponding private returns. Knowledge spills over to other potential users of knowledge and enhances the productivity of future researchers. The study of Coe and Helpman (1995) suggests rather large estimates for the social returns to R&D. Within a country, they estimate the return to investment to be around 100% for society as a whole. Taking international R&D spillovers into account, this figure increases to 130% for the world as a whole.[14]

All these findings provide a justification for the development of a growth model with endogenous technological change in which the social returns from innovation exceed the private ones.

2.2.2 Geography and Technology

Considering technological change as a crucial determinant of the growth process implies that the geographical dispersion of innovative activities is decisive for regional development. In an inter-country comparison within the EU we find pronounced differences in R&D intensities. Table 2.9 reveals strong disparities of R&D activities among EU countries. According to table 2.9 the majority of funds are spent in the private sector.

Table 2.9: R&D activities in EU countries (1990)

	B	DK	G	Gr	E	F	Irl	I	NL	P	UK
GDP per capita in ECU	105	139	128	35	69	115	66	103	102	35	93
Total Expenditures on R&D in % of GDP	85	77	141	24	44	121	46	69	103	25	111
Private Expenditures on R&D in % of GDP	95	65	155	8	40	114	42	59	85	9	113
Total employed scientists and engineers per 1000 employees	4.4	3.8	5.9	1.4	2.2	5.1	5.0	3.2	4.0	1.1	4.6
Scientists and engineers in the private sector per 1000 employees	2.4	1.5	3.8	0.2	0.6	2.3	1.3	1.3	1.6	0.1	2.8

The numbers in the first four rows are expressed relative to the respective average in the EU 12 countries. Source: Commission (1994, p.97)

[14] Coe et. al. (1997) find also substantial spillovers from developed to developing countries which are related to the volume of trade in differentiated inputs between the respective countries.

We can derive two basic stylized facts from table 2.9. First, R&D activities are more concentrated among the EU countries than per capita income. The unweighted standard deviation for total (private) expenditures on R&D amounts to 48.9% (61.6%). For R&D employment, we find a standard deviation of 40.2% and 65%, respectively. This compares to a standard deviation of per capita GDP of 36.8%. It is interesting to note the especially high geographical concentration of private R&D activities.

Second, we find a strong and significant relationship between per capita income and the R&D measures. We conduct simple linear regressions between total as well as private R&D expenditures on per capita GDP. For total (private) expenditures this yields a coefficient of 0.71 [4.21] (0.50 [3.90])[15] with an adjusted coefficient of determination of 0.63 (0.59). Regressing total (private) R&D employment on GDP per capita gives us 23.2 [3.36] (16.5 [3.32]) with adjusted $\bar{R}^2$ of 0.51 (0.50). A priori it is by no means clear in which direction the causal relationship points. We explore this statistical relationship in more detail in our theoretical analysis.

Looking at the regions in the EU, we find even more pronounced differences in R&D activities. A rather recent EU study revealed a strong concentration of R&D activities in some "R&D islands" (cf. Hilpert (1992)). These islands are small, mostly urban areas with a dense network of R&D laboratories and related firms. The main R&D-islands are in the Greater London area, Ile de France, Rotterdam/Amsterdam, the Ruhr area, Frankfurt, Stuttgart, Munich, Lyon/Grenoble, and Torino/Milano. We find a R&D belt in Europe (see figure 2.4). Three-fourths of European R&D activities are located in these centers. Audretsch and Feldman (1993) find a similar pattern for the US, where R&D activities are especially concentrated on the North East Coast and in California.

This picture is reinforced with a glance at the data of the location of R&D activities in the other, more peripheral member states of the EU (Greece, Ireland, Portugal, and Spain). In these countries, R&D activities are concentrated in very few regions. In Portugal, the share of the extended Lisbon area in R&D activities amounts to more than 70% of total national expenditures (see Commission (1987, 1991, 1994)). A similar pattern can be observed in Spain, where 50% of total R&D funds are allocated towards the region of Madrid, followed by 16% in the region of Cataluna. In Greece, 70% of private R&D expenditures are directed towards the region of Athens, and in Ireland,

[15] The numbers in square brackets indicate the respective t-statistics.

Figure 2.4: R&D islands in the EU

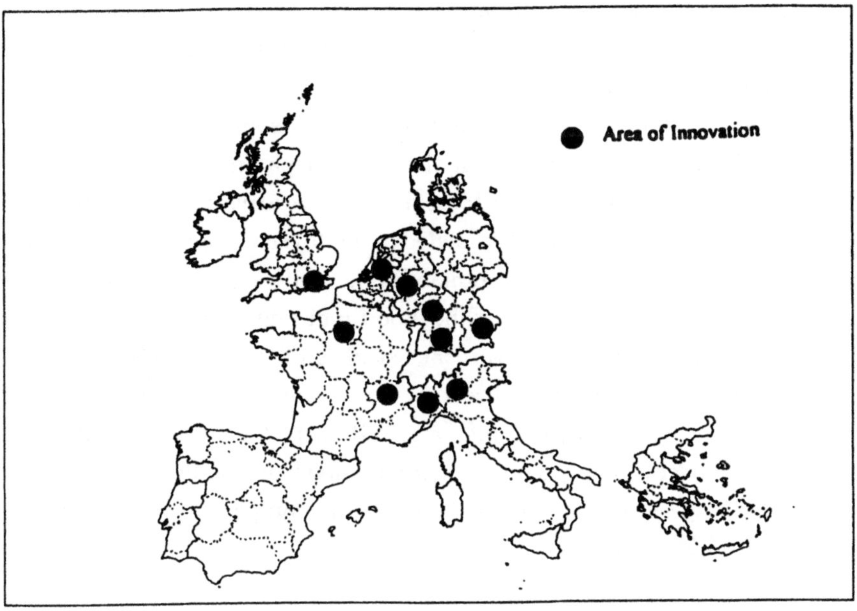

Source: Commission (1994, p. 100).

two-thirds of overall R&D expenditures are invested in the Eastern region. R&D is much more concentrated in these countries than population and income (cf. Commission (1994)). This concentration of the already rather low R&D budgets (relative to GDP) leaves the other regions with virtually no R&D activities. That is, we find a hierarchy of R&D locations. The regions in the core of Europe are followed by a small number of local centers in the less developed member states. The remaining regions constitute the R&D periphery.

One important characteristic of R&D centers is the existence of local R&D networks which facilitate the flow of knowledge. This observation already led Alfred Marshall (1920) to include local technological spillovers in his list of agglomeration advantages (i.e. forces leading to concentration of economic activity). The idea behind local knowledge spillovers is a rather simple one.

Closeness of firms and workers leads to faster and less costly transmission of ideas. The diffusion of knowledge has a local pattern. In reviewing agglomeration advantages, Krugman (1991a) argues that local technological spillovers are the least attractive agglomeration advantage for theoretical analysis, since these local knowledge spillovers leave "no paper trail" and, therefore, cannot be detected empirically.

Jaffe et al. (1993), however, point out that in some situations knowledge spillovers do leave a paper trail in the form of patent citations. Using US data, they link patent citations to regional innovative activities in order to detect direct evidence of local knowledge spillovers. They find surprisingly strong cross-citations at the regional level. This suggests that innovators use knowledge created in the neighborhood more intensively than knowledge from more distant locations. All other studies of local knowledge spillovers have concentrated on more indirect evidence and have not pointed to any other source of "paper trails" (cf. e.g. Glaeser et al. (1993), and Harhoff (1996)). The overall evidence for *regional* knowledge spillovers – at least at the present stage – seems to be less convincing compared to the existence of knowledge spillovers per se.

2.3 Summary

The objective of this chapter has been to highlight some stylized facts about interregional income, growth and specialization in an integration bloc (mainly the EU). Our analysis reveals that substantial differences in per capita income exist among regions in the EU. These differences are even more pronounced with respect to local R&D activities, the main driving force in the growth process. We detect a hierarchy of R&D activities among European regions with R&D being highly concentrated in the European core. Our theoretical framework will provide an explanation of such a concentration of R&D activities and localized growth based on innovative activities.

We have not been able to detect strong convergence among regions and countries in the European Community. We observe a decline in the speed of convergence in the post World-War II period. In our main period of investigation (1980-1995) we find a rather low rate of regional β-convergence and no σ-convergence.[16] Our investigation of income convergence does not support

[16] Thereby, our results are in the overall perspective in line with the ones of another recent study on the subject (see Busch et al. (1998)).

the hypothesis that regional integration fosters income convergence among participating countries and regions. This has rather strong implications for our theoretical analysis. Our finding of a non-positive relationship between integration and convergence is in contrast to the traditional, static integration literature. We will address this crucial empirical observation in our theoretical analysis. We overcome the shortcoming of the old integration theory in describing these observations by presenting various possible mechanisms by which integration may hamper rather than foster convergence.

Our analysis of the evolution of regional specialization patterns – which was admittedly conducted at a high level of aggregation – supports the hypothesis of Krugman (1991a) that integration may very well lead to more pronounced differences in regional specialization patterns. Our theoretical analysis will provide a wide array of reasons as to why this may happen.

Chapter 3

Brief Overview of Related Literature

3.1 Static Models of Regional Integration

The exemption of regional trading blocs from GATT rules was based on the conviction that the reduction of barriers to trade associated with the formation of regional integration blocs constitutes a move toward free trade and is consequently welfare improving. Viner (1950), however, showed that this general presumption is not true. Rather than depicting a uniform reduction of barriers to trade, trade liberalization in the course of regional integration is discriminatory. Producers in countries outside the integration bloc will not face lower barriers to trade and their imports into the integration bloc become more expensive relative to those of producers in partner countries. Viner pointed out that the net welfare effect of preferential trading clubs (free trade zones, custom unions) depends on the balance between trade creation and trade diversion.

This argument remained at the core of all theories of preferential trading clubs. Trade diversion in the course of trade liberalization in the trading club refers to the change of the origin of imports, shifting from the low-cost producer outside the club to the relatively inefficient producer in the partner country. In contrast, trade creation describes the replacement of domestic production through more imports from a less costly producer in the partner country. Whereas trade creation is beneficial, trade diversion distorts the international factor allocation and is, in general, harmful for participating countries.[1] The reduction of barriers to trade between the partner countries in the integration bloc takes place against the background of existing outside impediments to trade. A typical second-best problem arises.

The traditional three country, two goods models in the Vinerian tradition suffered from an important drawback. In this setting, the trade structure is necessarily asymmetric (at most one country is able to trade simultaneously with the other two nations). This drawback was partially overcome by the extensions of the product space, usually by introducing a third good. These extensions[2] also discuss the basic notion of trade creation and trade diversion and derive a number of interesting, but highly specific results. The outcome of these analyses hinges very much on the specific assumed trade pattern. This should not, however, be regarded as a disadvantage but rather as a consequence of a complex reality.

The above cited literature relied on non-decreasing returns-to-scale and perfect competition in all markets. In the tradition of Heckscher-Ohlin theory, these studies concentrate on the effects of preferential trading clubs on factor allocation in the presence of relative factor abundance differences. Consequently, changes in the scale of production and the degree of competition in imperfect markets are not considered. These effects are, however, very important in the course of regional integration.

Recently, a number of studies in the "new" trade theory literature has taken up this idea. They employ the notion of firms operating under firm-specific increasing returns-to-scale (cf. e.g. Venables (1987) and Venables/ Smith (1988)). In goods markets, monopolistic competition or an oligopolistic structure prevails. The general argument is that trade liberalization and the associated market extension from the point of view of an individual firm leads potentially to a better exploitation of economies of scale and a higher degree of competition.

Models of the "new" trade theory are still in the main-stream of international trade theory. That is, space as an economic dimension does not play any role. Countries are points in space. Trade between these points in space is costless, transport costs do not exist. Factor endowment in each country is assumed to be given. This shortcoming, which becomes more

---

[1] By introducing differentiated products, Ethier/Horn (1982) argue that a consumption gain effect arises. Consumers benefit through a larger available variety of consumption goods.

[2] For a short survey, see Lloyd (1982).

and more prevalent in the course of regional integration, was stressed by Krugman (1991a). He tried to merge international trade theory and regional economics by developing general equilibrium models of economic geography. For this purpose, interacting agglomeration economies and agglomeration diseconomies are embedded in a general equilibrium framework. In addition to allowing for mobile workers, he introduced transport costs combined with economies of scale. Krugman certainly deserves the credit for popularizing these kinds of models.[3]

A two-region general equilibrium framework allows for the determination of regional specialization patterns on the basis of agglomerative economies and diseconomies. Relative factor endowments of the regions are not the crucial factor determining regional production patterns.

Regional integration alters the relative strength of these forces. Location choices of firms and households are affected. In contrast to trade approaches with their given endowment assumption, in models of economic geography, trade liberalization in the course of regional integration can induce migration and, therefore, change each region's factor endowment.

These ideas lie at the heart of recent static models which lend themselves to an analysis of regional integration. In particular, Krugman/Venables (1990), Krugman (1991c) and Elizando/Krugman (1995) where among the first to follow this route of investigation. Addressing the enlargement of the European Community by integrating Spain and Portugal, Krugman and Venables (1990) point out that producers in the periphery do not necessarily gain a relative cost advantage. Rather, it is feasible that producers become attracted to the center due to a strengthening of the agglomerative forces. Krugman (1991c) looks at a related issue in a two-region approach, namely the deepening of regional integration. His basic result is that, starting from a realistic level of transport costs, a reduction in transport costs makes a core-periphery solution with industrial production in one region more likely. Once again, regional integration strengthens the agglomerative forces.[4] Krug-

[3] He was, however, not the first who developed this type of models. For example, Fujita (1988) and Rivera-Batiz (1988) have used models which have all the properties of general equilibrium approaches of economic geography.

[4] Krugman/Venables (1995) argue that this monotonicity result stems from the assumption of labour mobility in a regional context. Assuming immobility of labor gives them a non-monotone relation between agglomeration and (international) trade liberalization. Starting from high levels of trade barriers, trade liberalization leads to agglomeration. Eventually, however, continuing reductions in trade barriers lead in their model to a reindustrialization of the periphery.

man/Venables (1996) look at the adjustment costs of such type of processes. Puga and Venables (1997) stress the discriminatory character of preferential trading arrangements. They show that this type of trade liberalization pulls industries into the integrating countries and may cause further concentration of economic activity in the integration bloc.

Elizondo/Krugman (1995) investigate the regional impact of closer integration in the world economy. With an extension of the relevant market range, the size of the domestic market becomes less important. The relative (and absolute) attractiveness of the domestic center decreases. The agglomerative forces are weakened and production is shifted away from the domestic center to the domestic periphery. [5]

In a nutshell, the development of static approaches to regional integration over time begins with the analysis in the traditional trade theory literature with perfect competition, leading up to the consideration of economies of scale and imperfect competition in "new" trade theory. More recently, various authors employing models of economic geography have focused on the impact of regional integration on regional specialization patterns.

In our analysis of regional integration in this study, we combine the major elements of the above discussed literature (partial character of regional integration, trade diversion versus trade creation, scale economies, aspects of economic geography) and embed them in a dynamic framework, i.e. an endogenous growth framework.[6]

This allows for an analysis of a wide variety of aspects of regional integration. But before we turn to this analysis, let us consider the relationship between international integration (integration of a country in the world market) and growth.[7]

[5] A further example of a study in which geography plays a role can be found in Wooton (1988) who analyzes the implications of factor mobility in a common market. This study relies, however, on perfect competition in all markets.

[6] Puga/Venables (1996) also look at the evolution of industry location in the course of economic development by using a model of economic geography. They leave, however, issues of an endogenous development of the economies under investigation aside.

[7] Walz (1997a) provides a survey of all aspects of the dynamic effects of economic integration (i.e. regional as well as international integration).

3.2 Growth and International Integration

Static models completely neglect – per definition – the "rate effect" of regional integration. But this rate effect, i.e. the impact of policy changes on the rate of accumulation and the rate of income growth, can very well outperform the level effect of static analysis. In contrast to the static level effect which leads to a one-time jump in the income trajectory, the rate effect changes the slope of the income line. It is quite possible that the discounted impact on the growth rate is larger than a one-time jump in the income level. Policies with level effects which materialize in the short-run might, however, be considered politically more attractive than policies with pure rate effects. Policy makers might even be inclined to implement policies with a positive level and a negative rate effect, having a negative overall discounted welfare effect for private agents. That could be the case, for example, if the discount rate perceived by the policy maker is larger than the one of private agents. In any case, it is important to understand the growth rate effects of regional integration in the first place.

Until recently, theoretical tools to address these rate effects did not exist. Traditional neoclassical growth theory with its exogenously given rate of steady-state growth did not lend itself to this task. With the development of endogenous growth models this lack of a theoretical workhorse has been overcome. Recently, various authors have used this approach in order to analyse the relationship between *international* integration and growth. We will discuss these models in the next section in some detail.

Later on, we will argue that there are important differences between regional and international integration. Therefore, it is not feasible to transfer the results of these studies to an analysis of regional integration. Rather, it is necessary to adopt a quite different basic framework. Nevertheless, it is helpful to look at the basic mechanisms behind these models. Therefore, the following discussion can be regarded as the basis for our discussion in the remaining part of the study.

3.2.1 Three Basic Mechanisms Linking Growth and Integration

The general feature of endogenous growth models is the (long-run) linearity of the accumulation equation with respect to the accumulable factor (cf. Sala-i-Martin (1990)). This contrasts with the neoclassical growth theory in which the accumulation equation (i.e. the accumulation equation of the physical capital stock) is concave in the accumulable factor. This results from diminishing returns of the macroeconomic production function with respect to physical capital.

Beginning with Romer (1986), researchers have developed a broad range of models sharing this linearity property. These models can be distinguished by their concentration on different accumulable factors (human capital, physical capital, knowledge capital (technological change)). The literature relating international integration to growth, however, has almost exclusively employed growth models with endogenous technological change. This is partly a consequence of the opinion, shared by most observers, that technological change is the main driving force of economic growth. In the absence of technological change, capital accumulation would be subject to diminishing returns and would finally approach a stationary steady-state. Hence, the rate of technological change also governs the rate of capital accumulation (cf. Grossman/Helpman (1994)). Furthermore, endogenizing technological change in a growth framework is regarded as the most important merit of endogenous growth theory (cf. Solow (1994)). The rate of technological change is also considered to be influenced most in the course of integration. Owing to their much richer microstructure growth models with endogenous technological change allow allow for the analysis of important aspects of economic integration and are therefore most suitable for this task. The general idea is that integration changes the cost and demand situation for potential innovators, thereby altering the incentives to innovate and consequently, the rate of technological change and growth.

The basic growth models with endogenous technological change have been developed by Aghion/Howitt (1992), Grossman/Helpman (1990) and Romer (1990). The main common pillars of these models are the following. Research and development (R&D) is undertaken by rational, forward-looking firms. Innovators of new and better products and processes achieve (temporary) monopoly positions in the respective market segment, allowing them to earn positive profits during this time period, which compensate them for the initial R&D costs. Market entry in this segment is limited since it requires the possession of private knowledge about the respective blueprint. Hence, imperfect competition prevails in the dynamic general equilibrium and creates an incentive for private firms to accumulate costly knowledge.

The following discussion of the long-run effects of integration is pursued against the background of a dynamic general equilibrium model with horizontally (rather than vertically) differentiated products, which lends itself most easily to the incorporation of various issues related to integration (knowledge transfers, tariffs, non-tariff barriers, labor migration etc.). Horizontally differentiated products are either used as inputs in a final good or as consumption goods. The development of new goods by means of R&D enlarges the available variety of goods. This, in turn, improves the well-being of consumers (who value variety) or enhances productivity in final-goods production through an increased division of labor. Many, although not all results carry over to the model with vertically differentiated products and quality improvements.[8]

Broadly speaking, integration alters the steady-state growth rate of participating countries if the accumulation equation is changed. With endogenous technological change this implies that in order for integration policies to influence the steady-state growth rate, the R&D function must be affected in one way or the other. The R&D or accumulation function is the strategic equation with respect to the long-run effects of integration. In the literature, there are two basic specifications of the R&D function which generate ongoing growth. In the first one, the *knowledge-driven specification*,[9] the rate of change of the number of known differentiated goods ($\dot{n}$) is a linear function of human capital employed in this sector (H_n) and the level of public knowledge $(W = n)$[10]

$$\dot{n} = H_n W. \tag{3.1}$$

R&D has partially the characteristics of a public good, creating spillovers in knowledge for future innovators. This dynamic externality prevents the rate of return from falling. The second specification, the lab equipment formulation uses the notion that R&D is created using unskilled labor (L_n), human capital (H_n) and the quantity x_n of each of the available differentiated inputs:

$$\dot{n} = (L_n)^{1-\alpha-\beta}(H_n)^{\beta} \int_0^n x_n(j)^{\alpha} dj \quad 0 < \alpha, \beta < 1. \tag{3.2}$$

In the lab equipment case, intermediate goods and industrial final goods are produced following the same production function as for the creation of new blueprints. Increasing the number of differentiated inputs leads to a higher degree of specialization and productivity in R&D. The function is

[8]For the basic model, see Aghion/Howitt (1992) and Grossman/Helpman (1991a).

[9]The terminology is borrowed from Rivera-Batiz/Romer (1991a).

[10]The following equations refer to a closed economy.

homogenous of degree two with respect to H_n, L_n, x_n, and n. With both specifications (the knowledge-driven and the lab equipment one), the accumulation equation displays constant returns with respect to the accumulable factor (n). In the knowledge-driven model, R&D costs amount to $c_n = w_H/n$ and in the lab equipment case to $c_n = B(w_L)^{\frac{1-\alpha-\beta}{1-\alpha}}(w_H)^{\frac{\beta}{1-\alpha}}/n$ with w_L and w_H denoting factor rewards for unskilled labor and skilled labor capital, respectively (note that $p_x = c_n$). The price of each input is represented by p_x whereas B is a positive constant.

The decisive difference between the two formulations is the way in which a larger number of intermediate goods leads to higher productivity in the R&D sector. The knowledge specification operates through the spillover of public knowledge which enhances the productivity of future researchers. In the lab equipment case, R&D productivity increases through a larger degree of the division of labor in the R&D laboratory.

The economic mechanisms behind the dynamic effects of integration can be best explained with the help of a no-arbitrage condition. This no-arbitrage condition describes the intertemporal equilibrium and the incentives to undertake innovative activities. Potential innovators will continue investing in R&D as long as the expected rate of return is larger than the costs of capital. Denoting the flow of profits from monopolistic firms by G, we derive the following no-arbitrage condition: [11]

$$\frac{G}{P} + \frac{\dot{P}}{P} = \rho, \tag{3.3}$$

with P describing the value of existing firms. With free entry, innovators undertake innovation until $c_n = P$. Choosing the numeraire such that, for example, consumption expenditures are equal to one implies that in the steady-state factor prices have to be constant as well. Hence, we obtain the following modified steady-state no-arbitrage condition:

$$\frac{G}{P} - \rho = g, \tag{3.4}$$

where $g := \dot{n}/n$ denotes the rate of innovation. In equilibrium, private households are willing to finance R&D investment if the expected rate of return equals their subjective discount rate ρ. Profits per share (G/c_n) have to be corrected for expected capital losses which arise due to the permanent development of new inputs, i.e. more competition leads to a decrease in the

[11] In later chapters we integrate the no-arbitrage condition in a general equilibrium framework.

costs of new R&D investment, and hence the value of existing firms. With a standard CES production function for final goods (see eq. (3.2)) or a Dixit-Stiglitz utility function, producers of differentiated goods face a constant demand elasticity, $\epsilon = 1/(1-\alpha)$. For example, with differentiated inputs and our normalization, we obtain for a setting with a single consumption good sector (which has the same production function as the R&D-sector in the lab equipment case) the demand function for an input of variety v:

$$x(v) = \frac{p_x(v)^{-\epsilon}}{\int_0^n p_x(v')^{1-\epsilon} dv'}, \tag{3.5}$$

with $p_x(v)$ denoting the price of the v-th variety of the intermediate good (see Helpman/Krugman (1985)). The optimal price is a mark-up on unit costs. In a symmetric equilibrium, we obtain for the instantaneous profits $G = (p_x - c_x)x = (1-\alpha)/n$. With R&D-costs declining linearly in the number of differentiated goods, the rate of profits, G/c_n stays the same.

The no-arbitrage condition is reminiscent of the accumulation equation in a traditional Solow model. The rate of growth of the accumulable factor is equal to the difference between the factor's productivity and the subjective discount rate. But here, in contrast to the traditional neoclassical model productivity of the accumulable factor is constant and growth does not peter out (as long as $G/c_n > \rho$).

Now we can address the impact of integration on the growth rate of the participating economies in general terms. The literature on the dynamic effects of integration distinguishes three types of potential effects or mechanisms on growth: the **redundancy effect**, the **integration or scale effect**[12] and the **allocation effect**.

The **redundancy effect** refers to the avoidance of duplicative R&D in different countries. An overlap in R&D exists if some products are developed and produced in both countries. The total "effective" number of different intermediate products can be expressed as $n = n^A + \varrho n^B$. The parameter ϱ $(0 < \varrho < 1)$ measures the extent of the R&D overlap in both countries. More precisely, it denotes varieties produced in B which are already manufactured in country A (assuming implicitely that country A has a larger differentiated product sector). With $\varrho = 0$, firms in country B produce only a subset

[12] In the following we prefer the term scale effect rather than integration effect since the latter is rather confusing with regard to our subject. Furthermore, this effect is based on increasing returns to scale in the accumulation equation (3.1) and hence, is more appropriately described by the former.

of differentiated goods already manufactured in A. Eliminating duplicative R&D leads to an increase in n. With the exception of pure national knowledge spillovers ($W^i = n^i$) in the knowledge-driven formulation, R&D-costs decrease in both formulations. In the knowledge-driven model, the level of public knowledge increases, whereas in the lab equipment formulation, the productive impact of a larger range of available differentiated inputs leads to a decrease in R&D costs.

The **scale effect** works through the integration of the R&D sector and the manufacturing sectors of the economies in the presence of increasing returns-to-scale in the accumulation equation (i.e. the R&D functions (3.1) and (3.2)). The intersectoral allocation of resources is held constant (this implies in most set-ups constant intersectoral employment levels). In the presence of increasing returns-to-scale in the accumulation function, doubling all inputs proportionally means that R&D output increases by a factor larger than two. Hence, replicating two identical economies leads to an innovation rate larger than the sum of the two individuals ones. In the next section, we will investigate which integration policies achieve this result.

Most integration policies have an **allocation effect** which describes the change in sectoral and international resource allocation as a consequence of integration. A shift of resources (L_n and/or H_n) into (out of) the R&D sector increases (decreases) the rate of knowledge accumulation and growth. In the remaining chapters of the study, we often rely on this effect when we discuss the long-run implications of different regional integration policies. In the next section, we address the growth effects of different international integration steps in more detail.

3.2.2 The Long-run Effects of International Integration

What are the growth rate effects of different international integration policies? Our answer to this question is based on the approach of Rivera-Batiz/Romer (1991a). They proposed the artificial division between the international flow of ideas (international knowledge spillovers) and the international exchange of goods as well as factors of production.[13]

First, the liberalization of the international diffusion of knowledge is addressed. Then, we discuss the different aspects of product market integration. Finally, we investigate some aspects of liberalizing factor flows. Re-

[13] In reality, however, the flow of goods and labor can almost never be separated from the flow of knowledge.

versing this order of policy experiments would create stability problems in the knowledge-driven approach (see Devereux/Lapham (1994) and Grossman/Helpman (1991b, chapter 8)). In the presence of local knowledge spillovers and traded differentiated inputs, multiplicity of equilibria emerges with a corner solution being approached in the long-run (see also section 4.7). In other words, integrating two identical economies by allowing trade in goods but not in knowledge leads to an asymmetry between the two countries. Innovating activities take place in one country only. Which country this will be depends on history and small initial shocks.

Allowing for international flows of ideas between two countries is equivalent to an integration of the two R&D sectors (see Grossman/Helpman (1991b, chapter 9), Rivera-Batiz/Romer (1991a)). This might trigger a scale effect in the R&D sector. The pool of public knowledge (W) which innovators can draw upon increases, implying a higher productivity of reseachers and lower R&D costs. In the knowledge-driven case, the expected return on R&D investment increases. Lower R&D costs lead to faster innovation and growth (see eq. (3.4)). Allowing for international diffusion of knowledge is growth-enhancing. The increase in the growth rate is more pronounced if the R&D overlap is small ($W^i = n^i + \varrho n^j$). Knowledge flows, however, have no growth rate effect in the lab equipment formulation. R&D costs are unchanged after free knowledge flows are allowed for and the innovation rate remains unchanged.

The overlap in the creation of new goods is eliminated with the integration of product markets. International trade makes it unprofitable to "discover" an already existing good for the second time. Given the existence of an R&D overlap without trade, this redundancy effect of trade liberalization contributes potentially to lower R&D costs and consequently to faster innovation and growth as a glance at the no-arbitrage condition reveals. In the knowledge-driven model, a necessary condition for the redundancy effect to occur is some kind of international spillovers. With purely national spillovers ($W^i = n^i$), eliminating duplicative research leaves the productivity in the R&D sectors and hence the speed of innovation unchanged. The redundancy effect can be observed in these models in the transition from autarky to free trade, i.e. it occurs even if high barriers to trade prevail after the abolition of autarky. Lowering barriers to trade from a tariff well below prohibitive levels, hence, has no effect in this respect.

The second potential effect of opening product markets to international trade is the scale effect in the manufacturing sector, i.e. the enlargement of the market size for the producers. The increasing number of consumers is, however, accompanied by a larger number of competitors. As has been shown by Rivera-Batiz/Romer (1991a) and Grossman/Helpman (1991b) employing the knowledge-driven set-up, these two effects just balance. This becomes most obvious with two identical economies. The number of consumers and the number of competitors double. Market enlargement and fiercer competition compensate each other. Profits per firm (G) remain unchanged. The incentive to innovate is unchanged. This implies that with no initial R&D overlap and in the absence of an allocation effect, free trade has no growth rate effect: " ... the integration of product markets will have no effect on the long-run growth rates in either country." (Rivera-Batiz/Romer (1991b, 245)). This result hinges, however, on the specific R&D function. With the lab equipment formulation, enlarging the product market for innovators leads to lower R&D costs and consequently to faster innovation and growth. Innovation becomes more profitable and market entry takes place until the higher innovation rate brings the no-arbitrage condition back into equilibrium. Whether free flow of goods or knowledge has a positive scale effect on growth depends very much on the specification of the R&D function.

Matters are different if we look at two countries with unequal innovation rates and national knowledge spillovers. This situation is analyzed in Feenstra (1990). National knowledge spillovers imply either natural or artificial barriers impeding the free flow of ideas across national borders. Against this background, Feenstra (1990) shows that the competitive situation of innovators in the smaller country (say country B) worsens over time after the integration of product markets. They face a larger number of foreign competitors in the producer market while R&D costs in the smaller country are declining less rapidly: $((G^A/c_n^A) > (G^B/c_n^B) \rightarrow g^A > g^B)$. Hence, profits per share in the smaller country decrease over time. Relative to the autarky situation, the innovation rate of the small country decreases, whereas innovation in the larger country takes place at a faster pace for a transition period and falls back to the autarky level in the steady-state.

Grossman/Helpman (1991c) investigate the implication of trade if knowledge and goods flows cannot be separated from each other for a small country. The extent of international knowledge spillovers is a positive function of the trade volume. Trade liberalization leads to a higher trade volume and, consequently, to a larger pool of public knowledge which domestic innovators can draw on. R&D costs decline and the speed of knowledge accumulation and growth accelerates.

Let us now turn to the third mechanism describing the relationship between integration and growth: the *allocation effect* of trade liberalization. In general, innovation and growth increase through this channel if more resources are shifted into the R&D sector (i.e. L_n and/or H_n increase). In this reallocation process, the marginal product of skilled labor outside the dynamic sector declines relatively, leading to a shift of skilled workers into the dynamic sector. The profit rate of innovation (G/c_n) rises. But when does this occur and are there situations in which the allocation effect is negative?

First, let us look at similar countries with factor endowments which do not differ too greatly and of similar size such that no economic activity is concentrated in one country only. All the following arguments rest on the knowledge-driven R&D model. The specific form of the R&D function is not as important in the discussion of the allocation effects as it was with the integration and redundancy effects.

Grossman/Helpman (1990) provide an example showing that, even in the presence of international knowledge spillovers, trade liberalization between similar countries can lead to a deterioration of the growth performance. Rivera-Batiz/Romer (1991b) embed this argument in a more general framework and show that the growth rate of the two countries is a non-monotone function of the tariff rate. When tariffs are small, a reduction in tariffs leads to faster growth. Only with tariffs exceeding a critical rate, reductions worsen the growth performance. In an extension of this argument, Rivera-Batiz/Xie (1992) show that the critical tariff rate is a positive function of the number of countries involved in tariff reduction. They conclude that, with realistic parameter constellations, tariff reductions always enhance growth. But it should be noted that this argument applies either to a general tariff reduction or to a one-sector world and is derived for perfectly symmetric countries. A sector-specific trade policy reducing tariffs for traditional goods, increases consumption and production of this good. This attracts resources at the expense of the dynamic sector. Wage rates rise, R&D costs increase and the expected profit rate of innovative investment erodes (see eq. (3.3)). The rates of innovation and growth decline.

Once more, matters are different in the case of dissimilar countries. With both countries innovating in the presence of free trade, Rivera-Batiz/Xie (1993) obtain an in-between result. As in the standard Heckscher-Ohlin model, opening of trade leads to an increase in the reward to skilled workers employed in final-goods production in the country which is well-endowed with this factor (country A). Resources are shifted out of the R&D sector and R&D costs increase. The incentive to innovate declines in A. The reverse pattern holds in country B. The overall effect on innovation and growth rates depends on the extent of knowledge diffusion. The overall growth rate effect is only positive with strong diffusion of technology. With national knowledge spillovers (i.e only national reseachers benefit from previous knowledge accumulation), the worldwide growth rate effect is negative.

In a two-sector world, innovation in the country abundantly endowed with unskilled labor may cease altogether. This country completely specializes in the traditional sector (see Grossman/Helpman (1991b, chapter 9)). But it is important to stress that the output growth rate and/or the innovation rate are not adequate welfare measures. Even if innovation ceases completely in one country this country still might gain through free trade through the supply of more or cheaper goods.

This is also the bottom line in Young (1991). Using an endogenous growth model with learning by doing, he investigates the dynamic effects of free trade between a developed and a less developed economy. With free trade, the developing country (the developed country) experiences a rate of technological progress which is less or equal (larger or equal) than the one under autarky. Despite the potentially lower rate of technological change, the static efficiency gains may lead to a higher welfare level in the developing country.

Finally, we briefly turn to other integration policies. By incorporating financial intermediation in a growth model with endogenous technological change, Blackburn/Hung (1993) investigate the impact of financial liberalization on growth. Financial intermediaries monitor the activities of innovating firms. Whereas growth leads to more financial development, financial deepening has no effect on steady-state growth.

Rivera-Batiz/Xie (1993) look at the implications of migration between two dissimilar countries. They show that migration of unskilled labor from the low-wage country (with abundant unskilled labor) to the high-wage country (with a relative scarcity of unskilled labor) leads to slower innovation and less growth. Marginal productivity of skilled workers in the final-goods sector and the demand for final goods in the high-wage country increase, leading to higher wages for skilled workers. This, in turn, implies higher R&D costs, profits per share (G/c_n) decrease and innovation slows down (see eq. (3.4)).

With similar countries, free flow of knowledge and goods are perfect substitutes for factor flows. That is, with free knowledge diffussion and free trade, allowing for free factor mobility has no growth rate effect.

3.2.3 International versus Regional Integration

One of the basic insights of static analyses of regional integration is that international and regional integration are different issues, leading in many cases to different results. Deeper regional integration involves important asymmetries. In contrast to uniform liberalization steps in the course of international integration, regional integration is per definition discriminatory. Liberalization only takes place among a subset of countries, leaving the relationship with other countries unchanged (implying thereby a relative deterioration with respect to the openness to these countries outside the integration bloc). Capturing the asymmetry associated with this discriminatory character of integration requires at least a three-country setting. The same is true for the enlargement process which has been more and more prominent in recent years, especially due to the planned and realized extensions of the EU (see CEPR (1992)) and NAFTA.[14]

The second important distinction refers to the way the structure of participating countries is modelled properly. The main idea is that with an increasing degree of regional integration, the paradigm of international trade theory is no longer adequate. That is, with a sufficiently high degree of factor mobility, the assumption of given factor endowments as used in international trade theory is not suitable. Especially the mobility of physical capital but also of skilled labor comes to one's mind. Therefore, location choices of firms and mobile factors of production have to be taken into account. Taking aspects of regional economics, location theory and economic geography into account[15] allows for the determination of countries' specialization via the interaction of agglomeration advantages and disadvantages. In the analysis of international integration, however, countries are considered to be points in space. Besides state-imposed barriers to trade, the exchange of goods between countries is costless. Barriers to migration are prohibitive.

Taking in a regional context costs of overcoming space into account (i.e.

[14]Despite the importance of this development, there exist very few (formal) analyses of this process and its impact on *all* participating countries.

[15]Since in our context the difference between these terms is not that important, we use them in the following as synonymous.

transport and transaction costs), requires an explicit analysis of location choices. Combining the costs of overcoming space with increasing returns-to-scale at the firm level creates non-footless industries.[16] If it is costly to relocate the production site and transport costs exist, the extent of the local market plays an important role.

All these elements of economic geography allow for the emergence of various interesting features of the development of production and employment in different geographical areas.[17] Due to the existence of agglomerative forces, concentration of economic activity is worthwhile for firms and workers. By clustering together, economic agents create a positive spatial externality. If this externality is strong enough, a cumulative and circular causation process might arise[18] after which economic activity in non-footless industries is concentrated completely in one country. History and path-dependence matter.

Analyzing regional integration policies against this background is quite different from the analysis of international integration. In the latter case, countries are symmetric or their specialization patterns are determined through relative factor abundance. With regional integration, the determinants of countries' specialization patterns (agglomeration economies and diseconomies) are directly affected. The results discussed in the previous section provide a first insight into the general mechanism, but cannot be carried over to our subject.

---

[16]The term "industry" is used in this work in a very general sense, simply describing sectors of the economy. It can stand for a service as well as for a manufacturing industry. For example, when talking later on about high-tech industries , we can find even more examples in the service than in the manufacturing sector.

[17]The incorporation of aspects of economic geography also allows for an investigation of the impact of integration on different regions in one country.

[18]This is an old idea in regional economics, see Perroux (1955).

Chapter 4

Growth and Economic Geography

4.1 The Basic Elements

In the introductory section, we have argued that an analysis of the long-run implications of regional integration has to be based on an endogenous regional growth model. But how should the basic structure of such a model look?

Apparently it should use a growth mechanism which allows for an endogenously determined, positive growth rate in the long-run equilibrium. A growth process which is driven by an exogenous force is not adequate for our purpose since by definition any growth rate effects of regional integration policies are excluded in such a framework. For reasons outlined in the previous sections we choose to use a growth framework based on endogenous technological change and knowledge spillovers.[1]

As a second essential input, we have to introduce the interaction between agglomeration advantages and disadvantages.[2] This depicts the regional aspect of the approach. In contrast to traditional trade theory, each country's comparative advantage, and hence, their specialization and trade

[1]Other recent models of localized growth employ the notion of externalities in the aggregate capital stock (see Palivos/Wang (1996)) and population growth (see Black/Henderson (1999)). By being more closely focused on urban or city growth, these approaches are, however, less suitable to our objective of analyzing long-run effects of regional integration.

[2]Various authors employ the expressions centripetal and centrifugal forces.

patterns, are endogenously determined. They are not given via their relative endowments with immobile factors of production. Besides determining the countries' specialization as well as the interregional trade structure, the interaction between these forces also provides an explanation of the spatial concentration of economic activity.

Agglomeration advantages describe the positive effects of spatial proximity of agents on the same market side (producers or consumers) and/or on different sides of the market. Savings in transport costs, the local availability of differentiated consumption goods or differentiated inputs (labor, producer goods and services) and local technological spillovers are the most prominent sources of agglomeration advantages (cf. Fujita (1988), Krugman (1991a,b,c), Rivera-Batiz (1988), and Stahl (1987)). Further possible agglomeration advantages arise from the provision of local public goods (cf. Walz/Wellisch (1996)).

Most agglomeration disadvantages can be reduced to the immobility of factors of production (land, labor, environmental quality etc., cf. Schulz (1995)). As a further agglomeration disadvantage which affects the location choices of producers, different degrees of local competition have to be mentioned.[3]

In a world with constant returns-to-scale production functions and homogeneously distributed resources, concentration of economic activity does not occur (cf. Starrett (1978)). Since an unequal distribution of resources is observed and hence has to be explained, the introduction of scale economies as the fundamental prerequisite for the concentration of economic activity in space is usually considered a necessity.

We follow this notion by introducing economies of scale in the production of intermediate goods. Countries are modeled as points in space. Space as an economic dimension is introduced via transport or transaction costs which have to be paid for the exchange of goods and services between countries. The existence of economies of scale at the firm level, however, invalidates perfect competition and price-taking in this industry. Rather, monopolistic competition prevails.

Imperfect competition supports both parts of our framework, i.e. the endogenous growth mechanism as well as the regional aspects. With monopolistic competition, firms earn pure profits which, in turn, enable them to

[3]For a recent and extensive survey of the economics of agglomeration as well as the recent literature see Fujita/Thisse (1996).

repay their initial investment. Thus, imperfect competition and economies of scale are important, if not essential building blocks of our endogenous growth framework as well as of our regional approach.

The decisive agglomeration advantage stems from the combination of transport costs and returns-to-scale in the production of differentiated intermediate goods. Differentiated intermediate goods are used in an industrial final good. It is advantageous for the producers of industrial final goods to locate in the country with the larger number of locally produced intermediate goods in order to save transport costs. The intermediate goods can also be termed as producer goods and services. Examples for the latter are legal, financial, consulting, and maintenance services. In turn, the larger final-goods market induces new intermediate goods producers to locate there as well. Due to increasing returns-to-scale at the firm level, each producer serves the entire market from one production site.

The agglomeration advantage is offset by the limited supply of an immobile factor of production in each country. An additional agglomeration disadvantage results from the more intense price competition faced by intermediate goods producers in the country with the larger number of locally produced inputs.

The relative strength of the agglomeration advantages and disadvantages determines the countries' specialization patterns. If the agglomeration advantages are strong enough, a core-periphery pattern with complete concentration of the differentiated-goods industry can be observed.

4.2 A Two-Country Model

The model economy consists of two countries, A and B.[4] In these two countries, two final goods are produced with two basic factors of production and a set of intermediate products.

Each of the two countries is endowed with a stock of an immobile factor of production L of equal size ($\bar{L}^A = \bar{L}^B = \bar{L}$).[5] immobile factors including immobile, unskilled labor, land, as well as local infrastructure. We thereby capture the productive character of local infrastructure and stress the im-

[4] For matters of concreteness, we refer to the geographical entities in our study as countries rather than regions even if in the course of regional integration the boundary between the two terms dissolves more and more.

[5] Walz (1996c) allows for asymmetric countries in this set-up.

portance of the limited supply of land and local labor as an agglomeration disadvantage.[6]

In addition, a given stock of a perfectly mobile production factor between countries is supplied inelastically in the two countries as a whole. We refer to the mobile factor as skilled labor whereas the immobile factor is considered to be unskilled labor. The fixed supply of skilled labor is equal to $\bar{H}$. This displays the notion that skilled labor is considered to be more mobile than unskilled workers. Alternatively, the mobile factor of production could be described as a given stock of mobile physical capital.

All factors of production, even if they are internationally immobile, can move freely between the sectors in a country.

We distinguish between a traditional consumption good Z and a modern, industrial final good Y. Both are freely traded. Households share the intertemporal utility function

$$U_t = \int_t^{\infty} e^{-\rho(\tau - t)} \left[\sigma ln C_Y(\tau) + (1-\sigma) ln C_Z(\tau) d\tau\right], \qquad (4.1)$$

with $C_Y(\tau)$ and $C_Z(\tau)$ representing the consumption levels of the two final goods. [7] Financial capital is assumed to be perfectly mobile between countries. The instantaneous, risk-free rate of interest is identical in both countries ($r^A = r^B = r$).

Denoting the assets of households at time t by $A(t)$ and their labor income by $V(t)$, we can write the intertemporal budget constraint as:

$$\int_t^{\infty} e^{-[R(\tau)-R(t)]} [p_Y(\tau) C_Y(\tau) + p_Z(\tau) C_Z(\tau)] d\tau \leq \int_t^{\infty} e^{-[R(\tau)-R(t)]} V(\tau) d\tau + A(t), \qquad (4.2)$$

where $R(a) = \int_0^a r(\tau) d\tau$ represents the cumulated rate of interest from 0 to a.

Due to time separability in eq. 4.1, households can solve their maximization problem in two separate steps. Let static consumption expenditures

[6] Assuming a fixed supply of the immobile factor is certainly an oversimplification, especially with regard to local infrastructure. Allowing, however, for accumulation of this factor would not change our results at all, as long as the *relative* supply of this factor between the countries stays the same. See also the discussion in section 4.5. For that reason and to keep the model as simple as possible, we chose to use the assumption of a constant supply of the immobile factor.

[7] Since all households share the same preferences, for notational reasons we do not distinguish between individual and aggregate variables.

be E. Due to the free tradability of final goods, $p_Y^A = p_Y^B = p_Y$ as well as $p_Z^A = p_Z^B = p_Z$ holds. Hence, as a solution to the static maximization problem, we find:

$$p_Y C_Y = \sigma E \tag{4.3}$$

and

$$p_Z C_Z = (1 - \sigma) E. \tag{4.4}$$

Inserting these equations in the dynamic programming problem consisting of (4.1) and (4.2) yields the optimal consumption expenditure path[8]

$$\frac{\dot{E}}{E} = r - \rho. \tag{4.5}$$

Along the optimal spending path, the intertemporal budget constraint must hold with equality. Since the model lacks a monetary instrument, we can normalize prices such that E is equal to one at every moment in time. This implies that $r(t) = \rho$ for all t holds. This requires that, along the optimal path, the value of assets of households can not exceed $1/\rho$ (see (4.2)).

Mobile households also have to decide upon their place of residence. They choose to live and work in the country with the highest remuneration of skilled labor. This follows from the absence of migration costs and identical prices of consumption goods in the two countries.

We can now turn to the production side of the model economy. It consists of two sectors. In one sector, the traditional good Z is produced with skilled and unskilled labor only (H_Z and L_Z respectively):

$$Z^i = (L_Z^i)^\delta (H_Z^i)^{1-\delta} \qquad 0 < \delta < 1, \qquad i = A, B. \tag{4.6}$$

The modern industrial sector is vertically structured. Producers of the industrial final good employ the two basic factors of production as well. In addition, they make use of a set of differentiated products.[9] We use the

[8]For a derivation, see e.g. Barro/Sala-i-Martin (1995).

[9]Using the notion of differentiated producer goods rather than differentiated consumer goods has various advantages. First, it reflects the fact that the volume of trade in differentiated intermediates is much more prominent than in consumer goods (cf. Ethier (1982)). Secondly, this route allows for an analysis of the relationship of location choices in vertically structured sectors. Thirdly, and most important, using the notion of differentiated consumer goods would complicate the analysis in the presence of utility-maximizing migration decisions immensely. Mobile households have an incentive to locate in the country with a larger number of locally produced differentiated consumer goods (cf. Stahl (1983)). In our dynamic general equilibrium setting, this drives a wedge between wages for skilled

functional form introduced by Ethier (1982):

$$Y^i = (L_Y^i)^\alpha (H_Y^i)^\beta \left(\int_0^n \tilde{x}^i(v)^\gamma dv \right)^{\frac{1-\alpha-\beta}{\gamma}} \qquad 0 < \alpha, \beta, \gamma < 1, \tag{4.7}$$

with L_Y^i, H_Y^i, and $\tilde{x}^i(v)$ representing inputs of unskilled and skilled labor, as well as of the differentiated product v ($v \in 0, n$). The total number of known intermediate goods is denoted by n. Differentiated products stand for producer goods and services such as differentiated industrial inputs, technical and financial consulting etc. The larger the set of these producer goods and services, the larger the productivity of final goods producers. This reflects the notion of productivity gains through the division of labor.

The production of these intermediate goods and services requires skilled labor:

$$x^i(j) = a_x^{-1} H_x^i(j), \qquad i = A, B; j = 1, ..., n. \tag{4.8}$$

In addition, intermediate goods producers must possess the respective production blueprint in order to be able to assemble the intermediate good. This blueprint can be acquired by the producing firm by investing in R&D.[10]

Research and development activities result in two outcomes. On the one hand, specific private knowledge in the form of the blueprint emerges from the R&D activities. On the other hand, R&D activities create general public knowledge which increases the productivity of future researchers. This spillover of knowledge from R&D is the growth engine in our model. Since we assume international knowledge spillovers, this does not influence the location decisions of firms. We write the R&D function as:

$$\dot{n}^i = H_n^i W. \tag{4.9}$$

Given the stock of non-depreciating knowledge W, innovators in country i, employing H_n^i skilled workers, are able to develop $\dot{n}^i$ new intermediate products. We follow the literature on endogenous growth (cf. Grossman/Helpman

labor in the two countries which changes over time. Furthermore, since mobile workers receive income from their asset holdings in addition to their labor income holdings, the functional distribution of assets is decisive for the location of mobile workers. In order to keep the analysis tractable, we have chosen to look at the case of differentiated intermediate producer goods and services. But, in contrast to Grossman/Helpman (1991a) who abstract from transport costs and factor mobility, our analysis of the intermediate product case does not carry over straightforwardly to the differentiated consumer good case.

[10] An alternative way of receiving the blueprint is to sign a licensing contract with the innovator. In the absence of informational friction and with free entry in the bidding process for the blueprint, the two alternatives yield the same outcome.

(1991a), Romer (1991) and Sala-i-Martin (1990)) by imposing linearity on the accumulation equation. This is done in the simplest way by setting $W = n$. It is straightforward to introduce depreciation of the knowledge stock. This would not change our results as long as the depreciation rate is not so large that it makes investment unprofitable. The accumulation equation would read: $\dot{n}^i = a_n H_n^i W(1-\delta)$ with δ being the depreciation rate. In this case, the net measures can be deduced by simply multiplying the gross variables by $(1-\delta)$. Thereby, we get a constant rate of return of R&D investment. If this rate of return is larger than capital costs, firms have to pay to finance R&D investment ongoing R&D is profitable, and we find a balanced steady-state with a positive rate of innovation.[11]

"Discovering" an already known product variety is not profitable since the resulting duopolistic profits are strictly lower than those from discovering an unkown intermediate good. Even if imitative costs are lower than innovation costs, the employment of Bertrand-strategies in the post-entry game reduces profits for imitators to a very low level. Note that in the presence of transport costs duopolistic profits are – in contrast to other models in the literature (cf. e.g. Grossman/Helpman (1991a), Dinopolous et al. (1994)) – still positive. But, if imitative costs are also significant, Bertrand-strategies in the post-entry game are a credible entry deterrence measure. In order to avoid a very cumbersome discussion, we allow for infinite patent protection of initial innovators.[12]

An important assumption in our entire study is that private knowledge is not tradeable. A differentiated product developed in, say, country A has to be produced in country A. This assumption can be justified by information and control costs associated with the geographical separation of R&D and the production of intermediate goods (cf. Horstmann/Markusen (1989)). In the course of international licensing enforcement, problems arise for the licensee who might have problems enforcing a non-production claim for the R&D firm. Formation of multinational firms (MNC's) is associated with additional set-up costs arising from the geographical separation of production and R&D.

In our stylized model, economic incentives for international licensing and the formation of MNC's do not exist.[13] Therefore, very small costs arising from complete geographical separation of R&D and production make trade

[11] For a detailed discussion of this point see Barro/Sala-i-Martin (1992).

[12] Walz (1995a) contains a detailed analysis of costly innovation and imitation processes.

[13] See for an analysis of the relation between growth and MNCs, Baldwin et al. (1998) and Walz (1997c) .

in private knowledge unprofitable. Relaxing this assumption, however, leaves our main results in place. We refer to this fact later on. Assuming sufficiently large set-up costs for additional plants makes production from one location more profitable. In a nutshell, each variety of producer goods and services is produced by one firm in the country where the R&D for the development of this specific variety was undertaken.

With this description of the basic set-up at hand, we can now look at the optimal behavior of producers. With perfect competition in the two final-goods industries, marginal cost pricing prevails. With cost-minimizing behavior we get:

$$p_Y^i = B_Y (w_L^i)^\alpha (w_H^i)^\beta \left(\int_0^n (\tilde{p}_x^i(v))^{1-\epsilon} dv \right)^{\frac{1-\alpha-\beta}{1-\epsilon}}, \quad B_Y > 0, \tag{4.10}$$

and

$$p_Z^i = B_Z (w_L^i)^\delta (w_H^i)^{1-\delta}, \quad B_Z > 0, \tag{4.11}$$

with $\epsilon := 1/(1-\gamma) > 1$ representing the elasticity of demand for producer goods and w_L^i and w_H^i standing for the wage rate of skilled and unskilled labor in country i. With perfect mobility of skilled workers, $w_H^A = w_H^B = w_H$ as long as a corner solution with all skilled workers residing in one country does not exist. We can exclude this latter case by noting that this would leave all immobile workers in the respective countries unemployed. The variable $\tilde{p}_x^i$ denotes prices, Y-producers located in i have to pay for intermediate goods.

It is costly to trade producer goods and services across national borders. We assume (symmetric) transport costs of the iceberg type. Of one unit shipped from, say, country A to country B, only k units $(0 < k < 1)$ arrive and $(1-k)$ units vanish.[14] The iceberg type formulation leaves the elasticity of demand unchanged and attributes resources costs for the transport sector to the production location. With the introduction of transport costs, the local availability of producer goods and services matters. In regional economics this is often mentioned as a crucial determinant for regional development (cf. Fujita (1990) and Rivera-Batiz (1988)).[15] We borrow this basic idea and introduce it in our dynamic general equilibrium framework.

[14] Since we allow for transport costs in the intermediate goods sector we need to distinguish between variables which relate to the production side and those which denote prices and quantities Y-producers have to pay and use in production. We write the latter variables with a tilde which will not appear at the former.

[15] This hypothesis is discussed in Hansen (1990). See for empirical tests of the importance of local asset-sharing von Hagen/Hammond (1994).

In a broader interpretation, costs for shipping goods across borders can also be understood as transaction costs of technological adaption. It is easier to implement technologically advanced products if production takes place locally. This depicts the advantage of close contact with engineers, scientists and skilled workers of firms prdoducing final and intermediate goods. Suppose, for instance, that problems arise in producing with a specific differentiated input. Then, it is less costly to solve the problem if the firm producing intermediate goods is located in the same geographical area as when the two firms are geographically far apart. One could think of production stillstands due to the time it takes for engineers to travel between the two locations, the travel costs etc.. With producer services, these costs of distance are even more obvious and pronounced.

Let $p_x^{i,j}$ and $x^{i,j}$ denote the producer price and the output of an intermediate product produced in country j and used in country i. We derive the following relationship between between user and producer prices

$$\tilde{p}_x^{i,j} = \begin{cases} p_x^{i,j} & \text{if} \quad i = j \\ p_x^{i,j}/k & \text{if} \quad i \neq j \end{cases} \tag{4.12}$$

as well as between output and input levels[16]

$$\tilde{x}^{i,j} = \begin{cases} x^{i,j} & \text{if} \quad i = j \\ x^{i,j}k & \text{if} \quad i \neq j. \end{cases} \tag{4.13}$$

Intermediate goods producers in i maximize their monopolistic profits from selling their product of variety v in both markets:

$$G^i(v) = (p_x^i - c_x^i)(x^A(v) + x^B(v)), \tag{4.14}$$

with $c_x^i = a_x w_H$ (hence, $c_x^A = c_x^B$) and the total demand for each variety $x^A(v) + x^B(v)$ being derived from cost-minimizing factor demand of Y-producers. Applying Shephard's Lemma to (4.10) and taking (4.3) into account yields:

$$x_i^A(v) + x_i^B(v) = \frac{(1-\alpha-\beta)(p_x^i)^{-\epsilon}}{\int_0^n (\tilde{p}_x^{i,j}(v'))^{1-\epsilon} dv'} p_Y Y^i + \frac{(1-\alpha-\beta)(p_x^i)^{-\epsilon} k^{\epsilon-1}}{\int_0^n (\tilde{p}_x^{i,j}(v'))^{1-\epsilon} dv'} p_Y Y^j. \tag{4.15}$$

[16] Variables with a single superscript refer to the location of production (with a variable without a tilde) and to the location of consumption (with a variable with a tilde), respectively.

Maximizing (4.14) with respect to p_x^i and taking (4.15) into account yields the optimal producer price:

$$p_x^{i,j}(v) = p_x^{i,i} = p_x^i = \frac{c_x}{\gamma}. \tag{4.16}$$

Optimal producer prices are the same irrespective of whether the respective variety is used domestically or exported. Intermediate goods producers charge a constant mark-up over costs. As a consequence of this mark-up pricing, instantaneous profits arise in the intermediate goods sector. With free entry in the R&D sector, these pure static profits are, in a dynamic sense, arbitraged away. Entry takes place as long as the costs of innovation in country i, $c_n^i = w_H/n$, are smaller than the expected gain of successful innovators, P^i. In equilibrium with positive innovative activities, $c_n^i = P^i$. The "price" an innovator receives from R&D at time t is just equal to the discounted flow of instantaneous profits:

$$P^i(t) = \int_0^n e^{-r(\tau-t)} G^i(\tau) d\tau. \tag{4.17}$$

The value of a firm which has acquired a new blueprint at time t is $P^i(t)$. This implies that the firm's value is determined by its fundamentals. This implicitly assumes the absence of real asset bubbles. Speculative asset bubbles, however, can never arise in our framework, in which infinitively living households maximize their utility function by taking their intertemporal budget constraint into account (cf. Blanchard/Fischer (1989) and the appendix to this chapter).

Differentiating (4.12) with respect to time gives us a no-abitrage condition which has to hold at every moment in time in order to ensure capital-market equilibrium:

$$\frac{G^i}{P^i} + \frac{\dot{P}^i}{P^i} = r = \rho. \tag{4.18}$$

In order to close the basic set-up we need to state the factor-market clearing conditions for skilled as well as unskilled labor, and the international market-clearing conditions for final goods. The latter can by expressed with eqs. (4.3) and (4.4) simply by

$$p_Y(Y^A + Y^B) = \sigma, \tag{4.19}$$
$$p_Z(Z^A + Z^B) = 1 - \sigma. \tag{4.20}$$

The factor-market clearing condition requires that the national demand for unskilled labor and the economywide demand for skilled labor of the respective industries exhaust the fixed factor supply:

$$\bar{L}^i = L_Z^i + L_Y^i \tag{4.21}$$

and

$$\bar{H} = \sum_i (H_Z^i + H_Y^i + H_x^i + H_n^i), \tag{4.22}$$

with H_x^i denoting total employment in the intermediate goods sector in country i.

Before we proceed, let us restate the two basic mechanisms in our approach. The first one, driving the growth process, is based on knowledge spillovers. These spillovers of knowledge continuously decrease the costs of innovation, thereby offsetting the fall of profits in the course of the permanent increase in the number of intermediate goods (see (4.15) and (4.18)). In contrast to Solow growth models, this prevents the rate of return of accumulation from falling below the rate of time preference. The profit rate rather approaches a constant in the steady-state. Permanent innovation is profitable as long as the factor endowment of the economy is large enough to support a rate of return which is larger than the cost of capital.

The second mechanism, discussed in more detail in the next subsections, is the interaction of agglomeration advantages and disadvantages which govern the location of industry and of mobile workers in the two countries. The agglomeration advantage consists of the combination of economies of scale at the firm level and transport costs. The agglomeration disadvantage is the fixed supply of an immobile factor.

For both mechanisms, increasing returns to scale are crucial. It allows firms to recover their initial R&D costs and forces them to produce in a single plant. In this regard we diverge completely from traditional approaches of regional growth (cf. e.g. Borts/Stein (1964), Siebert (1969), and Richardson (1978)).

4.3 Short-Run Equilibrium

In this section we look at the short-run equilibrium for a given number of known blueprints of intermediate goods in each country. The number of locally produced differentiated inputs in the two countries, n^A and n^B, is constant. Consequently, the number of intermediate goods and services in country A relative to those in country B, $\mu := n^A/n^B$ is constant as well. In the next section we investigate the evolution of μ over time and determine the properties of the long-run equilibrium.

In the short-run equilibrium factor and goods markets clear. We distinguish between two cases with respect to the relative number of intermediate goods, μ. Either, $\mu = 1$ or $\mu \neq 1$. The latter case can be divided in two subcases with $\mu > 1$ and $\mu < 1$ which are, however, symmetric.

In order to determine the countries' specialization patterns in the short-run equilibrium, as well as the relative wage rates for unskilled immobile workers, we have to take into account the cost situation in the final goods production of each country. Note that the factor costs of the mobile factor are the same in either country. The traditional good is produced in both countries if, and only if,

$$\omega := \frac{w_L^A}{w_L^B} = 1. \tag{4.23}$$

With $\omega > 1$ ($\omega < 1$), this footless industry is located entirely in country B (A). For a given μ the industrial final good is produced in both countries if $c_Y^A = c_Y^B$. With (4.10), (4.12), and (4.16), this holds if, and only if,

$$\omega = \left(\frac{\mu + k^{\epsilon-1}}{\mu k^{\epsilon-1} + 1}\right)^{\theta} := \Psi^{\theta}, \tag{4.24}$$

with $\theta := (1 - \alpha - \beta)(1 - \gamma)/(\gamma\alpha) > 0$. In the presence of transport costs for producer goods and services, it is more attractive for Y-producers to locate in the country with the larger number of locally produced inputs. The other country can compensate for this disadvantage only by a lower wage rate in order to stay competitive in this industry. This reflects the lower productivity of unskilled labor in Y-production. Now, we can analyze the properties of the short-run equilibrium.

With (4.23) and (4.24) we can establish

Proposition 4.3.1 *Suppose that the relative number of locally produced goods in the two countries is equal. Hence, in the short-run equilibrium $\omega = 1$.*

Proof: Suppose $\omega \neq 1$. Thus, the two final goods are produced in the low-wage country only (see (4.23) and (4.24)), leaving unskilled labor in the other country unemployed. This does not constitute a short-run equilibrium.
Q.e.d.

With $\mu = 1$, neither country has any comparative advantage. The countries' specialization patterns are indeterminate.

Furthermore, we find

Lemma 4.3.1 *The country with a larger number of locally produced intermediate goods n^i has a wage rate w_L^i for unskilled workers which is at least as large as the respective wage rate in the other country.*

Proof: Suppose $\mu > 1$. Then $\omega < 1$ implies $L_Y^B = L_Z^B = 0$ (see (4.23) and (4.24)). This, however, violates the factor-market clearing condition in country B (cf. (4.21)). The case $\mu < 1$ is symmetric. Q.e.d.
In the following we impose

Assumption 4.1 $1 < \xi := \alpha\sigma/(\delta(1-\sigma) < \infty$.

This assumption states that the industrial final goods sector is – compared to the traditional final goods sector – large enough that the former sector's demand for unskilled labor is larger than that of the traditional sector. This assumption excludes the possibility that, with equal wages ($\omega = 1$), the industrial final good is exclusively produced in the country with a larger number of inputs. This assumption gives us dynamics which reveal the interaction of agglomeration advantages and disadvantages over time.[17] In footnotes we handle situations in which assumption 4.1 fails to hold.[18]

We establish

Proposition 4.3.2 *Given assumption 4.1, $\mu > 1$ ($\mu < 1$) implies $\omega > 1$ ($\omega < 1$). The country with the larger number of locally produced goods specializes completely in the industrial sector. The traditional final good is exclusively produced in the low-wage country.*

Proof: i.) Suppose $\mu > 1$ and $\omega = 1$. Then $p_Y^A < p_Y^B$ and $p_Z^A = p_Z^B$ (see (4.23) and (4.24)), implying together with Shephards Lemmas used in the unit cost functions of the final-goods sectors $\bar{L}^A = \frac{\sigma\alpha}{w_L} + \frac{s_Z^A\delta(1-\sigma)}{w_L}$ and $\bar{L}^B = \frac{(1-s_Z^A)\delta(1-\sigma)}{w_L}$ with $s_Z^A = Z^A/(Z^A + Z^B)$ being the market share of country A in Z-production. Since $\bar{L}^A = \bar{L}^B$ and assumption 4.1 holds, both factor-market clearing conditions cannot hold simultaneously. Hence, with $\mu > 1$, $\omega = 1$ does not represent a short-run equilibrium. The case of $\mu < 1$ is symmetric. With $\omega \neq 1$, the low-wage country is the exclusive producer of Z. Q.e.d.

[17] With $\xi \leq 1$, the country with an initial advantage (country i) will become the technological leader (s_Y^i) and will remain so forever. Innovation takes place in this country only. Transitional dynamics are absent and factor-price equalization prevails.

[18] For a detailed discussion, see Walz (1996c).

For the case of $\mu \neq 1$ we can derive the market share of the two countries in the short-run equilibrium. Since the cases $\mu > 1$ and $\mu < 1$ are symmetric, we choose to investigate only the former case in the following. With $\mu > 1$, $s_Z^A = 0$ ($s_Z^B = 1$) (see proposition 4.3.2). Hence, solving the two factor market clearing conditions for unskilled labor yields

$$s_Y^A = \frac{\xi + 1}{\xi(\Psi^{-\theta} + 1)} \tag{4.25}$$

$$s_Y^B = \frac{\xi\Psi^{-\theta} - 1}{\xi(1 + \Psi^{-\theta})}. \tag{4.26}$$

The country with an advantage with respect to the number of locally produced inputs has a larger market share in Y-production ($s_Y^A > s_Y^B$).

Against the background of the short-run equilibrium, we can now analyze the evolution of μ over time.

4.4 The Steady-State

In this section we investigate the countries' specialization, trade and growth patterns in the long-run. A decisive question in this respect is, in which country the development and production of new intermediate products takes place.

The steady-state equilibrium is defined such that all nominal variables grow at a constant rate. Since we chose $E = 1$, this requires that wages are constant over time in the long-run equilibrium. This can best be seen by rewriting the factor-market clearing conditions. With the help of Shephard's Lemma applied to (4.10) and (4.11) and making use of (4.9), (4.12), (4.13), as well as of (4.14), we arrive at:

$$\bar{L}^i = \frac{\alpha\sigma s_Y^i}{w_L^i} + \frac{(1-\alpha)\delta s_Z^i}{w_L^i} \tag{4.27}$$

and

$$\bar{H} = \frac{\Delta}{w_H} + g, \tag{4.28}$$

with $\Delta = \beta\sigma + \sigma(1-\alpha-\beta)\gamma + (1-\delta)(1-\sigma)$. Constant wage rates imply that the intersectoral resource allocation does not change over time.

We can distinguish between two types of steady-state equilibria: one in which innovation takes place only in one country, and one in which innovative activities are undertaken in both countries. We refer to the first as a *core-periphery pattern* and call the second one an *interior solution*. Let us first (and mainly) look at the latter.

Potential innovators decide on their location on the basis of the expected relative profitability in the two countries. Note that with perfect mobility of skilled workers and equal R&D productivity in both countries, innovators in both countries face identical R&D costs.

With free entry in the R&D sector and positive overall innovative activities (later we impose a condition for this to hold), $P^i = c_n^i = w_H/n$. This implies $\frac{\dot{P}^i}{P^i} = \frac{\dot{w}_H}{w_H} - g$, with $g = \frac{\dot{n}}{n}$ denoting the overall innovation rate. In a long-run equilibrium with innovation taking place in both countries, the relative number of intermediate goods produced in A compared to B, μ, has to be constant. This implies that the rate of innovation has to be the same in both countries ($\frac{\dot{n}^A}{n^A} := g^A = g^B := \frac{\dot{n}^B}{n^B} = g$).

A look at (4.18) reveals that potential innovators will choose to locate in both countries in the long-run if, and only if, $G^A = G^B$. There are three potential candidates for an interior solution. The first candidate is the case with an equal number of intermediate producers in both countries ($\mu^* = 1$) and equal market shares of the countries in the production of final goods ($s_Y^A = s_Y^B = s_Z^A = s_Z^B = 0.5$). This constellation obeys all short-run equilibrium conditions and allows for equal profits in intermediate goods production in either country. It constitutes a symmetric long-run equilibrium. In addition to this symmetric candidate, asymmetric candidates for a long-run equilibrium with $\mu^* > 1$ and $\mu^* < 1$ exist. Since both asymmetric cases are symmetric to each other, in the following we analyze only the $\mu > 1$ case explicitly.

Using (4.15) and (4.16) in (4.14) enables us to write the profit differential as:

$$G^A - G^B = \frac{(1-\alpha-\beta)(1-\gamma)\sigma}{n^B + n^A k^{\epsilon-1}} \left[s_Y^A \Psi^{-1} - s_Y^B \right]. \tag{4.29}$$

With $\mu > 1$, $\omega > 1$ and $s_Z^B = 1$ (see Proposition 4.3.2). Hence, using (4.25), (4.26) and (4.15) in (4.14) we find for (4.29):

$$G^A - G^B = \Xi(1 + \xi(1 - \Psi^\eta) + \Psi), \tag{4.30}$$

with $\Xi := \frac{(1-\alpha-\beta)(1-\gamma)\sigma(1-k^{\epsilon-1})}{(n^B + n^A k^{\epsilon-1})\xi\Psi(1+\Psi^\theta)}$ and $\eta =: 1-\theta$.

We prove in the appendix:

Proposition 4.4.1 *The symmetric steady-state equilibrium (with $\mu = 1$) is unstable. A necessary condition for the existence of an interior asymmetric equilibrium is $\eta > 0$. With $\eta > 0$, a (locally) stable interior solution exists if* $\xi > \frac{k^{1-\epsilon}+1}{k^{(1-\epsilon)\eta}-1}$.

The intuition behind the condition $\eta > 0$ is the following. There are two basic forces governing the location of intermediate goods production.

On the one hand, in the presence of transport costs, intermediate goods production is the more profitable, the larger the local demand for intermediate products, i.e. the larger the local production of industrial final goods. Final goods producers, in turn, have an incentive to locate near their suppliers of inputs in order to save transport costs. This in turn attracts new intermediate goods producers. In order to illustrate this demand effect, which is reflected in s_Y^A and s_Y^B in (4.29), we suppose that μ is increasing. To isolate the demand effect, we hold Ψ constant. Let us start start from a position with equal profitability of research in both countries, i.e., $G^A = G^B$. The increase in μ attracts more final-goods producers into country A. The market share of country A in Y-production, s_Y^A, increases, whereas s_Y^B decreases (see (4.25) and (4.26)). The larger final-goods market in A makes, in turn, intermediate-goods production in A relatively more profitable (see (4.29)). New innovators locate in country A. Hence, we get a circular causation argument which calls for a complete concentration of the industrial sector and especially of producer goods and services in one country. This effect displays the centripetal or agglomerative force in our model.

On the other hand, however, intermediate goods producers would like to produce in the country with little competition rather than in the country with fierce competition in prices. Competition is the lower, the smaller the number of locally produced intermediate goods and services. This effect is depicted by the factor Ψ^{-1} in (4.29). If only a small number of intermediate goods and services are produced domestically, a large share has to be imported at a high sales prices due to transport costs (see (4.12) together with (4.16)). This is the centrifugal force or agglomeration disadvantage in our approach calling for a dispersed location of intermediate goods.

Whenever the first force, the demand effect, dominates, a core-periphery pattern emerges. If, however, the second force, the competition effect, is strong enough to compensate the demand effect for some μ, a stable interior solution (intermediate goods are produced in both countries) arises. With

$\eta < 0$, the demand effect is stronger than the competition effect.

We establish

Corollary 4.1 *With $\eta < 0$, an asymmetric interior solution does not exist. Intermediate goods production becomes completely concentrated in one country.*

Let us now address the growth process in the overall economy. With permanent innovation, the growth process becomes visible through permanent decreases in the industrial final good's price. The growth rate of utility is proportional to the innovation rate g. With (4.1), (4.3), (4.4) and (4.18), we get $\hat{V} = g\sigma(1-\alpha-\beta)(1-\gamma)/\gamma$, the growth rate of instantaneous utility. The growth rate of output and utility is proportional to the innovation rate.

Note that the output growth rates of the two countries are different even in the interior solution case, due to the complete concentration of traditional good production in one country. The lagging country has a lower output growth rate than the unionwide average. Naturally, the other country's output growth rate is higher than the unionwide average. Even in a core-periphery situation, the output growth rate of the periphery is positive as long as it produces the industrial good. In this case, the periphery benefits via trade from the permanent development of new inputs in the center, leading to productivity increases in the periphery.

It is important to note that, irrespective of the geographical location of innovation and the production of producer goods and services, *consumers* in both countries benefit to the same extent from the growth process. Since prices are also internationally identical, consumers are indifferent as to whether e.g. the home country is the center region or the foreign country. Mobile households are – by definition – also indifferent with respect to their income situation. Hence, they experience the same utility level in both regions. This is, however, not at all true for the immobile households. They prefer to live in the center country, experiencing a higher wage rate than they would living in the periphery. That is, there exists a large incentive for political lobbying to influence the market outcome and the respective specialization pattern by means of government intervention.

Finally, we are now able to derive the overall innovation rate. Using (4.3), (4.14)-(4.16) (4.28), and (4.30) in (4.18) gives us, after some calculations:

$$g = \frac{\bar{H}\Phi - \rho\Delta}{\Phi + \Delta}, \tag{4.31}$$

with $\Phi = (1-\alpha-\beta)(1-\gamma)\sigma$.

That is, if the endowment with skilled workers (used in the R&D sector) is sufficiently large compared to the rate of time preference (the price households, claim for abstaining from consumption), there is ongoing product development. For the rest of our study we assume that the countries' factor endowments are large enough to support a positive steady-state growth and innovation rate. For this, $\bar{H} > \rho\Delta/\Phi$ has to hold.

4.5 The Role of Physical Capital Accumulation

In the traditional neoclassical growth model (cf. Solow (1956) and Cass (1965)) as well as in traditional regional growth theory (cf. Borts/Stein (1964), Richardson (1973)), the accumulation of physical capital plays a decisive role. We have so far neglected physical capital completely in our model of regional growth.

We followed the notion that the (permanent) accumulation of knowledge is possible, whereas the same is not true with respect to the accumulation of physical capital (cf. Romer (1992)). The pure accumulation of physical capital implies a pile-up of physical machines which is obviously limited. One could argue that the accumulation of physical capital is possible since new and more costly machinery is more productive without being "larger" in a physical sense. This, however, implicitly assumes the existence of technological change, i.e. of knowledge accumulation embodied in physical capital.

"Ordinary" physical capital accumulation takes place under decreasing returns-to-scale, the standard assumption of traditional growth theory. In the absence of knowledge accumulation, the rate of return on physical capital accumulation decreases with the stock of physical capital. After having reached the subjective rate of time preference (the necessary reward households demand in order to abstain from consumption), capital accumulation and growth ceases. Without technological progress, the rate of per capita growth is zero in the steady-state. Hence, in order to derive an endogenous growth path, a growth engine other than from physical capital accumulation is required.

Adding physical capital accumulation to our approach outlined in the previous subsections is, however, a straightforward exercise. In this subsection we introduce physical capital. We argue that this does not change our qualitative results. It simply adds more realism to our model of regional growth. However, it increases the computational complexity of the model significantly without yielding interesting additional insights. For that reason we choose to rely for the rest of the study on the model without physical capital.

We basically adopt the same demand structure of the economy as in section 4.2. By introducing physical capital, we extend the range of assets households can purchase. Households can invest in firms buying machinery which, in turn, is used in the production process. Equivalently, households can buy shares of innovating firms. In the absence of aggregate uncertainty, they are indifferent between holding shares of innovative firms and of firms investing in physical capital if the returns of the two assets are equal.

We assume that physical capital (K) is used in the traditonal goods sector, as well as in the production process of industrial final goods and differentiated intermediate goods. We express the production function for these three industries as:

$$Z = (L_Z^i)^{\iota}(K_Z^i)^{1-\iota} \quad 0 < \iota < 1 \tag{4.32}$$

and

$$Y^i = (L_Y^i)^{\alpha}(K_Y^i)^{\beta}\left(\int_0^n \tilde{x}^i(v)^{\gamma} dv\right)^{\frac{1-\alpha-\beta}{\gamma}} \quad 0 < \alpha, \beta, \gamma < 1, \tag{4.33}$$

as well as

$$x^i = (H_x^i)^{\nu}(K_x^i)^{1-\nu} \quad 0 < \nu < 1, \tag{4.34}$$

with K_Z, K_Y, K_x denoting the input of physical capital in the respective sectors. The accumulation equation of knowledge is given by (4.9).

Physical capital is internationally mobile. Consequently, the rental rate of physical capital r^K is the same in either country. Investors in physical capital purchase industrial final goods and transform them one-to-one into machinery. This implicitly allows for technological change embodied in machinery. Taking the goods-market clearing condition into account, we can write the accumulation equation of physical capital

$$\begin{aligned} \dot{K} &= Y - C_Y \\ &= Y - \tfrac{(1-\sigma)}{p_Y}. \end{aligned} \tag{4.35}$$

This is reminiscent of the accumulation equation in the traditional growth model. The output function (Y) has diminishing returns with respect to physical capital (see (4.33)). The decisive difference, however, is the fact that ongoing knowledge accumulation permanently increases the productivity of Y-production and, hence, of new machinery. This offsets the decrease in the rate of return on physical capital due to diminishing returns. As we will see in a moment, this allows for the permanent accumulation of physical capital.

The additional value to a firm purchasing an additional unit of physical capital is equal to the discounted sum of the rent of this additional unit:

$$P_K(t) = \int_t^{\infty} e^{-r(\tau-t)} r^K(\tau) d\tau. \tag{4.36}$$

With free entry, $P_K = p_Y$ holds. Differentiating (4.36) with respect to time and using the free entry condition yields the free-entry, no-arbitrage condition for firms investing in physical capital:

$$\frac{r^K}{p_Y} - \frac{\dot{p}_Y}{p_Y} = r = \rho. \tag{4.37}$$

Since capital is freely traded, all results with respect to location choices of firms and households, as well as the determinants of these decisions remain the same as in section 4.2. Let us now take a closer look at the aggregate growth process. With the help of the production functions, we can derive factor-market clearing conditions from the cost-minimizing behavior of firms. Cost-minimizing input demand of firms yields together with (4.9), (4.31) and (4.33)

$$K = \frac{(1-\iota)(1-\sigma) + (\beta + (1-\nu)p_Y Y)}{r^K}, \tag{4.38}$$

$$\bar{H} = \frac{(1-\alpha-\beta)\nu p_Y Y}{w_H} + g. \tag{4.39}$$

Furthermore, taking (4.29) into account provides the steady-state no-arbitrage condition for innovators:

$$\frac{\Phi p_Y Y}{w_H} - g = \rho. \tag{4.40}$$

By combining (4.39) and (4.40), we can derive the steady-state innovation rate:

$$g = \frac{\Phi \bar{H} - \bar{\Delta}\rho}{\bar{\Delta} + \Phi}, \tag{4.41}$$

with $\bar{\Delta} = (1-\alpha-\beta)\nu\sigma$. Comparing this equation to (4.31) reveals that the introduction of physical capital changed neither the determinants of regional specialization patterns nor the pattern of the aggregate growth process.

What additional insights do we gain from introducing physical capital? There are basically two important lessons which can be drawn from this exercise. *First*, in contrast to traditional growth approaches, physical capital will be accumulated at a positive rate in the steady-state. This can be seen as follows. In the steady-state, the wage rate for human capital has to be constant since otherwise the total value of innovating firms would grow either without bound, thus violating the households' transversality condition, or shrink to zero, thereby violating agents expectations about a positive growth path (see Grossman/Helpman (1991a)). Constant intersectoral allocation in the steady-state requires $p_Y Y$ to be constant as well (see (4.38)).

With (4.35), we find that the steady-state capital-output ratio has to be constant as well. Note that we get from (4.32) and (4.33)

$$p_Y^i = C(w_L^i)^\alpha (r^K)^\beta \left(\int_0^n (\tilde{p}_x^{1-\epsilon} \right)^{\frac{1-\alpha-\beta}{1-\epsilon}})$$

and

$$p_x^i = D(w_H)^\iota (r^K)^{1-\iota}.$$

In the steady-state, $\hat{r}^K = \hat{p}_Y$ (see (4.37)). All this together with (4.4) implies $g^K := \frac{\dot{K}}{K} = \frac{\dot{Y}}{Y} = g\theta\beta$. The permanent growth process initiated by the accumulation of knowledge carries over to the accumulation of physical capital. That is, it suffices for only one accumulation equation to exhibit constant returns with respect to the accumulable factor.[19]

The *second* additional result is closely related to the first one. Since physical capital is used in traditional goods production, the permanent productivity increases caused by the permanent development of new intermediate goods "spill over" to the traditional goods sector. These permanent productivity increases are transmitted via the higher productivity of new machinery (embodied technological progress). The lower price of new machinery leads to a decrease in the rental rate of physical capital r^K. The price of the traditional good decreases at the rate $(1-\iota)g^K$.

In order to keep the computational complexity of the model at the simplest possible level, for the rest of our study we return to our basic model without physical capital.

[19] This general insight was pointed out and derived rigorously for the first time in Rebelo (1990).

4.6 Appendix

Appendix 1: Instability of Symmetric Equilibrium

We start with $\mu = 1$ and $s_Y^A = s_Y^B = s_Z^A = s_Z^B = 0$ and hence $G^A = G^B$. Now suppose a small deviation from this equilibrium to $\mu_1 = 1 + \varepsilon$ with ε being a very small but positive number. Along the path towards the symmetric equilbrium, $G^A > G^B$ and hence $P^A > P^B$. Innovation occurs only in country A. The symmetric equilibrium can not be reached anymore after a disturbance.

Appendix 2: Existence and Uniqueness of Interior Solutions

In an asymmetric interior solution,

$$M := 1 + \xi(1 - \Psi^{\eta}) + \Psi = 0 \tag{A.4.1}$$

has to be fulfilled. We have to distinguish between two cases: i.) $\eta < 0$ and ii.) $\eta > 0$.

ad i.) With $\eta < 0$ and $\mu > 1$, $\Psi^{\eta} < 1$. M is always positive. An interior solution does not exist. That is, $\eta > 0$ is a necessary condition for the existence of an interior solution.

With $\eta > 0$, M is positive for μ slightly larger than 1. For $\mu > 1$, M reaches an extremum, $\bar{\mu}$, being defined implicitly by $M^{'} = \dfrac{\partial M}{\partial \mu} = \Psi^{'}(-\xi\eta\Psi^{-\theta} + 1) = 0$ with $\Psi^{'} = \frac{\partial \Psi}{\partial \mu} := \frac{(1-k^{2(\epsilon-1)})}{(\mu k^{\epsilon-1}+1)^2} > 0$. Since $\frac{\partial^2 M(\bar{\mu})}{(\partial \mu)^2} = \left((\Psi^{'})^2(\theta\xi\eta\Psi^{-(1+\theta)}\right) > 0$, $\bar{\mu}$, if it exists, is a minimum. Then, M has a negative slope for $1 < \mu < \bar{\mu}$ and it slopes upward for $\mu > \bar{\mu}$. An interior equilibrium exists if μ^* exists with $M(\mu^*) = 0$.

There may be two possible equilibria if M cuts the μ-axes twice. At the second equilibrium with $\mu > 1$, μ_2 $(1 < \mu_1 < \bar{\mu} < \mu_2)$, which will be discussed below, the M-function has a positive slope. A sufficient condition for the existence and a necessary condition for the uniqueness of an interior equilibrium with $\mu > 1$ is $M(\mu = \infty) < 0$, i.e. $\xi > \dfrac{k^{1-\epsilon} + 1}{k^{(1-\epsilon)\eta} - 1}$.

Appendix 3: Stability of Asymmetric Interior Solution

In order to analyze the stability of an interior solution with $\eta > 0$, we use the phase diagram in Figure 4.1. which displays the equilibrium dynamics of the economy. We explicitly analyze the case of $\mu^* > 1$ only and concentrate on the transition towards the equilibrium for $\mu < \mu^*$. The case of $\mu^* < 1$ as well as the situation for $\mu > \mu^*$ is symmetric. With the no-arbitrage condition (4.18) in the two countries, we find that $\dot{\mu} > (<)0$ for $\mu < (>)\mu^*$. For $\mu < (>)\mu^*$, innovation takes place in country A (B) only. For $\mu = \mu^*$, $(G^A - G^B = 0)$, $g^A = g^B$ implies $\dot{\mu} = 0$. Let us define $N^A = nP_A$, the total value of firms if all firms are valued as in country A. Hence, $\dot{N}^A/N^A = g + \dot{P}_A/P_A$. Using (4.12)-(4.16) in (4.18) yields, together with (4.28) and $\dot{n}^B = 0$, for the case $1 < \mu < \mu^*$

$$\dot{N}^A = N^A(\bar{H} + \rho) - L(\mu), \tag{A.4.2}$$

with $L = \Delta + \frac{(1-\alpha-\beta)(1-\gamma)\sigma}{\xi(1+\Psi^\theta)}\left[\frac{\Psi^\theta(\mu+1)(1+\xi)}{\mu + k^{\epsilon-1}} + \frac{(\xi - \Psi^\theta)k^{\epsilon-1}(\mu+1)}{1+\mu k^{\epsilon-1}}\right]$.

We only look at the case to the left of μ_1^* $(\mu < \mu_1^*)$ and note that the case to the right is symmetric. Without loss of generality of the stability property, we have drawn the $\dot{w}_H = 0$-line with a negative slope in $\mu - N^A$-space. With (4.31), $\dot{\mu} = 0$ is a vertical line. The arrows indicate the direction of movement of the economy.

Figure 4.1 reveals that the economy converges on a unique (saddle) path (TF) towards the equilibrium point F. All other trajectories can be ruled out for the equilibrium dynamics. They lead either to an ever-decreasing N^A and or to an ever-increasing N^A with an infinite value of innovating firms. The first case violates agents is asssociated with unfulfilled expectations (the value of firms with strictly positive profits declines to zero), and the second case violates the intertemporal budget constraint (or equivalently the transversality condition of the consumers' maximization problem). Hence, TT displays the unique trajectory leading to the equilibrium. Starting from any initial point, agents jump onto the saddle path.

Let us briefly consider the second possible interior equilibrium. With $\mu > (<)\mu_2^*$, $\dot{\mu} > (<)0$. That is, only a small deviation away from the equilibrium, i.e. $\mu > (<)\mu_2^*$ leads to innovation taking place only in country A (B). μ_2^* can never be reached after a small pertubation. It is an unstable equilibrium.

Figure 4.1: The equilibrium dynamics

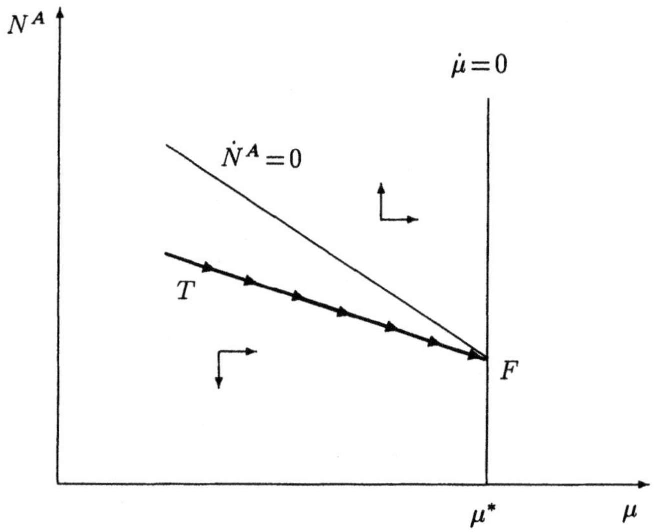

Appendix 4: Stability of a Corner Solution

In the following we derive the saddle path property of the corner solution. We do this for the case of $g^B = 0$. The situation where innovation only takes place in country B is symmetric. Let $z = n^A/n$ be the share of intermediate goods in country A. In the long-run equilibrium, $\mu^* = \infty$ and $z^* = 1$. Differentiating z with respect to time yields:

$$\frac{\dot{z}}{z} = (1 - z)g^A. \tag{A.4.3}$$

With the help of (4.28) we can replace g^A in (A.4.4):

$$\dot{z} = (1 - z)(H - \frac{\Delta}{N^A}). \tag{A.4.4}$$

Taking $\mu = z/(1 - z)$ in (A.4.4) into account gives us, together with (A.4.5), two differential equations in $z - N^A$ dimension. Linearizing these two differential equations and evaluating them at the equilibrium point (z^*, N^{A*}), we find that the determinant of the Jacobian matrix is negative. That is, the corner solution is approached on a unique trajectory (see Lorenz (1989)). We could also use the same graphical argument as for the interior solution.

Appendix 5: Local Technological Spillovers

In the regional economics literature, local technological spillovers are considered to be one of the main reasons for spatial concentration of production. We briefly show that, in our basic model, purely local technological spillovers represent an initial agglomerative force which excludes the possibility of any stable interior solution.

With local knowledge spillovers, the R&D functions are expressed by:

$$\dot{n}^i = H_n^i n^i, \qquad \text{(A.4.5)}$$

whereby local knowledge is equated with the number of locally known blueprints. Successful R&D exclusively benefits future researchers in the same country. Hence, R&D-costs are equal to $c_n^i = \frac{w_H}{n^i}$. Inserting these costs into the no-arbitrage conditions reveals that a steady-state with a constant μ, requiring $g^A = g^B$ calls for

$$(\mu + \xi(\mu - \Psi^\eta) + \Psi) = 0. \qquad \text{(A.4.6)}$$

Since $\mu > \Psi^\eta$, this equation can never be fulfilled. An asymmetric interior solution does not exist. The symmetric equilibrium is unstable in this case as well.

Adding local technological spillovers to the advantage of the local availability of differentiated inputs always leads always to a core-periphery pattern.

4.7 Summary

In this section we developed a dynamic general equilibrium model of economic geography by combining an endogenous growth approach with elements of regional economics. The resulting model could be termed an endogenous regional growth approach. The model depicts a wide variety of regional specialization and growth patterns. A core-periphery pattern with innovation concentrated in one country only, as well as an interior solution with active innovation sectors in both countries, may emerge. Common to all settings is the existence of multiple equilibria. The initial advantage of a country is reinforced over time.[20] Thereby, the model provides a rigorous formalization of

[20] See Walz (1996c) for a framework in which asymmetric factor endowments of regions can give rise to the uniqueness of the long-run equilibrium.

the idea of cumulative causation often stressed in regional economics.[21] The interaction of agglomeration advantages (local availability of differentiated inputs) and agglomeration disadvantages (given supply of immobile factor of production) is decisive for regional growth and the evolution of specialization patterns. The relative strength of these forces determine whether an interior solution or a core-periphery pattern results.

The theoretical framework is based on the idea that technological change is the driving force behind the growth process. This takes into account the results of growth accounting exercises discussed in subsection 2.2. In the absence of technological change accumulation of physical capital runs into diminishing returns and hence, leads to a falling rate of profits. Investment in physical capital ceases in the long run. Only permanent technological improvements keep the rate of profit on investments in physical capital from falling. The innovation rate governs the rate at which physical capital is accumulated. It suffices to look at the implications of regional integration on the rate of technological change.

The analysis of local technological spillovers reveals very strong agglomerative forces leading always to a core-periphery pattern. This extreme feature of local technological spillovers together with the apparent difficulty to measure this effects empirically (see section 2.2) are the justification for concentrating on the local availability of differentiated inputs as the main centripetal force in our framework.

Our framework has two decisive advantages in comparison to traditional regional growth theory and static approaches of economic geography. First, it provides for an endogenous determination of regional innovation and growth processes, as well as of the overall growth rate. This opens the possibility of investigating the influence of policy measures (here: regional integration measures) on the countries' growth patterns and the unionwide growth rate. Secondly, rather than on relying on ad-hoc dynamics of static analysis (cf. e.g. Krugman (1992)), we derive the evolution of the economy on the basis of rational, maximizing and forward-looking agents. This is considered to be a decisive advantage (cf. Lucas (1987)). In addition, this model allows for a coherent analysis of the effects of regional integration on specialization and trade patterns in a setting which takes location and migration decisions of firms and workers explicitly into account. Hence, we are able to overcome

[21] Matsuyama (1995) provides an extensive survey of models predicting cumulative processes as well as the basic mechanism behind them.

the two major shortcomings of the existing literature on regional integration: the neglect of growth rate effects, as well as of aspects of economic geography.

Integration policies alter the determinants of location and migration decisions, as well as the incentives to invest in the accumulation of factors of production. Analyzing the channels by which different integration steps and measures change these decisions of private agents is the objective of the remaining parts of the study.

Chapter 5

Deeper Regional Integration

Deeper regional integration is associated with the reduction of barriers to trade and factor flows. Barriers to trade are reduced between the members of the integration bloc and might be altered vis-à-vis the rest of the world. At more advanced stages (especially in a common market or an economic union), regional integration is accompanied by policies jointly pursued by the member states in the integration bloc. With respect to trade liberalization, a wide variety of measures are adopted in the course of integration. Trade liberalization is not at all limited to tariff reductions. In later stages of integration, the removal of non-tariff barriers comes to the fore. Technical, administrative, safety, and health regulations, as well as discriminatory national procurement policies are considered to be far more important than tariffs (cf. e.g. Commission (1988b)). The creation of the European Common Market (Europe 1992) was in most respects equivalent to the reduction of such non-tariff impediments to inner-community trade. In the following sections as well as in chapter 6, we look at trade liberalization via tariff reductions, as well as via lower non-tariff barriers to trade.

In this chapter, we focus on three major aspects of deeper regional integration and look at their long-run implications. First, we focus on the impact of tariff reduction and migration liberalization among the members of an integration bloc, investigating this in a two-country framework. Secondly, we look at the discriminatory character of trade liberalization in integration blocs by extending our approach to a three-region framework. Thirdly, we analyze policies typically introduced or pursued in the course of regional integration. The first two topics are also at the center of traditional, static analysis of regional integration. We will investigate them against the background of a dynamic general equilibrium framework.

We adopt a modified version of our basic regional growth approach presented in chapter 4. This modified two-country model allows us to investigate the implications of tariff reductions between the two countries and a gradual relaxation of state-imposed migration barriers. In the integration literature, many authors have stressed the importance of trade liberalization for the growth performance of participating countries (e.g. El-Agraa (1994)). But due to the lack of an appropriate growth framework, this hypothesis has never been approached in a rigorous manner.

In contrast to international dynamic models, the tariff level not only affects the incentive to accumulate knowledge, but might also change the relative importance of agglomeration advantages and disadvantages. This, in turn, alters the specialization and trade patterns of countries. Our regional growth framework also has the very significant advantage of allowing the investigation of trade liberalization in a wide variety of circumstances. We do not have to limit ourselves to an analysis of two entirely symmetric countries as Rivera-Batiz/Romer (1991b). Rather, we are able to depict a varying degree of asymmetry between the countries. We can even look at a complete core-periphery situation with innovative activities concentrated only in one country. In contrast to Grossman/Helpman (1990), we are not restricted to small departures from the free-trade equilibrium. This is important since it turns out that, in many cases, the effects of trade liberalization hinges on the starting position.

Within a two-country model, one of the main characteristics of regional integration is hidden, namely its partial and discriminatory character. This feature has been at the heart of most of the integration discussion. In order to address this aspect, we extend our basic set-up to a simple three-country framework in section 5.2. Whereas in section 5.1 we take a closer look at the effects of regional integration relating to the countries in the integration bloc, in section 5.2, we focus on the discriminatory character of regional integration. Two countries form the integration bloc which is linked with the rest of the world via trade. A reduction of inner-union trade barriers not only influences the countries in the integration bloc, but also alters their relationship to the rest of the world. The creation of a customs union might even lead to higher external barriers to trade. Once again, changes in impediments to trade affect the specialization patterns of all three countries. We look at the implication for growth, specialization, and trade patterns. An extensive analysis discusses the welfare implications of partial trade liberalization.

Section 5.3 deals with our third major issue, the impact of policies pursued in an integration bloc. Most prominent examples are the common agricultural policy in the EU and regional policy measures. In the EU, for example, the objective to reduce regional disparities can be traced back to the treaty of Rome. We ask whether the employed instruments reach their immediate goal and look at the side effects of these policies on regional specialization and trade patterns, as well as on the growth effects. Thereby, we once again follow our two-country regional growth approach.

5.1 Liberalization in a Two-Country Setting

5.1.1 A Two-Country Integration Bloc

We study an integration bloc consisting of two countries, A and B. The structure of the two-country model in this section is similar to the one of our basic model in chapter 4.[1] To keep matters simple, we assume that households in both countries consume only the industrial final good, Y, and share the following intertemporal utility function:

$$U_t = \int_t^\infty e^{-\rho(\tau - t)} ln C_Y(\tau) d\tau. \tag{5.1}$$

The optimal consumption expenditure path of households is described by (4.5). For the static demand function, we simply derive:

$$p_Y C_Y = E. \tag{5.2}$$

Once again, we choose the normalization of prices such that E equals one at every moment in time. Hence, the return of internationally mobile financial capital which households claim in order to abstain from consumption is equal to their rate of time preference.

The endowment of each country with immobile, unskilled labor is $\bar{L}^i$ $(i = A, B)$. Endowment with this factor may differ between the two countries.

[1] The discussion in this subsection is based on Walz (1995b).

The other factor of production, skilled labor, is perfectly mobile between the two countries.

We maintain the production function of the industrial final good. Producers in the final-goods sector employ skilled and unskilled labor, as well as differentiated intermediate products:

$$Y^i = (L_Y^i)^\alpha (H_Y^i)^\beta \left[\int_0^n x^i(v)^\gamma dv\right]^{\frac{1-\alpha-\beta}{\gamma}} . \tag{5.3}$$

Intermediate-goods producers and innovating firms employ skilled labor only (see (4.8) and (4.9)). Production of differentiated inputs as well as of R&D activities are more human capital intensive than final-goods production. Our simple model exhibits a one-sector structure with vertically differentiated production.

In contrast to the output of the two other subsectors, R&D output is not traded. This, however, applies only to the R&D output accruing to private investors and is due to information and control costs of international licensing and the establishment of vertically integrated MNC's. Since in this model there are no gains arising from geographical separation, small costs suffice to rule out the internationalization of innovative activities and intermediate-goods production as a profitable alternative.

Trade in differentiated products is burdened with *ad valorem* tariffs, imposed symmetrically by governments in A and B.[2] Tariffs drive a wedge between the prices final-goods producers have to pay for imported goods, $\tilde{p}_x$, and the proceed per unit of producers in country i, p_x^i. By denoting the *ad valorem* tax rate as κ, we derive the following relationship:

$$\tilde{p}_x^{i,j} = \begin{cases} p_x^{i,j} & \text{if} \quad i = j, \\ p_x^{i,j}/\bar{\kappa} & \text{if} \quad i \neq j, \end{cases} \tag{5.4}$$

[2]For simplicity we assume that no tariffs are levied on final-goods production. This can be justified by the observation that the volume of trade and, hence, the importance of barriers to trade is much more pronounced in the intermediate-goods sector, where the bulk of trade is of intra-industrial nature. Final goods, in contrast, are only shipped in one direction. With symmetric countries, our results are completely unaffected by the introduction of tariffs in this sector as well. The volume of final-goods trade is nil, only intra-industry trade of differentiated products takes place. The introduction of barriers to final-goods trade would drive a wedge between international consumption prices. Then the migration decisions would depend on the countries' specialization and trade patterns, which are a function of the migration decision and the initial distribution of financial assets across individuals. To avoid this very complex circular relationship, we chose to refrain from trade barriers in final-goods trade.

with $\bar{\kappa} = (1+\kappa)^{-1}$. The revenues arising from tariffs for the two governments are redistributed to households in a lump-sum manner. The public budget is balanced in present value terms. Since the model obeys the Ricardo-Barro property (Barro (1974)), this leaves the optimal intertemporal allocation unaltered.

Applying Shephard's Lemma to the unit cost function of final-goods producers (see (4.10)), we can derive the demand function faced by each intermediate-goods producer. Noting that with tariffs the quantities produced and demanded exactly match each other, we can express total output of producer v as:

$$x^i(v) = \frac{p_x^{i,j}(v)^{-\epsilon}}{\int_0^n \tilde{p}_x^{i,j}(v')^{1-\epsilon} dv'}(1-\alpha-\beta)p_Y Y^i + \frac{p_x^{i,j}(v)^{-\epsilon} k^{\epsilon}}{\int_0^n \tilde{p}_x^{i,j}(v')^{1-\epsilon} dv}(1-\alpha-\beta)p_Y Y^j. \tag{5.5}$$

Intermediate-goods producers maximize their profits $G^i = (p_x^i - c_x^i)x_i(v)$ by choosing their optimal producer price:

$$p_x^{i,j} = p_x^{i,i} = p_x^i = \frac{c_x^i}{\gamma}, \tag{5.6}$$

where $c_x^i = w_H a_x$. The price per unit sold is independent of the country where the final good is used.

With free entry in the innovation sector, the following no-arbitrage conditions prevail in the country with an active R&D-sector:

$$\frac{G^i}{c_n^i} + \frac{\dot{c}_n^i}{c_n^i} = \rho. \tag{5.7}$$

Since at least some skilled workers reside in either country to guarantee profitable employment opportunities for unskilled labor, and since final-goods prices are equalized across countries, wage rates for skilled labor have to be the same in both countries as well.

Factor-market and goods-market clearing complete the basic set-up. Final-goods market clearing simply requires $p_Y C_Y = 1$. Since the only employment opportunity for unskilled labor is in the final-goods sector, factor-market clearing for unskilled labor requires

$$\bar{L}^i = L_Y^i, \tag{5.8}$$

whereas for skilled labor (4.22) has to hold.

5.1.2 Specialization Patterns in the Integration Bloc

In the present model, Y-production has to take place in both countries at every moment in time in order to ensure factor-market clearing for unskilled labor (see (5.8)). This, in turn, requires that Y-producers in both countries work under equal cost conditions ($c_Y^A = c_Y^B$). Tariffs create a cost advantage for Y-producers in the country with the larger number of locally produced intermediate goods. Hence, lower wages for unskilled labor in the country with the smaller "technological" base must compensate for the disadvantage of local Y-producers. Relation (4.24) must hold to guarantee competitiveness for Y-producers in both countries with k replaced by $\bar{\kappa}$. Cost-minimizing behavior of final-goods producing firms gives us, together with (5.3), the factor demand function $L_Y^i = \alpha s_Y^i / w_L^i$. Inserting the modified relative wage equation and the factor-demand function for unskilled labor in (5.8) yields the following relation which ensures simultaneous factor-market clearing for immobile labor in both countries:

$$\frac{s_Y^A}{s_Y^B} = \left(\frac{\mu + \bar{\kappa}^{\epsilon-1}}{1 + \mu\bar{\kappa}^{\epsilon-1}}\right)^{\theta} f, \tag{5.9}$$

with $f = \bar{L}^A / \bar{L}^B$ denoting the relative endowment of country A with unskilled labor compared to the endowment of country B. The larger the number of locally produced intermediate goods and the larger the relative endowment with unskilled labor, the larger the share of the respective country in Y-production. This number of locally produced intermediate goods is, however, as we will see in a moment, endogenous. Rather, the relative long-run equilibrium number of differentiated goods in country i is positively related to this country's factor endowment.

Let us now turn to the long-run equilibrium properties of the two-country integration bloc. On the basis of the steady-state equilibrium, we then can look at the long-run effects of integration policies. This is done via comparative dynamics.

With identical innovation costs, innovators will undertake R&D and subsequent production of intermediate goods in both countries if, and only if, $G^A = G^B$. This follows directly from the no-arbitrage condition (5.7). Using (5.5), (5.6), and (5.9) in the profit functions yields:

$$G^A - G^B = \Xi \left[f \left(\frac{1 + \mu\bar{\kappa}^{\epsilon-1}}{\mu + \bar{\kappa}^{\epsilon-1}}\right)^{\eta} - 1 \right], \tag{5.10}$$

with $\Xi = \dfrac{s_Y^B(1-\alpha-\beta)(1-\gamma)(1-k^\epsilon)}{n^B + n^A \bar{\kappa}^{\epsilon-1}}$.
An interior solution emerges if the term in brackets vanishes for a positive and finite μ. As in our basic regional growth model, the profit differential reflects the interaction between agglomeration advantages (closeness to the market) and disadvantages (intense competition).

By employing a similar stability analysis as in chapter 4, we find that an interior solution is stable for $\eta > 0$. With $\eta < 0$, $G^A > (<) G^B$ for $\mu > (<)\mu^*$. Hence, after a small deviation from the interior equilibrium (say due to a country-specific shock) this equilibrium can no longer be approached. It is unstable. Innovation takes place in one country only, and a corner solution arises in which one country specializes completely in the final-goods sector. The other country, the innovative center, is the sole location of R&D activities. Intermediate-goods production is concentrated there. Therefore, we assume in the following that $\eta > 0$. Solving in our one sector setting explicitly for the long-run equilibrium μ in the interior solution gives us:

$$\mu^* = \frac{\tilde{f} - \bar{\kappa}^{\epsilon-1}}{1 - \tilde{f}\bar{\kappa}^{\epsilon-1}}, \tag{5.11}$$

with $\tilde{f} = (L^A/L^B)^{\frac{1}{\eta}}$. If the endowment differences are not too large, i.e. f is sufficiently close to one, an interior solution exists. Otherwise the "larger" economy becomes the innovative center, whereas the "smaller" country specializes completely in final-goods production.
With (5.10) we can establish

Proposition 5.1.1 *For $\bar{\kappa}^{(\epsilon-1)\eta} < f < \bar{\kappa}^{(1-\epsilon)\eta}$ and $\eta > 0$ a unique and saddle path stable interior solution exists. If endowment differences are pronounced ($f > \bar{\kappa}^{(1-\epsilon)\eta}$ or $f < \bar{\kappa}^{(\epsilon-1)\eta}$), the country with the larger immobile resource base emerges in the long-run as the innovative center. With $\eta < 0$, a core-periphery pattern emerges as well.*

With an interior solution, the country with the larger immobile resource base will have the larger number of locally produced intermediate products ($\mu^* > (<)1$) for $f > (<)1$). Only with an equal number of immobile workers living in both economies, does $\mu = 1$ constitute the long-run equilibrium. The larger immobile working force allows for the larger share of final-goods production and, consequently, for the larger domestic market for intermediate goods. Additional intermediate-goods production is attracted as long as the negative effect of fiercer price competition does not outweigh the advantage of the larger local market. With $f = \mu = 1$, $s_Y^A = s_Y^B = 0.5$.

The capital accounts of the economies are balanced if financial assets are distributed equally among households. Then, trade must be balanced as well. In this perfectly symmetric world, only intra-industry trade in differentiated inputs takes place. Final goods are not exchanged between the two countries. Input producers sell the larger share of their output in the domestic market. This follows directly from the existence of tariffs which discriminate against the imports of differentiated inputs (see (5.5)). The more asymmetric the countries (with respect to f), the more geographically concentrated intermediate-goods production and the smaller the volume of intra-industry trade becomes.

Inserting (5.11) in (5.9) reveals that, with an interior solution, the share of final goods in the long-run equilibrium is

$$\frac{s_Y^A}{s_Y^B} = \tilde{f}. \tag{5.12}$$

Finally the innovation rate must be derived explicitly before turning to the discussion of the integration process. For this reason, we rewrite the profit rate of potential innovators in country i with the help of (5.2) and (5.5) to

$$\frac{G^i}{c_n^i} = \frac{\Phi_1}{w_H}\left(\frac{s_Y^i(1+\mu^i)}{\mu^i + \bar{\kappa}^{\epsilon-1}} + \frac{s_Y^j(1+\mu^i)\bar{\kappa}^{\epsilon}}{1+\mu^i\bar{\kappa}^{\epsilon-1}}\right), \tag{5.13}$$

with $\mu^i = n^i/n^j$ and $\Phi_1 = (1-\alpha-\beta)(1-\gamma)$.

With the help of the factor-market clearing condition for skilled labor, we eliminate w_H in (5.13). Using (5.5) in (4.22) we find a modified version of the market clearing condition: [3]

$$\bar{H} = \frac{\beta}{w_H} + \frac{(1-\alpha-\beta)\gamma}{w_H}\left(\frac{s_Y^A(\mu+\bar{\kappa}^{\epsilon})}{\mu+\bar{\kappa}^{\epsilon-1}} + \frac{s_Y^B(1+\mu\bar{\kappa}^{\epsilon})}{1+\mu\bar{\kappa}^{\epsilon-1}}\right) + g. \tag{5.14}$$

[3] At this point it is necessary to point out a decisive difference between transport costs as chosen in chapter 4 and tariffs in the present section. In contrast to tariffs, transport costs have quantity effects. That is, transport costs display resource costs which require additional production. With tariffs, $x^i = \tilde{x}^i$, whereas with transport costs, $x^{i,j} = \tilde{x}^{i,j}/k$ if $i \neq j$. With transport costs, the innovation rate in the interior solution case would be independent of the degree of integration (level of transport costs). The term $\bar{\kappa}^{\epsilon}$ in (5.13) and (5.14) is replaced with $\bar{\kappa}^{\epsilon-1}$. Neither the factor-market clearing condition nor the profit rate of firms in the two innovating countries depends on transport costs. Quantity and price effects compensate each other. Intermediate-goods producers face lower demand for their product from abroad. But with transport costs type barriers to trade, the associated additional production balances the negative demand effect.

Note that in the steady-state equilibrium, all nominal variables grow at the same rate as nominal aggregate expenditures E, i.e. at a zero rate. Therefore, costs of R&D decrease at the overall rate of innovation ($\dot{c}_n/c_n = -g$). Using (5.12) and (5.13) in (5.9) enables us to derive the steady-state rate of innovation. We distinguish between the two cases with superscripts I for interior solution C for core-periphery setting:

$$g^s = \frac{\bar{H}\Phi_1\Delta^s - \rho}{1 + \Phi_1\Delta^s}, \quad (s = I, C), \tag{5.15}$$

with

$$\Delta^I = \left\{\beta\left(\frac{1+\bar{\kappa}^{\epsilon-1}}{1+\bar{\kappa}^{\epsilon}}\right) + (1-\alpha-\beta)\gamma\right\}^{-1}.$$

For the sake of concreteness, in the rest of the section we look at core-periphery patterns with country B representing the innovative center (innovation takes places exclusively in B or relatively concentrated in B). Then we obtain:

$$\Delta^C = \left\{\beta\left(\frac{1+\bar{\kappa}^{(\epsilon-1)\theta}f^{-1}}{\bar{\kappa}+\bar{\kappa}^{(\epsilon-1)\theta}f^{-1}}\right) + (1-\alpha-\beta)\gamma\right\}^{-1}.$$

5.1.3 Trade Liberalization

Now, we are prepared to investigate the impact of trade liberalization on countries' growth performance as well as their specialization and production pattern. The steady-state output growth rate, g^Y, is proportional to the steady-state innovation rate g: $g^Y = (1-\alpha-\beta)(1-\gamma)\gamma g$ (see (5.3)). It suffices to look at the innovation rate.

Let us begin with the **interior solution** case. Trade liberalization, i.e. an increase in $\bar{\kappa}$, brings about a weakening of the agglomeration disadvantage. The relative degree of price competition is altered in favor of the country with the larger number of locally produced inputs. An increased relative concentration of intermediate-goods producers can be observed in the new steady-state (see (5.11)):

$$\frac{\partial\mu^*}{\partial\bar{\kappa}} = \frac{(\epsilon-1)\bar{\kappa}^{\epsilon-2}(\tilde{f}^2-1)}{(1-\tilde{f}\bar{\kappa}^{\epsilon-1})^2}. \tag{5.16}$$

For $f > 1 (< 1)$, this expression is positive (negative). The share of industrial final goods is left unchanged (see (5.12)). The same is true for the relative wage rate, ω, which can be expressed in the interior solution case as:

$$\omega = f^{\frac{\theta}{\eta}}. \tag{5.17}$$

The induced change in the relative number of differentiated inputs just compensates for the change in relative productivity of the immobile factor as a direct consequence of tariff reductions.

We can state:

Proposition 5.1.2 *Regional integration via trade liberalization leads to a further concentration of production in the interior solution case. The relative productivity of the immobile factor stays the same in the course of trade liberalization.*

A reduction in tariffs makes a center-periphery pattern more likely (see propositions 5.1.1 and 5.1.2). Inter-industry trade remains the same. This follows from the unchanged international production patterns in the final-goods sector. The effect on intra-industry trade is less obvious. Since inter-industry trade is unchanged, we can trace the impact on intra-industry trade by looking at the change in the gross flow of the value of differentiated intermediate products: $n^A p_x^A x^{B,A} + n^B p_x^B x^{A,B} := T_{II}$. Using (5.5), (5.12), and (5.14) we arrive at:

$$T_{II} = (1 - \alpha - \beta) \left[\frac{1}{\bar{\kappa}^{-1} + \bar{\kappa}^{-\epsilon}} \right]. \tag{5.18}$$

This expression increases with $\bar{\kappa}$. Intra–industry trade increases with trade liberalization. We establish

Proposition 5.1.3 *With an interior steady-state solution, tariff reductions lead to an expansion of trade. However, only intra-industry trade benefits from trade expansion. Inter-industry trade takes place at the same level.*

The growth rate effects of tariff reduction are our third focus. Differentiating (5.15) with respect to $\bar{\kappa}$, we obtain

$$\text{sign}\frac{\partial g^I}{\partial \bar{\kappa}} = \text{sign}\frac{\partial \Delta^I}{\partial \bar{\kappa}} = \text{sign}(1 + \epsilon\bar{\kappa} - \epsilon + \bar{\kappa}^{\epsilon}). \tag{5.19}$$

The term in brackets on the RHS of (5.19) is montonically increasing in $\bar{\kappa}$. With $\bar{\kappa} = 0$ ($\bar{\kappa} = 1$), the term is negative (positive). Hence, we can define a unique $\bar{\kappa}^I$ for which the term in brackets vanishes. Starting from $\bar{\kappa} > \bar{\kappa}^I$, trade liberalization leads to faster innovation and growth. Only with $\bar{\kappa} < \bar{\kappa}^I$, marginal tariff reductions lead to slower growth. In this case, the increase in competition due to more liberal trade overcompensates the positive effect of enhanced trade possibilities for intermediate-goods producers. Table 5.1 displays some examples for the critical $\bar{\kappa}^I$ and the correspending range of tariff rates for different values of the elasticity of demand.

Table 5.1: Numerical examples for the critical tariff level

ϵ	$\bar{\kappa}^I$	κ^I
1.5	0.25	300%
2	0,414	141%
3	0.596	68.2%
4	0.692	44.5%
5	0.753	32.8%
10	0.874	14.4%

The growth rate effect in this two-country model is based on an allocation effect. Starting from sufficiently low tariff levels, tariff reductions increase the productivity of skilled workers in the R&D sector. With international mobility of skilled labor, this shifts skilled workers into the more productive sector. The growth rate increases as a consequence of the allocation effect. The underlying reason for this allocation effect is the increase of sales opportunities for intermediate-goods producers. We can call this a market expansion effect.
We establish:

Proposition 5.1.4 *With an interior solution, the growth rate effect is non-monotone. Starting from a high (low) degree of integration (low (high) tariff levels) tariff reductions accelerate (slow down) steady-state growth. Skilled labor is allocated towards (away from) the dynamic sector.*

We now switch to a discussion of the impact of trade liberalization in the **core-periphery** case. Since the likelihood of a corner solution increases with trade liberalization, regime changes do not occur, given the initial core-periphery pattern between the two economies. In the intermediate-goods sector, production patterns remain the same. However, the periphery (country A) gains a higher market share in final-goods production. Country A looses some of its cost disadvantage. With smaller tariffs, the costs of imports for Y-producers in A decrease, and it becomes more profitable to shift production to country A. With (5.9), we find for $\mu = 0$:

$$\frac{s_Y^A}{s_Y^B} = \bar{\kappa}^{(\epsilon-1)\theta} f, \tag{5.20}$$

which increases with $\bar{\kappa}$. Overall production patterns become less concentrated.

The different impact of trade liberalization on the location of production sites between the two cases (I and C) stems from the different roles which barriers to trade play in the two sectors (intermediate-goods and final-goods production). Whereas for given μ tariffs display an agglomeration advantage in the final-goods sector, they represent an agglomeration disadvantage in the intermediate-goods sector (via price competition). This leads to an important conclusion which is contained in:

Proposition 5.1.5 *With a corner solution, trade liberalization leads to less asymmetric production patterns. Since barriers to trade represent agglomeration advantages in the final-goods sector (due to the market size effect) and agglomeration disadvantages in the intermediate-goods sector (due to the competition effect), a general case for the shift in production pattern cannot be made. Rather, trade liberalization affects sectors differently.*

In the interior solution case, the indirect effect on the intermediate-goods sector compensates the degglomerative impact of trade liberalization on the final-goods sector via the change in μ. In the core-periphery setting, the effect on the intermediate-goods sector by definition does not exist.

In our core-periphery setting, relative wages for immobile labor shift in favor of the periphery. The relative productivity of the immobile resource base in country A increases. All trade is of inter-industry nature. Trade expands. More intermediate goods are exported from B to A and relatively more final goods are imported into country B.

Potential dynamic effects of trade liberalization operate in this case via the allocation effect as well. The decisive question is, whether skilled labor is shifted towards or away from the R&D sector. Differentiating (5.15) with respect to $\bar{\kappa}$ gives us:

$$\text{sign}\frac{\partial g^C}{\partial \bar{\kappa}} = \text{sign}\frac{\partial \Delta^C}{\partial \bar{\kappa}} = \text{sign}[1 - (\epsilon - 1)\theta(\bar{\kappa}^{-1} - 1) + \bar{\kappa}^{(\epsilon-1)\theta} f]. \qquad (5.21)$$

Once again, the term in brackets at the RHS of (5.21) is increasing in $\bar{\kappa}$. With $\bar{\kappa} = 0$ ($\bar{\kappa} = 1$), the term in brackets is negative (positive). We define $\bar{\kappa}^C$ for which the term in brackets equals zero. Since the expression in (5.21) is monotone, a unique $\bar{\kappa}^C$ exists. As in our interior solution case, we find a non-monotone relationship between tariff levels and the growth rate. This non-monotonicity, however, holds only if $\bar{\kappa}^C$ exists, i.e. a core-periphery setting emerges with $\bar{\kappa} < \bar{\kappa}^C$. This is the case if the immobile resource bases of the two countries are sufficiently unequal. If for any $\bar{\kappa} < \bar{\kappa}^C$ an interior solution results, then tariff reduction in core-periphery patterns always accelerates growth.

Proposition 5.1.6 *In general, in a core-periphery setting the relationship between tariff levels and the steady-state growth rate is non-monotone. Starting from high (low) levels of protection, trade liberalization leads to a lower (higher) rate of growth. Trade liberalization between sufficiently integrated economies accelerates steady-state growth.*

5.1.4 Liberalization of Migration Barriers

Liberalization of Migration Barriers for Unskilled Labor

Suppose that the immobility of unskilled labor has two sources. On the one hand, natural barriers to migration (cultural differences between host and source country, friends, relatives, pecuniary costs of changing places) make it costly to migrate. On the other hand, state-imposed migration barriers add to the natural migration costs, making migration altogether prohibitively costly. Reducing state-imposed migration barriers may induce migration from the low- to the high-wage country. We assume that (natural) migration costs are not uniformly distributed across households. Migration is worthwhile in the absence of artificial, state-imposed migration barriers for some households. Then it is feasible to induce marginal immigration into the high-wage country by gradually relaxing barriers to migration for unskilled labor in the course of regional integration.

We investigate the impact of such a liberalization step on specialization and growth patterns. We start with the simple case, namely the interior solution case. In order to allow for a definitive international specialization pattern, we assume small but positive barriers to trade. Since country B is assumed to be the larger country, $\omega < 1$. That is, country B represents the immigration country. Migration reduces f.

Gradual relaxation of migration barriers for unskilled labor brings about a larger geographical concentration of intermediate-goods production (f decreases):

$$\frac{\partial \mu^*}{\partial f} = \frac{\eta^{-1} f^{\frac{1-\eta}{\eta}}}{(1 - \tilde{f}\bar{\kappa}^{\epsilon-1})}(1 - \bar{\kappa}^{2(\epsilon-1)})^2 > 0. \tag{5.22}$$

The same is true for final-goods production. The more unskilled workers reside in country B, the larger the pool of labor for final-goods producers, s_Y^B increases and ω declines (see (5.12) and (5.17)). The wage gap between the two countries widens even further. The incentive to migrate increases. Since the innovation rate is independent of f in the interior solution case, a reduction of migration barriers has no growth rate effect.

Matters are different with a core-periphery pattern. There, a reduction of f has a positive growth rate effect. Differentiating (5.15) with respect to f yields:

$$\text{sign}\frac{\partial g^C}{\partial f} = \text{sign}\frac{\partial \Delta^C}{\partial f} = \text{sign}(\bar{\kappa} - 1) < 0. \qquad (5.23)$$

The shift of immobile labor to the center country enhances the international allocation. The larger unskilled labor force enables Y-producers to locate themselves more closely to the intermediate-goods producers (which all produce in B). This, in turn, saves tariff costs. The productivity of skilled labor in the R&D sector in B increases. Skilled labor moves into this sector. The pace of innovation and output growth increases. The shift of final-goods production to country B can be seen from (5.20).
We can establish:

Proposition 5.1.7 *A reduction of migration barriers which induces immigration into the high wage country brings about a concentration of final goods as well as of intermediate-goods production in the interior solution case of intermediate-goods production. In the core-periphery (interior solution) setting, migration flows speed up (do not change) the growth process.*

Liberalization of Migration Barriers for Skilled Labor

A more liberal migration policy might also change migration flows of skilled labor.[4] In order to analyze the impact of such a policy, we depart from our assumption of perfect mobility of skilled labor and introduce marginal migration costs which are reduced to a zero level in the course of integration. In order to keep the analysis as simple as possible, we do not model

[4] Whereas here the division of the work force is given, Walz (1996b) considers the impact of a more liberal migration policy when the division of workers in skilled and unskilled workers is endogenously determined. In this model, however, a much simpler production structure is employed.

the migration decision of skilled workers as an explicit intertemporal utility maximization problem.[5] Rather, we allow for a wage gap between the two countries for skilled workers. Skilled workers from A are only willing to migrate to country B (which has a relatively more human-capital intensive production structure) if their migration costs are compensated by higher wages in B ($w_H^A := \bar{w}_H < w_H^B = \bar{w}_H\Gamma$ ($\Gamma > 1$)). With integration the wage gap vanishes and Γ becomes one.

Since the interior solution case proves to be extremely tedious with very few clear-cut results, we choose to present only the reduction of barriers to migration for skilled workers in the core-periphery setting. Country B is the innovative center. The wage gap makes Y-production as well as intermediate-goods production and R&D in B more costly. Hence, our condition for equal cost condition in final-goods production in both countries becomes:

$$\omega = \Gamma^{\beta}\left(\frac{\mu + \bar{\kappa}^{\epsilon-1}\Gamma^{1-\epsilon}}{\mu\bar{\kappa}^{\epsilon-1} + \Gamma^{1-\epsilon}}\right)^{\theta}. \tag{5.24}$$

The relative share in Y-production can then be expressed as:

$$\frac{s_Y^A}{s_Y^B} = \Gamma^{\beta}\left(\frac{\mu + \bar{\kappa}^{\epsilon-1}\Gamma^{1-\epsilon}}{\mu\bar{\kappa}^{\epsilon-1} + \Gamma^{1-\epsilon}}\right)^{\theta} f. \tag{5.25}$$

With a corner solution in B ($\mu = 0$), these two terms reduce to $\omega = \Gamma^{\beta}\bar{\kappa}^{(\epsilon-1)\theta}$ and $s_Y^A/s_Y^B = \Gamma^{\beta}\bar{\kappa}^{(\epsilon-1)\theta}f$. Inserting (5.4-5.6) into the profit function and the factor-market clearing condition for skilled labor and using the outcome in the no-arbitrage condition gives us a modified version of the steady-state innovation rate. In (5.15) Δ^C is replaced by

$$\tilde{\Delta}^C = \left[\beta\left(\frac{\Gamma^{1+\beta} + \bar{\kappa}^{(1-\epsilon)\theta}f^{-1}}{\Gamma^{\beta}\bar{\kappa} + \bar{\kappa}^{(1-\epsilon)\theta}f^{-1}}\right) + (1-\alpha-\beta)\gamma\right]^{-1}. \tag{5.26}$$

Now, we are in the position to evaluate the impact of a liberalization of migration restrictions for skilled workers. Γ decreases marginally to one. This yields $\partial\omega/\partial\Gamma > 0$ and $\partial(s_Y^A/s_Y^B)/\partial\Gamma > 0$. The elimination of impediments to migration shifts production into the center country. The international wage rate gap for skilled workers disappears and Y-production in B becomes relatively less costly. The relative cost reduction translates into a shift of

[5] In a dynamic context, migration costs are fixed costs which are weighted against expected future gains from migration. Hence, migration displays an investment decision which requires an intertemporal maximization approach (cf. Krugman (1991c)). Our approach is an abbreviated version of this much more complex decision process.

Y-production to B. Since intermediate-goods production is already perfectly concentrated, this implies a further increase in production pattern disparities between the two countries. Unskilled labor in A has to compensate for the non-availability of a local technological base to a larger extent.

Cost improvements in the innovative country, B, induce a more profitable environment for R&D:

$$\text{sign}\frac{\partial g^C}{\partial \Gamma}_{|\Gamma=1} = \text{sign}\frac{\partial \Delta^C}{\partial \Gamma}_{|\Gamma=1} = \text{sign}[-(\bar{\kappa} + \bar{\kappa}^{(1-\epsilon)\theta} + \beta\bar{\kappa}^{(1-\epsilon)\theta})(1-k))] < 0. \tag{5.27}$$

Liberalization of impediments to migration for skilled labor increases the relative productivity of skilled workers in the R&D sector. Skilled individuals can migrate more easily to B. The steady-state growth rate increases.
We can summarize:

Proposition 5.1.8 *Liberalization of barriers to migration for skilled labor in a core-periphery setting accelerates steady-state growth and leads to more pronounced concentration of production in the center country.*

5.1.5 Welfare Discussion

In our dynamic general equilibrium framework, the market allocation is not efficient. Integration potentially improves welfare. There are two distortions in the economy which are both affected by integration policies. On the one hand, due to imperfect competition and distorted trade in the intermediate-goods sector, inputs are not priced competitively and uniformely. Reducing the wedge between monopolistic and competitive prices represents a welfare gain. On the other hand, innovators do not internalize their positive contribution to the stock of knowledge capital which decreases costs of future innovators.[6] Hence, they underinvest in R&D. Whereas the first distortion

[6]Two additional external effects of an extra input brand exist. First, innovators do not take into account the extra gain in productivity of Y-producers associated with an additional input variety ("consumer-surplus" effect) into account. Secondly, a new input brand intensifies competition in the intermediate-goods sector and thereby diminishes the profitability of existing intermediate-goods producers (profit destruction effect). The "consumer surplus" effect leaves the economy with too little innovation and the profit destruction effect implies an overaccumulation of knowledge. Grossman/Helpman (1991, p. 82f), however, show that in models of increasing brand variety and a CES-function, these two effects exactly outweigh each other. The "net" externality is just equal to the knowledge spillover effect. See Benassy (1998) for further discussion of this issue.

represents a static inefficiency, the second externality displays a dynamic distortion influencing the slope of the expansion path.

Integration policies alter both sources of inefficiency. Before turning to the welfare position of different groups of agents in the two countries we first discuss the impact of integration on overall welfare. Integrating the intertemporal utility function and noting that $p_Y(t) = p_Y(0)e^{\frac{(1-\alpha-\beta)\gamma}{1-\gamma}}$, we obtain:

$$U_0 = \frac{1}{\rho}\left[-lnp_Y(0) + \frac{(1-\alpha-\beta)\gamma}{(1-\gamma)\rho}g\right]. \tag{5.28}$$

A reduction in the static distortion reduces $p_Y(0)$ whereas a dynamic welfare gain is achieved by increasing the rate of innovation, g.

Among all possible tariff levels, complete trade liberalization yields maximal welfare. This can be seen as follows. With $\bar{\kappa} = 1$ (i.e. in the absence of any tariffs), the additional artificial wedge between costs and monopolistic prices declines to $p_x = w_H/\gamma$. Therefore, the average ratio of monopolistic price and costs is minimal compared to other tariff levels. Furthermore, $\bar{\kappa} = 1$ (as well as $\bar{\kappa} = 0$) yields the maximum rate of innovation and growth among all tariff levels (see (5.15)). A Pareto-optimal solution, however, calls for even faster growth. Hence, in the absence of further policy intervention schemes, free trade is a second-best policy (and part of a first-best policy).

But what are the welfare effects of integration in our framework starting from any given degree of integration? Further concentration of final-goods and differentiated-inputs production for given or decreasing tariff levels enhances static efficiency. Distorting tariffs are reduced and the average price-cost margin in the intermediate-goods sector declines. If this is accompanied by an increase in steady-state growth, overall welfare improves. Therefore, trade liberalization (in an interior solution case) between closely integrated economies as well as liberalization of migration barriers for unskilled workers leads to a welfare gain. The static as well as the dynamic distortion are (partially) alleviated or left unchanged in the course of these integration measures.

In an interior solution, migration liberalization for unskilled labor improves welfare for all starting positions since the growth rate is not affected by the migration policy. A positive welfare effect also results with the liberalization of migration barriers for skilled labor in the core-periphery setting. Production concentration and the higher incentive to innovate reduce the static and the dynamic distortion. Among the cases discussed in the preceding analysis, only the liberalization of tariffs in a core-periphery setting has ambiguous static effects. The more strongly dispersed production pattern in the final-goods sector increases the average price which final-goods producers have to pay. This has to be contrasted with the direct effect of tariff reduction. Whenever the first (second) effect dominates, the static welfare effect is negative (positive). For all other settings we find a positive static welfare effect. Then, integration between already closely integrated economies increases overall welfare.

Finally, let us stress two important points with respect to the well-being of individual groups in the two economies. First, the positive impact of growth on consumer welfare is independent of the location of the growth process. That is, consumers are indifferent as to whether their home country or the foreign country is the faster growing one. Since, however, productivity of immobile factors of production depends on the local technological base, they have a strong incentive to ensure that their home country is the center country. Secondly, even with a positive overall welfare effect of integration, some groups of agents may lose since they experience a pronounced negative income effect. For example, with a core-periphery pattern and country B being the innovative center, immobile labor in country A experiences a drop in its relative income. Since in our two-country model an outside world does not exist, overall savings must be equal to overall investment. Factor income (labor income plus dividends, nG) minus savings (investment in R&D) must be equal to consumption expenditures: $w_L^A L^A + w_L^B L^B + w_H H + nG - w_H g = E$. Rewriting this equation with the help of the no-arbitrage condition and noting that $E = 1$ yields: $w_L^A = (1 - w_H(H + \rho))/(L^A + \omega^{-1} L^B)$. In situations with a positive growth rate effect, w_H increases (see (5.14)). Hence, with decreasing ω, unskilled workers in country A definitively experience a reduction of labor income. If their share in asset holdings is not too large and the discount rate sufficiently large (which puts a small weight on the dynamic welfare gain) the welfare of A's immobile workers drops. Hence, this group will oppose integration or claim compensating transfers.

5.1.6 Brief Summary

This section concentrated on the implications of regional integration steps for countries for which external relations are of minor importance. This allows us to neglect an outside world.

It turned out that integration between rather closely connected countries has a non-negative growth rate effect. Since the market provides too little new knowledge anyway, this is equivalent to a positive dynamic welfare effect.

Our distinction of general specialization patterns in a core-periphery setting and in an interior solution revealed the different roles of impediments to trade in different sectors of the economy. With respect to the intermediate-goods sector, lower impediments to trade strengthen the centripetal force. Trade liberalization leads to concentration of production patterns in the interior solution case. In the final-goods sector, in contrast, lower trade barriers for a given μ lead to less geographical concentration. With an interior solution, the concentration of intermediate-goods production just offsets this effect. With a core-periphery patter with a given μ (either 0 or ∞), final-goods production is shifted into the periphery. This indicates that barriers to trade do not point unanimously in the direction of agglomeration advantages or disadvantages. Rather, the spatial effects of trade liberalization call for a more detailed analysis.

5.2 Regional Integration as Partial Liberalization

A crucial characteristic of deeper regional integration is its partial and discriminatory character. Impediments to trade and factor flows are lowered only between the member states of the integration bloc. This partial liberalization policy discriminates against producers of countries which are not members of the integration bloc.

Suppose that country A imports from countries B and C which produce the good under consideration with equal costs and face the same level of barriers to trade. Then A and B form a free trade zone by lowering trade barriers between the two countries (or eliminating them altogether). Impediments to trade between A and B on the one hand and C on the other hand remain unchanged. Trade liberalization between A and B discriminates against C's producers. For consumers in A products from C become relatively more expensive compared to imports from B. Imports from B to A might be more competitive than C's imports, even if the latter produces with lower costs. (Partial) Trade liberalization in the course of regional integration does not necessarily lead to a more efficient international allocation. It might even deteriorate international efficiency. Welfare of countries engaging in regional integration might decline if it becomes optimal to switch to imports from high cost producers. This is the basic message of traditional analysis of the discriminatory character of regional integration (customs union literature).

The customs union literature has been limited to static welfare analysis and was almost exclusively concentrated on trade liberalization.[7] In the following section we extend the basic analysis of the customs union literature to a dynamic general equilibrium framework. Thereby, we take the potential dynamic effects into account. Furthermore, we look at the implications of the liberalization of factor flows. We ask whether or not the partial liberalization of factor flows always leads to an improvement of the international allocation (see also Walz (1997b)).

In order to address the implications of the discriminatory character of regional integration adequately, we develop a three-country dynamic general equilibrium approach. Rather than trying to establish a very general framework, we try to bring forward the main issues at stake with a fairly thrifty modeling approach. We look at a core-periphery pattern in the integration bloc with one country representing the innovative center. This facilitates the analysis considerably and allows us to highlight the major mechanisms at work.

5.2.1 A Three-Country Model

The model economy consists of three countries, A, B, and C. Countries A and B together form the integration bloc. Country C stands for the rest of the world (ROW). We adopt the basic structure of our model from chapter 4 but alter it in one important aspect. We assume that there is only one factor of production, immobile labor. $\bar{L}^i$ $(i = A, B, C)$ households reside in each country i. Each household is endowed with one unit of labor.

Hence, the consumers' optimal dynamic expenditure path can be expressed analogously to (4.5) as:

$$\frac{\dot{E}^i}{E^i} = r^i - \rho,$$

whereby E^i denotes aggregate consumption expenditures in country i. The static demand functions are equivalent to (4.3) and (4.4) with $E = E^A + E^B + E^C$ displaying worldwide consumption expenditures. The producers of

[7] An exception to the latter is Wooton (1988).

industrial final goods employ labor as well as differentiated inputs:

$$Y^i = A^i (L_Y^i)^\alpha \left(\int_0^n \tilde{x}^i(v)^\gamma dv \right)^{\frac{1-\alpha}{\gamma}}, \tag{5.29}$$

with A^i measuring productivity in Y-production in country i. In traditional- as well as intermediate-goods production, labor is the only factor of production. The parameters, a_x and a_Z display the labor-input coefficients in the intermediate- and traditional final-goods sector.

With perfect competition in the two final goods sectors we obtain the following pricing conditions:

$$p_Z^i = c_Z^i = a_Z w_L^i, \tag{5.30}$$

and

$$p_Y^i = c_Y^i = C^i (w_L^i)^\alpha \left(\int_0^n \tilde{p}_x^{i,j}(v)^{1-\epsilon} dv \right)^{\frac{1-\alpha}{1-\epsilon}}, \tag{5.31}$$

with $C^i = (A^i)^{-1}[(\frac{1-\alpha}{\alpha})^\alpha + \left(\frac{\alpha}{1-\alpha}\right)^{1-\alpha}]$.

Before regional integration takes place, it is costly to trade final goods as well as intermediate goods between either country. We assume that all trade barriers are of the non-tariff type, for example, voluntary export agreements, quotas, content protection, quality standards, health and technical regulations, government procurement policies, etc.[8] In fact, such barriers have become more and more widespread, despite the general reductions of tariffs worldwide achieved through GATT (cf. e.g. Nogues et al. (1985)). For example in the case of the EU, a number of studies indicate that the most important pre-1992 barriers to trade were of technical and administrative nature (industry standards, legal regulations, certification processes, border related controls etc., see, for example, Commission (1988)). Empirical evidence suggests that informal non-tariff barriers to trade (such as technical and administrative restrictions) are accompanied by significant resource costs (e.g. relabelling costs, redesigning costs, delay costs, registration costs, additional marketing costs, see Commission (1988a)).

We choose to model non-tariff barriers to trade similarly to transport costs (of the iceberg type), thereby stressing the resource loss associated with the impediment to trade. There are no revenues for the respective governments

[8] Anderson and Marcouiller (1998) even stress the issue of legal insecurity as an informal barrier to trade.

arising from the state-imposed barriers to trade.[9] In the final-goods sector, the level of barriers to trade between country j (the production location) and country i is represented by $\phi^{i,j}$. For simplicity let the barriers to trade faced by final-goods producers in countries A and B be the same when trading with the ROW ($\phi^{C,A} = \phi^{C,B}$ and $\phi^{A,C} = \phi^{B,C}$). Artificial, state-imposed barriers to trade in the intermediate-goods sector are depicted by ϕ_x^2 $(0 < \phi_x^2 < 1)$. Furthermore, following our original framework in chapter 4, we allow for "natural" barriers to trade (transport costs) in the intermediate-goods sector, k_x $(0 < k_x < 1)$. That is, total costs associated with trade in this sector are $\phi_x = k_x\phi_x^2$. With free trade $\phi_x^2 = 1$ and $\phi_x = k_x$. Hence, even with free trade, "natural" transport costs provide a source of comparative advantage.

Since barriers to trade do not alter the elasticity of demand for intermediate-goods producers, optimal producer prices are independent of the location of Y-producers using these inputs:

$$p_x^{j,i} = p_x^{i,i} = \frac{c_x^i}{\gamma}, \tag{5.32}$$

with $c_x^i = a_x^i w_L^i$, the production costs of intermediate goods.

Private knowledge resulting from investing in R&D according to:

$$\dot{n}^i = L_n^i n, \tag{5.33}$$

i.e. with international knowledge spillovers, is not traded between countries. Each intermediate-goods producer serves the worldwide market from only one location. Due to high fixed costs arising from the establishment of a foreign subsidiary, it is more profitable to choose the "arm's-length" alternative rather than the internal one (international foreign direct investment). Hence, potential innovators decide simultaneously on the location of innovation and intermediate-goods production. This decision, together with the principal decision to invest in innovation, is governed by the usual no-arbitrage condition. In the country with positive innovation,

$$\frac{nG^i}{w_L^i} + \frac{\dot{c}_n^i}{c_n^i} = r \tag{5.34}$$

has to hold. Since the price elasticity of demand for final goods equals one, the introduction of non-tariff barriers to trade in the final-goods sector does not alter the basic structure of demand functions. The price and the quantity

[9] This modeling approach is also pursued in Baldwin (1989, 279).

effects just cancel each other out.[10] We can express the goods-market clearing conditions as:

$$\sum_j p_Y^j Y^j = \sigma, \qquad (j = A, B, C), \tag{5.35}$$

and

$$\sum_j p_Z^j Z^j = 1 - \sigma, \tag{5.36}$$

with p_Z^j denoting producer prices of the respective good in country j.

Labor market equilibrium in each country is achieved if:

$$\bar{L}^i = L_x^i + L_n^i + L_Y^i + L_Z^i. \tag{5.37}$$

We can now turn to the long run equilibrium pattern of the three-country economy.

The Long Run Equilibrium

In order to keep the structure of the model as simple as possible, we assume that the ROW has a technological comparative advantage in Z-production due to low productivity in the production of the industrial final good and the intermediate good (i.e a small A^C and a large a_x^C). Hence, it specializes completely in Z-production. Furthermore, we look at a core-periphery pattern in the integration bloc. Country B is the innovating country; R&D is undertaken only there. This can be rationalized similarly to the explanation in section 5.1.

The integration bloc is incompletely specialized in the production of the two goods. The peripheral country in the integration bloc produces both final goods. We will provide conditions for this to hold in the steady-state in a moment. These assumptions on the specialization patterns facilitate the analysis considerably. Allowing for more general specialization patterns would, however, leave the basic results of our analysis unchanged as long as the integration bloc has a comparative advantage in the Y-sector and is

---

[10] Let, for example, p_Z denote the international price of the traditional final good and ϕ_Z the non-tariff barriers in the traditional-goods sector. Consumers' demand, e.g. in country A, for this good equals $(1-\sigma)E^A\phi_Z/p_Z$. Production abroad to meet this demand equals $(1-\sigma)E^A/p_Z$. That is, output and revenues of producers are independent of the location of consumers.

incompletely specialized. Against the background of the EU and NAFTA, this depicts a realistic scenario.

Trade barriers do not influence the goods-market clearing conditions (see (5.35) and (5.36)). However, they drive a wedge between producer prices in different countries. The ROW exports traditional final goods and imports the industrial final good. Country A, the periphery in the integration bloc, and the ROW compete with their traditional final goods production in country B. Hence, $c_Z^A/\phi^{B,A} = c_Z^C/\phi^{B,C}$ has to hold. This requires:

$$\bar{\omega}_{A,C} := \frac{w_L^A}{w_L^C} = \frac{\phi^{B,A}}{\phi^{B,C}}. \tag{5.38}$$

There are two possible trade patterns arising for country A. Either it exports final goods and imports intermediate products or, alternatively, it imports the industrial final goods as well as intermediate products. Since both scenarios yield the same qualitative result, for matters of concreteness we use the first alternative. Y-producers located in A and B compete with each other on world markets. This calls for:

$$c_Y^A = c_Y^B. \tag{5.39}$$

For relative wages this implies[11]

$$\omega = \frac{w_L^A}{w_L^B} = \phi_x^{\frac{1-\alpha}{\alpha}} < 1. \tag{5.40}$$

In the steady-state with a constant intersectoral allocation, all nominal variables grow at a proportional rate. Since we normalized prices such that $E = 1$, this implies $\dot{w}_L^i = 0, \forall i$.

Applying Shephard's Lemma to (5.31) and using (5.32) together with goods-market clearing conditions, we can write intermediate goods producers' output as:

$$x^A(v) = \frac{(1-\alpha)\sigma}{np_x^A}. \tag{5.41}$$

Hence, the profit rate of innovators in A equals $G^i/c_n^A = (1-\alpha)(1-\gamma)\sigma/w_L^A$. Applying Shephard's Lemma to (5.31) once again and using (5.41) to derive

[11] With the second scenario (country A being an importer of Y), $\phi^{B,A}c_Y^A = c_Y^B$ must hold. The relative wage equation reads as $\omega = \phi_x^{\frac{1-\alpha}{\alpha}}/\phi^{B,A}$. Using this relative wage equation instead of the one in (5.40) in the subsequent analysis reveals that the effects discussed below are reinforced by this change in the underlying trade patterns.

labor demand, we obtain the national full employment conditions by using the steady-state no-arbitrage condition:

$$L^A = \frac{(1-\alpha)s_Z^A}{w_L^A} + \frac{\alpha\sigma s_Y^A}{w_L^A}, \tag{5.42}$$

$$L^B = \frac{\sigma(1-\alpha)}{w_L^B} - \rho + \frac{\alpha\sigma s_Y^B}{w_L^B}, \tag{5.43}$$

$$L^C = \frac{(1-\sigma)s_Z^C}{w_L^C}, \tag{5.44}$$

with s_Z^i and s_Y^i denoting the market share of country i in traditional and industrial final-goods production.

After some calculations, we can derive the market share of country B from the pricing conditions and the labor-market clearing conditions:

$$\begin{aligned} s_Y^B &= \frac{\bar{f}(1-\sigma+\sigma\alpha) - \sigma(1-\alpha)\phi_x^{\frac{1-\alpha}{\alpha}}(\bar{\tau}+\tilde{f})}{\sigma\alpha\bar{f} + \phi_x^{\frac{1-\alpha}{\alpha}}(\bar{\tau}+\tilde{f})\sigma\alpha} \\ &:= S(\bar{f},\tilde{f},\bar{\tau},\phi_x), \end{aligned} \tag{5.45}$$

with $\bar{f} = (L^B+\rho)/L^C$, $\tilde{f} = L^A/L^C$, $\bar{\tau} = \phi^{A,C}/\phi^{A,B}$, and

$$\frac{\partial S}{\partial \bar{f}} > 0; \qquad \frac{\partial S}{\partial \phi_x} < 0; \qquad \frac{\partial S}{\partial \bar{\tau}} < 0; \qquad \frac{\partial S}{\partial \tilde{f}} < 0.$$

For the market share of country A in Z-production we obtain:

$$s_Z^A = \frac{(\bar{f}\phi_x^{\frac{\alpha-1}{\alpha}} + \tilde{f}) - \bar{\tau}(1-\alpha)/(1-\sigma)}{\bar{\tau} + f + \bar{f}\phi_x^{\frac{\alpha-1}{\alpha}}}. \tag{5.46}$$

We impose two technical assumptions, guaranteeing $s_Y^A > 0$ and $s_Z^A > 0$, respectively:

Assumption 5.2.1 $\qquad \frac{\sigma}{1-\sigma}\phi_x^{\frac{1-\alpha}{\alpha}} > \frac{L^B+\rho}{L^C},$

and

Assumption 5.2.2 $\qquad (\bar{f}+\tilde{f}) > \frac{\sigma}{1-\sigma}(1-\alpha).$

Both assumptions are simultaneously satisfied if the countries in the integration bloc are not too small compared to the ROW and the share of intermediate goods in total production $\sigma(1-\alpha)$ is not too large.

Now we can derive the steady-state innovation rate. With the no-arbitrage condition and the factor market clearing-condition of country A, the steady-state innovation rate can be expressed by:

$$\begin{aligned} g &= \frac{(1-\alpha)(1-\gamma)\sigma}{w_L^B} - \rho \\ &= \frac{(1-\alpha)(1-\gamma)\sigma(\bar{L}^A + \rho)}{\sigma(1-\alpha) + \alpha\sigma S} - \rho. \end{aligned} \tag{5.47}$$

The output growth rate is proportional to the innovation rate. The steady-state growth rate effects of regional integration can be deduced from (5.45) in combination with (5.47).

5.2.2 The Growth Effects of Regional Integration

We divide our analysis of the growth effects of regional integration into three steps. Firstly, we gradually relax barriers to trade between countries A and B. Then we look at the implications of a change in the impediments to trade with the rest of the world. Finally, we focus on the long run effects of migration. These three steps of regional integration follow along the lines of the standard definition of various forms of regional integration of an increasing degree: formation of a free trade zone (relaxation of internal barriers to trade), establishment of a customs union (adoption of a common external trade policy) and the creation of a common market (liberalization of factor flows).

With respect to trade liberalization between the two countries, we distinguish between barriers to trade in final goods and a reduction of barriers to trade for the exchange of intermediate goods. Liberalization of final-goods trade is equivalent to an increase in $\phi^{A,B}$ or to a decrease in $\bar{\tau}$. A glance at (5.45) and (5.47) reveals that the steady-state innovation and growth rate decline.

The intuition behind this result is the following. The reduction in barriers to trade between A and B in the final-goods sectors creates a cost advantage for Z-producers in A compared to their competitors in the ROW. Trade liberalization provides an incentive for consumers in B to demand a high share of Z-imports from producers in A, i.e. s_Z^A increases (see (5.46)). Trade is diverted from imports from the ROW into the integration bloc to trade flows between the member states. This trade diversion effect[12]

[12] It has to be noted that here trade diversion means that B imports more from the

shifts resources into the traditional-goods sector of A. This reallocation of resources from Y-production to Z-production in A induces a reallocation of resources in B as well. Resources are shifted out of the dynamic sector in B in order to free resources for the expansion of the Y-sector, s_Y^B increases. As in subsection 5.1, the allocation effect of integration alters the incentive to accumulate knowledge and invest in R&D. The allocation effect is based on the trade diversion effect in our three-country model. Steady-state innovation and growth rates decrease.

Just the reverse happens with a relaxation of barriers to trade in the intermediate-goods sector. With an increase in ϕ_x, trade of intermediate goods in the integration bloc is facilitated. Trade liberalization leads to trade creation. Y-producers in A become less costly and s_Y^A (s_Y^B) increases (decreases) (see (5.45)). This reallocation releases labor in country B which is employed in the R&D sector and w_L^B decreases.
We can establish:

Proposition 5.2.1 *Trade liberalization between the member states of the integration bloc in the trade of final goods leads to trade diversion and slows down steady-state growth. A reduction of the impediments to trade in the intermediate-goods sector has a trade creation effect and induces faster steady-state growth.*

The effect of a symmetric reduction in all areas of trade between A and B is ambiguous. Depending on the parameter constellation, the negative growth rate effect of trade liberalization in the consumption-good sector could dominate the positive effect of a reduction in non-tariff barriers to trade or vice versa.

External barriers to trade are altered in the course of the formation of a customs union. The direction of change of the average rate of protection is not clear-cut. Depending on the starting position and the details of the treaty, $\phi^{B,C}$ might increase or decrease. Suppose $\phi^{B,C}$ declines. This case also covers more protectionist behavior of the supranational body in the integration bloc (e.g. fortress Europe). With higher national external impediments to trade, Z-producers in the integration bloc – similarly to lower internal barriers to trade in the final-goods sector – gain a better competitive position relative

country with higher producer costs (A) but with reduced consumer prices. In contrast, however, to the classical trade diversion effect, where the loss of tax income just has a redistribution effect between consumers and the state, here, transport costs are actually saved, implying a ressource gain.

to their competitors in the ROW. Consumers in B have to pay higher prices for imports from the ROW. We observe a trade diversion effect. Country A's market share in the Z-sector expands (see (5.46)). The associated shift of resources away from the Y-sector into A causes B's market share in the industrial final-goods market to expand (see (5.45)). This occurs at the expense of the dynamic sector. Growth and innovation rates are lower in the new steady-state. Needless to say, lower external barriers to trade imply just the reverse result.
We establish:

Proposition 5.2.2 *Higher (lower) external barriers to trade induce a reallocation of resources leading to a higher (lower) share of Z-production in the integration bloc. Growth and innovation rates decrease (increase).*

Our results suggest that trade liberalization speeds up growth when the liberalization measures are accompanied by a trade creation effect. They lead to slower growth if they induce a trade diversion effect. This general result, however, requires a qualification. In our three-country setting, trade creation is equivalent to a displacement of Z-production in the integration bloc. This releases labor in countries A and B which can be employed in the dynamic sector. Even with immobile factors of production, the two countries are linked via the Y-sector. That is, our general result hinges on the assumption of the integration bloc having a comparative advantage in the more advanced sector and the fact that the periphery-country in the integration bloc is incompletely specialized. As already indicated above, this represents a realistic scenario against the background of the most prominent integration blocs, the EU and NAFTA.

Consider now the relaxation of barriers to migration between countries A and B. This can be interpreted as a move towards a customs union. Some barriers to trade (transport costs) are still present.
We state:

Proposition 5.2.3 *Relaxing barriers to migration in the integration bloc accelerates steady-state growth.*

Proof: By adding (5.42) and (5.43) we obtain with (5.40):

$$L^A+L^B+\rho=\frac{1}{w_L^B}\left[\sigma(1-\alpha)+\alpha\sigma(s_Y^B(1-\phi_x^{\frac{\alpha-1}{\alpha}})+\phi_x^{\frac{\alpha-1}{\alpha}})+(1-\sigma)s_Z^A\phi_x^{\frac{\alpha-1}{\alpha}}\right].$$

With migration from A to B, $\bar{f}$ increases whereas f decreases. Hence, s_Y^B increases (see (5.45)). We claim that w_L^B decreases. To prove this claim we suppose the contrary. Since the LHS of the above equation is constant, this requires that s_Z^A increase which, in turn, would lead to a decrease in s_Z^C and consequently to a lower w^C. But with constant barriers to trade, $w_L^B/w_L^C = \bar{\tau}^{-1}\phi_x^{\frac{\alpha-1}{\alpha}}$. A decrease in w_L^C requires a decrease in w_L^B as well. This violates our initial hypothesis of a non-decreasing w_L^B. The positive growth effect can be derived from the first line of (5.45) and the smaller w_L^B. Q.e.d.

The economics behind this result are straightforward. Migration increases the factor supply in country B while lowering it in country A. The additional labor force is partially employed in the Y-sector and partially in the R&D sector. That is, migration from the periphery to the innovative center country leads to an international allocation with a higher employment share in the dynamic sector.

5.2.3 Welfare Effects of Integration

Using our growth rate results from the preceding subsection, we can now address the welfare implications of regional integration in our three-country framework. We compare the welfare effects between the new and the old steady-state. Considering all three countries together, we find static as well as dynamic sources for a change in overall welfare. Static distortions arise from trade impediments due to the wedge between consumer and producer prices in the final-goods sector. In the intermediate-goods sector the difference between monopolistic prices and marginal costs is aggravated by non-tariff barriers to trade. Furthermore, trade impediments influence the dynamic distortion in the R&D sector. But, rather than looking at overall welfare, we address the welfare effects for each country. For this purpose, we express $\tilde{p}_Y^i(t)$ as $\tilde{p}_Y^i(0)e^{gt\frac{(\alpha-1)}{(\epsilon-1)}}$. With constant wage rates in the steady-state, we are able to integrate the intertemporal utility function to obtain:

$$U^i(0) = \frac{1}{\rho}\left[\bar{\sigma} + lnE^i - \sigma ln\tilde{p}_Y^i(0) - ln\tilde{p}_Z^i + \frac{\sigma(1-\alpha)}{\epsilon-1}\frac{g}{\rho}\right], \tag{5.48}$$

with $\bar{\sigma} = \sigma ln\sigma + (1-\sigma)ln(1-\sigma)$.

To simplify the analysis, we assume perfect mobility of financial capital between the countries in the integration bloc, but capital immobility between the ROW and the integration bloc. In the absence of R&D investment in the ROW, households in the ROW receive only labor income: $E^C = w_L^C$. In contrast, households residing in the integration bloc have two sources of income. In addition to wage income, they receive dividend payments. From the dividend payments accruing to households (nG^B), $\dot{n}c_n^B$ are reinvested in order to finance the development of new intermediate products. With the help of the no-arbitrage condition, we can write this expression as ρw_L^B. Denoting the share of individual households in total assets as $\tilde{s}$, we derive the individual consumption expenditure functions as: $E^B = w_L^B(1+\tilde{s}\rho)$ and $E^A = w_L^A + \rho\tilde{s}w_L^B$. In the steady-state with constant wages, consumption expenditures of households are constant as well.

With final-goods trade liberalization in the integration bloc, wages in country B and A increases (see (5.40), (5.43) and (5.45)). With s_Z^C decreasing, w_L^C decreases as well. Labor in the ROW becomes less competitive when it comes to final-goods production for the integration bloc.. Wages in the two member states rise proportionally (see (5.40)). Since $d\tilde{p}_Y^B = dw_L^B$ and $d\tilde{p}_Z^B < 0$ (w_L^C declines), the static welfare effect in country B is positive. Note that in contrast to the customs unions literature we look at a relaxation of non-tariff barriers to trade. The public budget is not affected by liberalization. Country A experiences a proportional increase in income and prices. Its static welfare effect is zero. Income and price effects exactly offset each other. Country C's static welfare effect is negative. The decrease in the price of Z only partially compensates the fall in income. Furthermore, $\tilde{p}_Y^C$ increases as a consequence of the rise in wages in the integration bloc. Total welfare effects can be obtained by adding the negative dynamic welfare effect to the static effects. We establish:

Proposition 5.2.4 *Liberalization of final-goods trade between the member states of the integration bloc leaves households in country A and the ROW worse off. Representative agents in the center country B experience opposing static and dynamic welfare effects and hence, an ambiguous net welfare effect.*

The reduction in barriers to trade in intermediate-goods trade improves the competitive position of Y-producers since it reduces their input prices. Due to competitive pressure, w_L^B decreases (see (5.45) and (5.43)). The better competitive environment leads to higher wages in country A after the increase in ϕ_x. This can be seen by noting the larger market share of the ROW in Z-production (see (5.46)). As a consequence of the shift of resources within the integration bloc into the R&D sector and away from traditional final-goods production, the ROW obtains a larger share in the latter. Together with (5.30) and (5.44), this implies the proportional increase of w_L^C and w_L^A. Hence, consumer prices for the traditional (industrial) final goods increase (decrease). The income effect in the ROW, having the same magnitude as the change in $\tilde{p}_Y^C$, is larger than the weighted price increases. This is a straightforward implication of the drop in prices of the industrial final good. The same would be true for households in A, but for their dividend income. Since dividends paid out of profits (arising in B) decline, the static welfare effect for A's households is ambiguous and depends on the share of dividends in income. Due to the negative income effect, B's households experience a static welfare loss. The static welfare effects have to be contrasted with a positive dynamic welfare effect. Liberalization of the trade in intermediate goods speeds up growth.

By comparing the welfare effects of liberalization of trade barriers on final goods and a reduction of barriers to migration on intermediate goods, we observe just the opposite effects. Inner-union welfare effects depend very much on the sector where trade liberalization is undertaken and the induced trade effect of the integration measures. It might very well be that the member states of the integration bloc lose in the course of regional integration.

Let us now turn to the imposition of additional external barriers to trade. With the higher external barriers to trade, A and the ROW experience the same static welfare effects as with an increase in $\phi^{A,B}$. The static welfare effect in B is zero. Income and prices increase proportionally. A negative dynamic welfare effect has to be added to the (zero) static welfare effects.

With a relaxation of barriers to migration between A and B, we find a completely different picture. Relative wages in all three countries stay the same, i.e., absolute wages decline to the same extent (see (5.38) and (5.40)). Hence, with constant barriers to trade, consumer price changes are equal to wage changes. Real income remains the same for all non-migrating households. Migrants realize a positive income effect. Otherwise they would not be willing to migrate in the presence of positive migration costs. These income gains have to be confronted with migration costs. At the margin, migrants do not realize any positive static welfare gains. However, all households experience a gain through the higher rate of innovation leading to a faster decrease in consumer prices in the industrial final good.

We summarize with

Proposition 5.2.5 *A less protectionist policy towards the ROW and the liberalization of inner-union barriers to trade both lead to an improvement of welfare for all households.*

5.2.4 Brief Summary

What are the general lessons to be learned from our analysis in this section? It became obvious that, as in static analysis, it is decisive to distinguish between integration measures with a trade diversion and polices with a trade creation effect. Given that the integration bloc has a comparative advantage in the more advanced sectors, the induced change in specialization patterns either brings about a shift of resources into the dynamic sector or away from the R&D sector. Whereas in the former case we observe a higher steady-state growth rate, the slope of the real income path becomes less steep in the second case. Our analysis goes a significant step beyond the static analysis of regional integration policies by showing that discriminatory liberalization might very well lead to a lower growth rate and a negative dynamic welfare effect. Hence, our model calls for a cautious point of view towards partial liberalization when only some countries move closer together while the links to other countries remain unchanged or become even more protectionist. In contrast to popular belief, partial liberalization in an integration bloc might even lead to a decrease in steady-state growth.

5.3 Regional Policies and Policy Harmonization in an Economic Union

At later stages of regional integration, public policies are more and more harmonized among the member states of the integration bloc. Formally speaking, conducting policies jointly is defined as the crucial factor in the transition from a common market to an economic union (cf. e.g. El-Agraa (1994)). Policies can be carried out jointly in two different manners: either by harmonizing national policies or by handing over the conduct of these policies to a supranational body, e.g. the EU Commission.

Furthermore, progressing regional integration is characterized by the increasing importance of regional policy. This is especially the case with enlarged integration blocs embracing more asymmetric countries and regions. In the EU, regional policy became substantially more important with the integration of Spain and Portugal. The broad target of regional policy is to reduce or even completely eliminate regional disparities (cf. Commission (1990)). This might be termed a "spatial equity" objective. The importance of regional policy is especially pronounced in the EU. Various layers of regional policy exist in the EU (cf. Waniek (1992), and Commission (1991)), embracing a large variety of different instruments. The main instruments are public provision of local infrastructure and investment in transport facilities, such as road and railway systems, and direct as well as indirect subsidies to producers in less developed regions.

The objective of this section is twofold. On the one hand, we look at the long-run implications of regional policy measures. We ask whether a trade-off between dynamic efficiency and "spatial equity" might arise. This potential trade-off has been stressed quite often by observers of regional policy (cf. e.g. Jensen-Butler (1993)), but this conjecture has never been verified in a formal model. We aim to close this gap. Broadly speaking, we judge regional policy measures with respect to two criteria. First, we ask whether the respective regional policy instruments are able to reduce regional disparities and lead to regional income convergence in the sense that the income gap in the new equilibrium has been narrowed. This verifies whether or not the regional policy objective is achieved by the respective instrument. Secondly, we look at the effects of regional policy on the unionwide steady-state growth rate. These two criteria together enable us to evaluate the potential trade-off between spatial equity and dynamic efficiency.

Our second objective in this section is to briefly address the long-run consequences of policy harmonization in an economic union. Among the wide variety of potential policy areas, we choose those which can be analyzed within the framework of our model: common agricultural policy, harmonization of environmental standards, a common currency and the harmonization of social policies.

We proceed as follows. In the next subsection (5.3.1) we outline a generalized version of our basic model in chapter 4. In subsection 5.3.2 we analyze the dynamic implications of regional policy measures. In 5.3.3 we look at the implications of the harmonization of policies at the union level.[13]

5.3.1 A Generalized Two-Country Model

We extend our basic model outlined in chapter 4 in one direction: We allow for different endowments of the two countries with the immobile factor $\bar{L}^i$.

The basic production and consumption structure is the same as in chapter 4. Hence, optimal consumer decisions are described in (4.3)-(4.5). Pricing

[13] Further issues in this respect are discussed in Walz (1996a).

conditions in the final-goods and intermediate-goods sectors are also the same as in chapter 4. Relative wages which allow for competitive production of the industrial final good are:

$$\omega = \left(\frac{\mu + k^{\epsilon-1}}{1 + \mu k^{\epsilon-1}} \right)^{\theta}, \tag{5.49}$$

see (4.24). Assuming $f < \xi$ ($f^{-1} < \xi$), with $f = \bar{L}^A / \bar{L}^B$. guarantees that factor price equalization for immobile labor does not display an equilibrium situation if $\mu > 1$ ($\mu < 1$). Simultaneous market clearing for unskilled labor in the two countries requires with equal wages $f s_Z^B = \xi + s_Z^A$. Even for $s_Z^A = 0$, the equality sign is excluded by our assumption. Hence, with $\mu > (<)1$, $\omega > (<)1$ and $s_Z^A = 0$ ($s_Z^B = 0$). To be specific, we assume $\mu > 1$ in our following argument. Together with the labor-market clearing conditions, we can write the share of the two countries in the industrial final goods sector as:

$$s_Y^A = \frac{f\omega(1+\xi)}{\xi(1+\omega f)}, \tag{5.50}$$

$$s_Y^B = \frac{\xi - f\omega}{\xi(1+\omega)}. \tag{5.51}$$

With the help of these equations we can derive the condition for an interior solution in which profit differentials between the two countries vanish. Similarly to (4.30), we obtain:

$$\text{sign}(G^A - G^B) = \text{sign}[\xi + 1 - f^{-1}\xi\Psi^{\eta} + \Psi] := M. \tag{5.52}$$

Once again, $\eta > 0$ is a necessary condition for the existence of an interior solution. An interior solution is obtained if the asymmetry between the two countries with respect to the immobile resource base is not too pronounced.

Regional specialization, trade and growth patterns depend on two factors: initial conditions with regard to the number of locally produced intermediate goods and factor endowment differences. In our simple approach with $f = 1$, the latter determinant for regional specialization patterns was absent. Loosely speaking, factor endowment differences are decisive if the country with the larger $\bar{L}^i$ is capable of offseting any initial disadvantage with respect to the relative number of locally produced inputs. This disadvantage consists of the lower productivity of its immobile factor on the one hand and on the other hand on the withdrawal of resources from Y-production due to the local production of the traditional final good. If the larger country is able to compensate for any initial disadvantage, a core-periphery pattern emerges with innovation taking place exclusively in the larger country. In this case a unique steady-state equilibrium exists. If, however, size differences are not too pronounced, multiple equilibria emerge and history matters. The country with the initial advantage (with regard to μ) specializes in the Y-sector whereas the other country produces the traditional final good. An extensive, more detailed and rigorous discussion of the different types of equilibria as well as the transitional dynamics can be found in Walz (1996c).

For our present purpose it suffices to distinguish between two basic settings. In the first setting an interior solution takes place. Suppose that the larger country (A) has an initial advantage. Then an interior solution emerges if M becomes zero for $\mu < \infty$. To ensure a unique steady-state equilibrium for $\mu(0) > 1$, $M(\infty)$ has to be negative. That is, $f < f^* = \frac{k^{(1-\epsilon)\eta}}{\xi k^{1-\epsilon}+\xi+1}$ has to hold.

The other type of equilibrium results when factor endowment differences are so large that $G^A - G^B < 0$ for any $\mu > 1$. Country B (the larger country) becomes the innovative center independently of initial conditions. This is the case if $G^A - G^B < 0$ for $\mu = 1$, and $s_Z^B = 1$. This holds true if $f^{-1} > \tilde{f}^{-1} = (\xi + 2)/\xi$.

In the main part of this section we consider the first scenario. We only allow for the second case when looking at the possibility of leapfrogging via regional policy.

With the help of the standard no-arbitrage condition in the country with an active innovative sector:

$$\frac{nG^i}{w_H} - g = \rho, \tag{5.53}$$

and the unionwide factor-market clearing condition for skilled labor:

$$\bar{H} = \frac{\beta\sigma + (1-\alpha-\beta)\sigma\gamma + (1-\sigma)(1-\delta)}{w_H} + g := \frac{\Delta}{w_H} + g, \tag{5.54}$$

as well as the aggregate profits $nG = (1-\alpha-\beta)(1-\gamma)\sigma = \Phi$ which results by inserting (4.29) in the profit function, we can derive the steady-state innovation rate as:

$$g = \frac{\bar{H}\Phi - \rho\Delta}{\Phi + \Delta}. \tag{5.55}$$

This relation seems to indicate that the immobile factor does not have any impact on the growth process at all. This is only true for the unionwide growth and innovation rate. The influence of a country's endowment with the immobile factor, however, can be decisive for the country's output growth performance. This can be seen most clearly for the cases where factor endowment unambiguously determines the national specialization and growth patterns. The output growth rate of the better endowed country is larger than the unionwide average (since it specializes completely in the vertically structured industrial sector), whereas the other country's output growth rate is below the unionwide growth rate.

Now, we can turn to the analysis of the long-run implications of policy measures for regional growth and specialization patterns.

5.3.2 Regional Policy

We concentrate on the following regional policy issues: subsidies to producers in the lagging country, infrastructure investment in the low-income country and the possibility of a policy-induced leapfrogging process. With the exception of the last issue, we look at the effects of marginal departures from the laissez-faire equilibrium. In the entire discussion we take the regional policy objective as given by the political process. We do not ask for a welfare-maximizing policy leading to a more efficient interregional allocation.

Subsidies to Producers in the Low Income Country

With $f < f^* = \frac{k^{(1-\epsilon)\eta}}{\xi k^{1-\epsilon}+\xi+1}$ and $\mu(0) > 1$, an interior solution arises with country A being the innovative center. Innovation, however, also takes place in country B. This will be the starting point of our analysis. The share of the dynamic sector (industrial final-goods and intermediate-goods production and R&D) is smaller in B than in A. This is due to the traditional goods production in B. Hence, output growth is lower in B compared to A.

With our stylized model we are able to capture three types of subsidies granted to producers in country B: settlement subsidies for intermediate-goods producers, production cost subsidies to intermediate-goods producer and subsidies to the traditional-goods sector. All these instruments are employed in a more or less pure manner in the EU. We assume that these subsidies are financed by means of lump-sum taxes imposed on all households. This leaves the intertemporal allocation and regional specialization as well as the growth process unaltered. We leave the implications of financing public expenditures via distortionary taxes aside.

A one-time subsidy which promotes the settlement of intermediate-goods producers in country B, ϕ_s^B, lowers fixed costs and increases profit rates of investors in country B. This strengthens the relative position of country B. The decisive term for the profit rate differential can be expressed as:

$$M(\phi_s^B) = \left[\frac{s_Y^A}{s_Y^B}\Psi^{-1} - \Theta_s^B\right],$$

with $\Theta_s^B = 1 - k^{\epsilon-1}(1-\phi_s^B)/(1-\phi_s^B - k^{\epsilon-1})$. Hence, $\partial M/\partial\phi_s^B < 0$. Since $\partial M/\partial\mu < 0$, we find:

$$\frac{d\mu}{d\phi_s^B} = -\left(\frac{\partial M/\partial\phi_s^B}{\partial M/\partial\mu}\right) < 0. \tag{5.56}$$

In the new steady-state, relatively more intermediate goods are produced in country B. The wage gap between the two countries decreases ($\partial\omega/\partial\mu > 0$). Hence, the subsidy achieves its objective of reducing regional income patterns. This must be paid for by a lower rate of growth? It turns out that just the reverse is true – the subsidy accelerates growth. Since the settlement subsidy is equivalent to an R&D-subsidy in B, this is not too surprising.

The growth enhancing effect of the subsidy can be shown as follows. Rewriting the profit function with the help of (5.52) yields for aggregate steady-state profits in A with an interior solution:

$$nG = \Phi\left[\frac{(\mu+1)}{\mu + (1-\phi_s^B)}\right] = \Phi(\mu(\phi_s^B), \phi_s^B), \tag{5.57}$$

whereby $d\Phi/d\phi_s^B$, evaluated at $\phi_s^B = 0$, is positive. The labor-market clearing condition for skilled workers is not affected by the subsidy. Hence, we find:

$$g(\phi_s^B) = \frac{\bar{H}\Phi(\phi_s^B) - \rho\Delta}{\Phi(\phi_s^B) + \Delta}. \tag{5.58}$$

This proves our conjecture. The settlement subsidy reduces regional disparities and accelerates growth. The same results emerge if we consider a subsidy to capital costs in country B, e.g. via state-owned banks granting cheap credit to innovators in B.

Granting *ad-valorem* cost subsidies to intermediate-goods producers in B, ϕ_x^B, reduces the production costs of producers of differentiated inputs in B to $c_x = (w_H a_x)(1-\phi_x^B)$. Leaving the elasticity of demand and hence the monopolistic mark-up unchanged, this translates into lower input prices which Y-producers have to pay for inputs from B: $\tilde{p}_x^B = \tilde{p}_x^A(1-\phi_x^B)$.

At a first glance, it seems that this type of subsidy does induce a shift of intermediate-goods production to the peripheral country B. But a second look reveals that this need not necessarily be the case. The input price-reducing subsidies increases the degree of price competition faced by B's local producers in the input sector. In other words an agglomeration diseconomy is weakened, thereby widening the center-country A's chance as the location for profitable input production. Depending on which of the two forces dominates, μ declines or increases with the cost subsidy. Analytically, this can be derived by taking $\tilde{p}_x^B$ into account in the profit differential. We obtain:

$$\operatorname{sign}(G^A - G^B) = \operatorname{sign}\left[\frac{s_Y^A}{s_Y^B}\Psi^{-1} - \frac{\Theta_x^B - k^{\epsilon-1}}{1-\Theta_x^B k^{\epsilon-1}}\right], \tag{5.59}$$

and consequently:

$$M(\phi_x^B) = \left[(\xi+1)(1-\Theta_x^B k^{\epsilon-1}) + (\tilde{\Psi} - f^{-1}\xi\tilde{\Psi}^\eta)(\Theta_x^B - k^{\epsilon-1})\right], \tag{5.60}$$

with $\tilde{\Psi} = \frac{\mu + k^{\epsilon-1}\Theta_x^B}{\Theta_x^B + \mu k^{\epsilon-1}}$ and $\Theta_x^B = (1-\phi_x^B)^{1-\epsilon}$.

Totally differentiating this expression reveals the two opposite forces:

$$\frac{d\mu}{d\phi_x^B} = \frac{-\partial\Theta_x^B/\partial\phi_x^B}{\partial M/\partial\mu} \qquad [\{\partial M/\partial\Theta_x^B(-\xi\eta f^{-1}\Psi^{-\theta}+1)(1-k^{\epsilon-1})\}$$
$$+\{-(\xi+1)k^{\epsilon-1} - \xi f^{-1}\Psi^\eta + M\}]. \tag{5.61}$$

The first fraction is definitively positive. The term in brackets is decisive for the change in μ. The first expression in braces is positive, since $\partial M/\partial\Theta_x^B < 0$ and $(-\xi\eta f^{-1}M^\theta + 1)$ is negative with an interior solution as well. The latter fact follows from the negative sign of $\partial M/\partial\mu$ (see also our general discussion in chapter 4). The positive term reflects the increasing price competition in country B. The second term in braces is negative (see the condition $M = 0$). It reflects the cost savings in B which benefit B as the location of new intermediate-goods producers. Whenever the second term dominates, the subsidy achieves its objective. But the subsidy does not achieve this goal in all cases. It might also lead to a larger gap in the production pattern.

Whereas the effect of the subsidy on regional specialization patterns is not clear-cut, we find an unambiguous growth rate effect. Growth slows down. This surprising result is based on an allocation effect. Resources are diverted into the intermediate-goods sector and away from the R&D sector. The positive direct effect on the profit rate in B is offset by the increase in price competition and the associated change in μ. Aggregate profits remain the same: $nG = \Phi$. The subsidies increases the demand for intermediate goods, driving up wages for skilled workers. Inserting (5.52) in the factor market clearing-condition yields after some calculations:

$$\begin{aligned}\bar{H} &= \frac{\beta\sigma + (1-\delta)(1-\sigma)}{w_H} + (1-\alpha-\beta)\gamma\sigma\left(\frac{\mu + (1-\phi_x^B)^{-1}}{\mu+1}\right) + g \\ &= \frac{\Delta(\phi_x^B)}{w_H} + g, \end{aligned} \tag{5.62}$$

whereby $\partial\Delta/\partial\phi_x^B$ is positive for a marginal deviation from a laissez-faire equilibrium.

Rewriting the innovation rate with the help of (5.53) reveals that the innovation rate decreases with ϕ_x^B:

$$g(\phi_x^B) = \frac{\bar{H}\Phi - \rho\Delta(\phi_x^B)}{\Phi + \Delta(\phi_x^B)}, \tag{5.63}$$

since $dg/d\phi_x^B < 0$.

The lower innovation rate slows down unionwide growth. We observe a potential trade-off between regional equity and dynamic efficiency. Even if the subsidy is able to fulfill the regional target by reducing regional disparities, this is achieved only at the cost of a reduced growth rate.

The third type of policy is employed most often, even if it is not always dubbed regional policy: subsidies to traditional-goods producers, ϕ_Z. Since traditional-goods producers are usually concentrated in lagging regions, such a policy instrument has a significant spatial character. An *ad-valorem* subsidy to traditional-goods producers for given net-of-subsidy costs leads to a decline in the prices consumer have to pay: $\tilde{p}_Z = c_Z(1-\phi_Z)$. This stimulates demand for the traditional good and, consequently, its production. The goods-market clearing condition changes to $p_Z Z = \tilde{p}_Z Z/(1-\phi_Z) = (1-\sigma)/(1-\phi_Z)$. Increased demand for traditional goods shifts resources into this sector. This can be verified by rewriting the factor-market clearing condition in country B as:

$$\bar{L}^B = \frac{\alpha\sigma s_Y^B}{w_L^B} + \frac{\delta(1-\sigma)/(1-\phi_Z)}{w_L^A}. \tag{5.64}$$

This can be abbreviated by the change in ξ to $\bar{\xi} := \xi(1-\phi_Z)$. This alters the equilibrium market share in either country to:

$$s_Y^A = \frac{f\omega(1+\bar{\xi})}{\bar{\xi}(1+\omega f)}, \tag{5.65}$$

$$s_Y^B = \frac{\bar{\xi} - f\omega}{\bar{\xi}(1+\omega f)}. \tag{5.66}$$

More unskilled workers are employed in B's traditional-goods sector, thereby withdrawing resources from local Y-production in B. This reduces the local market for B's intermediate-goods producers. With the reduced dimension of the local market, profitability of investment in country B declines. Replacing ξ by $\bar{\xi}$ in the modified interior solution condition shows that, in the new steady-state, relatively more differentiated inputs are located in A: $d\mu/d\phi_Z = (\xi(1 - f^{-1}\Psi^{\eta}))/(\partial M/\partial \mu) > 0$.

Besides sharpening regional disparities (ω increases as well (see (5.49)), the subsidy also imposes costs on the union as a whole in the form of a dynamic welfare loss. The reduction in the steady-state growth rate can be deduced from the factor market clearing-condition for skilled workers,

$$\bar{H} = \frac{\beta\sigma + \sigma(1-\alpha-\beta)\gamma + (1-\sigma)(1-\delta)/(1-\phi_Z)}{w_H} + g = \frac{\Delta(\phi_Z)}{w_H} + g, \tag{5.67}$$

in combination with the profit function of firms. With profits remaining unaltered, we obtain:

$$g = \frac{\bar{H}\Phi - \Delta(\phi_Z)}{\Phi + \Delta(\phi_Z)}. \tag{5.68}$$

This proves the negative growth rate effect of the subsidy granted to traditional-goods producers: $dg/d\phi_Z = (\partial g/\partial \Delta)/(d\Delta/d\phi_z) < 0$. The subsidy not only diverts immobile resources away from Y-production in country B, but also withdraws skilled labor from the dynamic sector on a unionwide scale.
We can establish:

Proposition 5.3.1 *Settlement subsidies to intermediate-goods producers in B reduce regional disparities and accelerate growth. With a cost subsidy for intermediate-goods production, a trade-off between "spatial equity" and dynamic efficiency might arise. A subsidy to traditional-goods producers widens regional income gaps and slows down growth. In general, we find that the more closely subsidies are directed towards the innovator in country B, the more likely they are to reduce regional disparities and enhance growth.*

Investment in Infrastructure

Next to direct subsidies to producers in the peripheral country, investment in infrastructure is the most prominent tool used by regional policy makers (see Capellini/Molle (1988)).

It proves useful to distinguish very sharply two different types of infrastructure investment undertaken in the periphery with the objective of reducing regional disparities. On the one hand, we look at investment in transport infrastructure facilitating the access from the periphery to the center and vice versa. On the other hand, we address the expansion of local infrastructure in country B. The decisive difference between the two instruments is their opposite effect on agglomeration advantages and disadvantages.

We interpret investment in country B's transport capacities as a reduction in transport costs, i.e. an increase in k. Investment in roads, railway systems and other means of transport, however, not only facilitate exports from B to A, but also from A to B. Intermediate-goods producers in B as well as in A benefit from this policy. Transport costs represent an agglomeration disadvantage in the intermediate-goods sector. They protect producers of differentiated inputs from import competition. Hence, lowering transport costs is equivalent to a reduction of the centrifugal force making innovation and investment in the center more attractive. Competition becomes more fierce in B, which more than offsets the higher profitability due to lower transport costs. Regional disparities increase. Totally differentiating (5.52) yields:

$$\frac{d\mu}{dk} = -\frac{\partial M/\partial k}{\partial M/\partial \mu} > 0, \tag{5.69}$$

with $\partial M/\partial k = (\partial M/\partial \Psi)(d\Psi/d\mu) > 0$. This results from the fact that lowering transport costs makes it easier to supply the peripheral market from the production location in the center. Looking, however, at $M = \frac{s_Y^A}{s_Y^B}\Psi^{-1} - 1$ reveals, together with (5.49) and (5.50), that Ψ and consequently market shares of both countries in Y-production as well as relative wages remain unchanged. The direct effect of the increase in k, indicating wage convergence, is exactly offset by the indirect effect of an increase in μ, implying wage divergence. This compensation effect also implies, that profits as well as the factor-market clearing condition for skilled labor is unaffected, leaving, therefore, the steady-state growth rate unchanged.

Matters are completely different when we look at the implications of investment in local infrastructure. For this purpose, we interpret the immobile factor as local infrastructure. There are two alternatives for the provision of local infrastructure. Either infrastructure is publicly provided and firms pay taxes which equal the marginal productivity of infrastructure, or local infrastructure is provided privately. Note that our immobile factor does not have any characteristics of a public good and can be provided privately without difficulty. At the same time, however, one has to note that in most industrialized countries, goods without any public good properties are provided by the state. Both alternatives leave our basic set-up in place. The productive impact of local infrastructure on private producers and its contribution to the growth process has been stressed in a number of theoretical (see e.g. Barro (1990)) as well as empirical papers (cf. e.g. Aschauer (1989)).

Regional policy via investment in local infrastructure can be depicted as an increase in $\bar{L}^B$, i.e. by a decrease in f. The limited supply of the immobile factor represents an agglomeration disadvantage. An increase of the periphery's endowment with the immobile factor strengthens the centrifugal force.

Totally differentiating (5.52) validates this assertion:

$$\frac{d\mu}{df^{-1}} = \frac{\xi \Psi^{\eta}}{\partial M / \partial \mu} < 0. \tag{5.70}$$

Relative wages decline and Y-production is shifted into the periphery (see (5.48)- (5.50)). The decrease in f leaves the incentive to undertake R&D investment unaltered. In other words, steady-state growth remains the same. We can establish:

Proposition 5.3.2 *With regional policy by means of investment in infrastructure in the periphery, it proves crucial to distinguish between investment in transport infrastructure and investment in local infrastructure. Both regional policy measures leave unionwide growth patterns unaltered. But, whereas investment in local infrastructure strengthens centrifugal forces leading to reduced regional disparities, investment in transport infrastructure in B reinforces the centripetal forces and, hence, sharpens regional disparities.*

Leapfrogging

In the preceding chapter, we restricted the analysis to regional policy instruments departing only marginally from the laissez-faire equilibrium. The general specialization patterns were left in place and a regime switch was excluded. In this subsection we relax this restriction and look explicitly at the possibility of a reversal of specialization patterns. We ask whether regional policy can induce a leapfrogging process with country B becoming the innovative leader.

The analysis is undertaken in light of the objective of many regional policy makers of narrowing the technological gap as much as possible. At the local level, regional governments are very much inclined to induce a switch of specialization which brings their immobile workers a better technological position and earns them higher relative wages. We suppose that local infrastructure in B is used as the instrument for achieving such a regime switch. Once again, we interpret $\bar{L}^i$ as a broad measure of immobile factors embracing local infrastructure as well as immobile labor. Expansion of B's local infrastructure leads to a decrease in f. Starting from a steady-state equilibrium with $\mu^* > 1$, $\bar{L}^B$ must be enlarged such that $G^A < G^B$ holds for all $\mu > 1$ in order for a regime-switch to occur. G^A is smaller than G^B for all $\mu > 1$ if $G^A < G^B$ with $\mu = 1$ and country B is the only producer of traditional goods. This follows from the fact that $G^A - G^B$ is decreasing in μ. The condition $G^A < G^B$ with $\mu = 1$ and $s_Z^B = 1$ is fulfilled if $f^{-1} > f_l^{-1} = (2+\xi)/\xi$. Increasing $\bar{L}^B$ so that this condition holds enables country B to serve the entire demand for traditional final goods and provides a large enough local market for industrial final goods for intermediate-goods producers willing to locate in B. Investment in country B proves profitable as long as $\mu > 1$. Increasing f^{-1} slightly above f_l^{-1} guarantees profitable investment in B even with $\mu = 1$. A sudden reversal of specialization patterns takes place with an additional investment in the development of new intermediate goods at $\mu = 1$. A policy induced regime switch can also be interpreted as the attempt to eliminate regional disparities altogether. We argue that even a small degree of overshooting brings about a complete reversal of specialization patterns and might even lead to a core-periphery patterns.

With $\mu = 1 - \varepsilon$ (ε being a very small but positive number), $\omega < 1$ for $p_Y^A = p_Y^B$. Traditional-goods production is shifted to country A. Country B becomes the innovative center. The remaining question is whether an interior solution with $\mu^* < 1$ constitutes the new steady-state equilibrium, or whether a core-periphery pattern emerges. To answer this question we need to derive the profit differential for situations with $\mu < 1$ and $s_Z^B = 0$. Therefore, we derive the market share of both countries in Y-production for this situation from the labor-market clearing conditions as:

$$s_Y^A = \frac{\xi f\omega - 1}{\xi(1+f\omega)} \tag{5.71}$$

and

$$s_Y^B = \frac{1+\xi}{\xi(1+f\omega)}. \tag{5.72}$$

Hence, we can rewrite the decisive profit differential term resulting from sign $(G^A - G^B) = $ sign $(s_Y^A\Psi^{-1} - s_Y^B)$ as:

$$M(\mu < 1) = f\xi\Psi^{-\eta} - \Psi^{-1} - 1 - \xi. \tag{5.73}$$

If $M(0) < 0$, a core-periphery pattern emerges. Since $M(0) = f\xi k^{(1-\epsilon)\eta} - k^{1-\epsilon} - 1 - \xi$, we obtain the following condition for an interior solution with $\mu^* < 1$: $f^{-1} < (f_I)^{-1} := (\xi k^{(1-\epsilon)\eta})/(k^{1-\epsilon} + 1 + \xi)$. The two conditions ($f^{-1} < (f_I)^{-1}$ and $f^{-1} > f_l^{-1}$) do not necessarily exclude each other. With a policy induced regime-switch a core-periphery might result. The larger ξ is, the more probable an interior solution becomes. Suppose, for example, $k = 0.7, \epsilon = 3$, and $\eta = 0.8$. Then with $\xi = 2$, $M(0) = -3.271$ and a core-periphery pattern results. With $\xi = 10$ we find $M(0) = 1.705$ and an interior solution ($\mu^* < 1$) emerges.

If traditional-goods production uses the immobile factor relatively intensively (small ξ), reversing specialization patterns via regional policy results in a core-periphery pattern with the initially lagging country taking over the role of the innovative core. For this to occur, it suffices to increase f^{-1} only marginally above f_l^{-1}. Regional policy aiming to reduce regional disparities completely runs the risk of inducing a complete reversal of specialization and growth patterns. Since the complete elimination of regional disparities is not feasible ($\mu = 1$ is an unstable equilibrium (see chapter 4)), a permanent switching of target countries (from B to A to B etc.) would be necessary. Since a reversal of specialization patterns leaves country A as the (relative) periphery (possibly even in a core-periphery pattern), this is not necessarily in the interest of central regional policy makers.
We establish:

Proposition 5.3.3 *Regional policy makers are able to induce a complete reversal of specialization patterns by enlarging f^{-1} slightly above $f_l^{-1} = (2+\xi)/\xi$. For a not too large ξ, this leads to a core-periphery pattern with even more pronounced regional disparities.*

5.3.3 Common Policies

From the wide variety of policy areas in which national policies can be harmonized, we can look only at a small subset of policy areas. Other policies require a substantially modified modeling approach.

We address the following issues. First, we briefly look at the implications of a common currency on the real economy in the union. Then, we investigate the effects of unionwide harmonization of environmental standards, and a common social policy imposing common working conditions in all member states of the union (Social Charta). Finally, we turn to an analysis of an agricultural policy pursued by the supranational body (e.g. the EU commission).

Let us begin with the introduction of a common currency. Before the currency union takes place, exporters face an at least partially flexible exchange rate. They are exposed to the risk of unanticipated exchange rate movements which have a negative impact on risk averse investors. If they hedge this risk away they have to bear the costs of the hedge. These costs can be significant especially with long-term investment. With a currency union, the costs for exporters decrease. It seems most appropriate to interpret this as a reduction in transport costs, i.e. as an increase in k. As our formal discussion in 5.3.2 revealed, a decrease in transport costs reduces the agglomeration disadvantages. Exports are facilitated and the relative importance of the larger local market in the center country (A) increases. We observe regional divergence with respect to regional production patterns. In the new steady-state, a relatively larger number of intermediate goods is produced in the center. Relative wages and market shares of countries in final-goods production remain, however, unchanged. The unionwide growth rate is unaffected.

Secondly, we consider a harmonization of environmental standards in the union. Typically, due to declining marginal utility of income, environmental controls are more strictly enforced in the high-income country (cf. e.g. Saint-Paul (1994)). Harmonization of environmental policies is then accompanied by an increase in standards in the low-income country and unchanged or even reduced standards in the high-income country. This can be captured in our model by including local environment in the broad measure of local productive factors. Harmonizing environmental standards reduces the degree to which local producers are allowed to pollute the environment (for which they have to pay an emission tax) to a greater extent in the periphery. The level of permitted pollution is reduced relatively more strongly. Hence, the relative amount of immobile resources available for final-goods producers diminishes and f increases. The competitive advantage of the periphery (country B) in the production sphere, stemming from lower preferences for a clean environment, are reduced or potentially eliminated. As the analysis of a varying f in the last subsection showed, this implies a lower relative number of differentiated goods being produced in the lagging country. Final-goods production is shifted towards the center and the relative factor price for the immobile factor in the periphery declines. The absolute factor price for the immobile resource, however, might increase due to the lower factor supply:

$$\bar{L}^B = \frac{\alpha\sigma s_Y^B}{w_L^B} + \frac{(1-\sigma)\xi}{w_L^B}. \tag{5.74}$$

Only if the decrease in s_Y^B more than offsets the decline in $\bar{L}^B$, we do observe a decrease in w_L^B.

Harmonizing social policy (minimum social standards) in the labor markets of the union is an integral part of a common social policy. Labor market policies have the most direct effects on regional factor prices and production patterns among the wide array of social policy measures. Hence, we limit our brief discussion of a common social policy to this subject. Social policies affecting the labor market embrace, e.g. in the EU common employment laws and common rules on working conditions. They are more or less equivalent to a compromise between existing standards in the union (cf. Collins (1994)). Many, if not most of social policy measures cause additional costs for the production factor factor labor (we look only at additional costs on immobile labor). Additional costs are equivalent to taxes on labor income. Additional costs on wages are more pronounced in the periphery than in the center. The impact of such a policy in our model is straightforward. Since the model works with gross wages (before taxes) and factors are supplied inelastically, gross wages are left unchanged. This simply follows from the fact that cost-minimizing firms in a competitive labor market are only willing to pay workers their marginal product. Since labor productivity stays the same, so do gross wages. Hence, the entire burden of social policy is carried by immobile workers in country B which experience a drop in their relative and absolute income. The same pattern would result if social policy places an additional burden on mobile workers. Production and growth patterns would stay the same, but net wages would be reduced. It is needless to say that a more elaborate analysis of such policies requires a more subtle modeling approach, including the possibility of regional unemployment, i.e. the interaction between unemployment and growth (cf. Aghion/Howitt (1994)). Our analysis can be considered as a very first step which highlights the fact that, in the presence of factor-market clearing and an inelastic supply of labor, the financial burden of social policy is imposed on workers.

Finally, we turn to the most prominent common policy in the EU, the common agricultural policy (CAP). The share of expenditures for the CAP as a percentage of the EU Commission's budget amounted to 58.6% in 1993 (cf. German Statistical Yearbook (1994)). The main difference between a national sectoral policy and one pursued at the supranational level is basically the higher support level for industries in low-income countries with a common policy. We already handled the impact of the CAP in the preceding subsection. It is equivalent to a subsidy directed at traditional-goods industries. We showed that such a policy increases regional disparities and reduces unionwide growth. Resources are shifted at the national as well as the unionwide level to the traditional-goods sector at the expense of the dynamic sectors (R&D and intermediate-goods production).

5.3.4 Brief Summary

There are three major policy implications emerging from this section. First, for regional policy purposes, the effect of a specific measure on agglomeration advantages and disadvantages has to be examined carefully. Many applied regional policy measures strengthen the centripetal rather than the centrifugal forces, thereby leading to more rather than less disparities among countries and regions.

Secondly, regional policy measures might also influence the overall incentive to invest. A potential trade-off between spatial equity and dynamic efficiency arises Policy makers often impose significant costs on the economy.

Thirdly, harmonization of policies in an economic union may very well contradict the regional policy objective by benefitting the center rather than the periphery country. This indirect effect, adding to the negative effect of centralization, creates a further need to justify harmonization and centralization of policies.

5.4 Summary

What are the main results of our analysis of a wide variety of aspects of deeper regional integration? We find a rather mixed picture with respect to the relationship between regional integration and growth. Our two-country model showed that general liberalization steps between sufficiently closely integrated economies always had a non-negative growth rate effect. Free trade produced the maximal steady-state growth rate. As in other static analyses, we found that deeper integration might lead to sharper regional disparities. This, however, is not a general characteristic of deeper regional integration, but rather depends on whether trade impediments display a centripetal or centrifugal force. Whereas trade impediments lead to an agglomeration advantage in the differentiated-goods sector, the very same trade impediment acts as an agglomeration disadvantage in the final-goods sector for a given relative number of intermediate products. Consequently, depending on the initial specialization patterns (core-periphery or interior solution), trade liberalization leads to more or less similar specialization patterns. Our analysis reveals that a general relationship between regional production patterns and trade liberalization does not exist.

In contrast, a liberalization of migration barriers leads to migration to the high-wage country and an even larger income gap. With sufficiently low costs to migration that could imply a complete depopulation of the low-wage region. Even if people are not willing to migrate at the beginning, the increased wage gap may induce a cumulative process ending with a complete concentration of households in the center country.

Stressing the discriminatory character of regional integration, we showed that the findings of static analysis are even reinforced in a dynamic setting. Liberalization measures leading to trade creation increase steady-state growth, whereas integration measures with a trade diverting effect decrease the steady-state growth rate. But it is important to note that this relationship between trade diversion and creation respectively and growth crucially depends on the general specialization patterns of the integration bloc compared to the rest of the world. Given that the integration bloc as a whole has a comparative advantage in the dynamic sector and is not completely specialized, the link between trade creation and faster growth on the one hand, and between trade diversion and slower growth on the other hand, holds. But with different specialization patterns (e.g the integration bloc having a comparative disadvantage in the dynamic sector) our relationship might be reversed.

Migration in the integration bloc induced by the liberalization of migration policies leads to a more efficient international allocation of resources. Migration flows associated with a shift of resources into the dynamic sector lead to faster growth and welfare improvements for all agents.

Our analysis suggests that, due to its discriminatory character, liberalization measures in the course of regional integration are by no means always growth-enhancing. Hence, our analysis adds to the caution with regard to regional integration stressed in static analysis. It goes even one step further by pointing out the possibility of growth reduction in the course of regional integration.

At later stages of integration, deeper regional integration is associated with harmonization of policies and the relatively more prominent role of regional policy. We have shown that, in a wide variety of cases, regional policy measures dampen the incentive for research in the union as a whole. Resources are shifted away from the dynamic sector and into the sectors of the periphery which are promoted by regional policy. These dynamic costs of regional policy add to the costs associated with distortionary financing of regional policy expenditures. Our analysis highlights the potential trade-off between a "spatial equity" objective (i.e. a reduction of regional income disparities) and dynamic efficiency. Furthermore, we discovered that, in many cases, regional policy does not even achieve its foremost objective, namely to equalize income and specialization patterns across regions. Rather, by strengthening agglomeration advantages, regional policy deteriorates the relative position of the periphery. This is particularly obvious with respect to the support of traditional industries in the lagging country, but also true for investment in transport infrastructure. Our analysis reveals that it is important to look at the precise impact of regional policy measures on centripetal and centrifugal forces. Whereas investment in local infrastructure in the periphery reduced regional disparities, a seemingly closely related measure, investment in the periphery's transport infrastructure, has just the opposite effect. Our analysis calls for a very cautious view with respect to regional policy. Even if one accepts the notion of a reduction of regional disparities (which is very often not based on efficiency considerations), the associated costs and the necessity (as well as the difficulty) of evaluating the impact on agglomeration advantages and disadvantages casts strong doubts on the feasibilty of developing an adequate regional policy strategy.

By examining the long-run implications of policy harmonization, we find that many of these policies have potential effects on unionwide as well as regional growth patterns. Harmonization brings about a restriction of the possibility of adjusting policies to each country's need. Our first step towards an analysis of the long-run consequences of common policies revealed that it is worthwhile to investigate the long-run consequences of the transition from a common market to an economic union on the regional as well as on the unionwide growth process in order to assess the potential costs of such policy measures.

Chapter 6

Enlarging the Integration Bloc

Along side deeper regional integration among a given number of member states, the enlargement of an existing trading bloc displays the second major form of regional integration. With enlargement, in contrast to a deepening of integration, barriers to trade, factor flows and other regional integration measures between 'old' members of the integration bloc remain the same. Rather, the number of member states increases and the relationship between old and new members is altered.

In order to distinguish enlargement from the deepening of integration adequately, we need to analyze the enlargement process in at least a three-country framework. This enables us to leave the relationship already established between the members unchanged, while altering the two countries' relationship vis-à-vis the entrant. A two-country model can not encompass the decisive impact of the enlargement process on the relationship among already established members.

The most prominent example of an integration bloc where enlargement has played an important role is, once again, the EU. Consisting initially of six founding countries, it has expanded steadily ever since. After the fourth enlargement step which entailed the inclusion of the former EFTA-countries Austria, Sweden, and Finland, it now includes fifteen member states. There is a long list of countries willing to enter in the foreseeable future. In particular, integration of Central and Eastern European countries is on the political agenda. In 1998, the EU started official negotiations for accessesion with Polen, Hungary, the Czech Republic, Slovenia and Estonia (see Berliner Morgenpost (1998)). In addition, Roumania, Slovakia, Latvia, Lithuania and Bulgaria have applied for membership in the European Union. In Central and Northern Europe, Norway and to a lesser extent Switzerland are the two candidates most likely to join the EU in the not too distant future. Furthermore, with the formal Turkish application for membership, the announced reapplication of Malta as well as with the official negotiotations for accession between the EU and Cyprus, a potential for EU enlargement to the South direction is on the way.

In other integration blocs, enlargement also plays a decisive role. One of the most recent examples is the integration of Mexico into the US-Canadian free trade agreement via the creation of NAFTA. More recently, talks have been started on expanding NAFTA through the inclusion of Chile. Even further reaching agreements of closer economic cooperation between the countries of the Western Hemisphere are targeted towards an enlargement of NAFTA across basically the entire American continent (see Financial Times (1994)).

The above mentioned potential and actual entrants fall into two broad classes of countries. The first group consists of developed, high-income countries like Sweden, Austria, and Switzerland. The second group of countries embraces candidates such as Poland, Hungary, Turkey and Mexico, constituting lagging economies with a relatively low income per capita and specialization patterns oriented more towards the traditional sector. We will discuss these two groups separately.

In the following, we look at the consequences from the integration of a country belonging to either group. In section 6.1, we extend our basic framework to a three-country setting. With the help of this three-country model, we analyze the gradual integration of a less-developed country into an integration bloc, consisting initially of two countries with endogenously determined specialization patterns. We focus on the growth effect of integration and the impact of enlargement on the relationship between the two 'old' member countries.[1] In section 6.2, we look at an enlargement scenario with an advanced country as the candidate for integration. In contrast to section 6.1, innovation as well as production in advanced sectors takes place in the third country which becomes integrated in stages.

[1] Thereby, we draw on the analysis in Walz (1998).

In sections 6.1 and 6.2, the relative specialization patterns among the three countries are unaffected by the enlargement process. A country which was initially producing traditional goods will continue to do so after integration has taken place, although it may be doing that to a lesser extent. Complete reversals of specialization patterns among two of the three countries are excluded.

In section 6.3, we allow for a complete endogeneity of specialization patterns. We ask whether or not enlargement can induce a leapfrogging process. Suppose that the integration bloc consists of an industrial core (France/Germany/ Benelux) and a relative periphery (Southern Europe) where traditional production as well as some innovative activities take place. Before integration, the candidate for integration (an Eastern European country) is completely specialized in the traditional sector. Enlarging the integration bloc by gradually integrating the third country changes relative prices and the relative competitiveness of participating countries. We investigate the conditions under which the newly integrated country is brought into a better position for local innovation, such that the initial specialization patterns between the relative periphery and the entrant switch. If such a situation arises, the periphery in the integration bloc loses its dynamic sector, which is shifted into the newly entering country. Through the integration of Eastern Europe, Southern European countries lose their initial advantage.

6.1 Integrating a Lagging Country

In a large number of cases, the technological level of the candidate for integration was or will be significantly lower compared to the established member states of the integration bloc. In the history of the EC, enlargement steps integrating Greece, Ireland, Spain, and Portugal are obvious examples. Future cases may include the integration of Central and Eastern European countries as well as Turkey. The most recent example of enlargement via integration of a technically less advanced country (compared to the incumbent ones), however, is the formation of NAFTA with the incorporation of Mexico into the free trade zone between Canada and the US.

These examples reveal two important facts. First, there may be pronounced differences of interest between the "old" member states of the integration bloc. Secondly, the enlargement process often takes place stepwise. Usually free trade agreements are signed before the possibility of a full membership with free factor flow is addressed. Examples are the free trade agreements between the EU and Turkey, as well as some Central and Eastern European countries (Poland, Hungary). A similar pattern can be observed with respect to the establishment of NAFTA. Rather than allowing for free labor mobility, only gradual trade liberalization was agreed upon. According to neoclassical trade theory (Heckscher-Ohlin model), trade and factor mobility are substitutes. The same allocation as with free trade in goods is achieved with free mobility of one factor (cf. Razin/Sadka (1992)). Hence, the question remains as to why countries are reluctant to allow for free labor migration while at the same time signing free trade agreements. In the following, we will provide a possible explanation for this behavior.

With our subsequent analysis of the enlargement process via integration of a technologically lagging country, we want to investigate the consequences of this form of the integration process on specialization, trade, and growth patterns. These are decisive issues for policy makers. The change in specialization and trade patterns indicates the degree of the reallocation of resources which can be expected, as well as the relative position of the country in the world economy. Potential winners and losers can be determined. Positive (negative) growth effects imply dynamic welfare gains (losses). Different effects of the enlargement process can be seen as the rationale of different points of view of "old" countries towards this process.[2]

This section is divided in three parts. In the first one, we outline the three-country equilibrium for given trade and migration barriers. We adopt our basic framework from chapter 4 and extend it to a three-country setting. In the second part, we concentrate on the implications of trade liberalization vis-à-vis the third country. The third subsection addresses the second step of the enlargement process: the relaxation of barriers to migration. Wethereby distinguish between the liberalization of migration barriers for different types of worker-households.

[2] Wellisch and Walz (1998) discuss an alternative explanation for the reluctance of especially rich countries to allow for free labor migration while at the same time signing free trade agreements. They argue that migration will distort the optimal national redistribution policy while trade of goods will not. It is shown that even when the two integration steps are equivalent in the absence of state activities, migration turns out to be the inferior integration step compared to trade liberalization due to this distortion of national redistribution policies.

6.1.1 Three-Country Equilibrium

The economy consists of three countries, A, B, and C. Countries A and B together form the initial common market. Country C is the candidate for integration. In the common market all state-imposed barriers to migration and trade have been eliminated.

However, barriers to trade between country C and the countries in the common market exist. Migration between country C and the common market is prohibited by artificial, state-imposed migration barriers. In the course of the enlargement process, artificial barriers to trade and factor flows will be eliminated gradually and stepwise. We consider a two-factor, two-sector setting. One factor, skilled labor, is perfectly mobile between countries in the absence of artificial barriers to migration. Skilled workers do not face any natural barriers to migration. Their costs from moving from country A to B and vice versa are zero. In contrast, the second factor of production, unskilled labor, faces specific positive natural migration costs which make migration in the common market not worthwhile. Hence, even without artificial migration costs, unskilled workers do not migrate across borders in the common market at the given factor price difference.

Barriers to trade between country C and the integration bloc are of the non-tariff type. Using the same argument as in chapter 5.2, we model these non-tariff barriers to trade similarly to transport costs. In order to depict our hypothesis of the integration of a technologically lagging country, we assume that country C has a technological disadvantage in the industrial sector. This technological inferiority is so pronounced that country C specializes completely in Z-production.[3] Furthermore, we assume that the countries in the initial common market are, taken together, incompletely specialized. At least one country will contain Z-producers as well.

Households in all three countries consume the two final goods: the industrial final good Y and and the traditional final good Z. They share identical intertemporal preferences, expressed by:

$$U_t = \int_t^{\infty} e^{-\rho(\tau - t)}(\sigma ln C_Y(\tau) + (1-\sigma) ln C_Z(\tau))d\tau. \qquad (6.1)$$

[3]We could also derive country C's specialization pattern from its relative factor endowment, i.e., the relative scarcity of skilled labor and country C's relative position with respect to the initial number of locally produced intermediate goods. But since we want to focus on a scenario with country C being the traditional goods producer, we use the simplest manner of modelling this set-up. The possibility of a change in specialization patterns of country C in the course of regional integration is considered in subsection 6.3.

Two-stage maximization yields the familiar static demand functions, as well as the dynamic optimal consumption expenditure path in each country:

$$\tilde{p}_Y^i C_Y^i = \sigma E^i, \qquad (i = A, B, C), \tag{6.2}$$

$$\tilde{p}_Z^i C_Z^i = (1 - \sigma) E^i, \tag{6.3}$$

and

$$\frac{\dot{E}^i}{E^i} = r^i - \rho. \tag{6.4}$$

Since the optimization problem for all households in each country is identical, these functions can be interpreted as aggregate demand functions with $\tilde{p}_Y^i$ and $\tilde{p}_Z^i$ denoting the prices which consumers have to pay for the respective final good. Mobility of financial capital implies $r^A = r^B = r^C = r$. With identical optimal consumption expenditure paths and perfect mobility of financial capital, we can add up the Euler equation in (6.4) to $\dot{E}/E = r(t) - \rho$. Normalizing worldwide consumption expenditures to unity, this implies $r(t) = \rho$ at every moment in time.[4]

Production functions of all activities are the same as in chapter 4 (see (4.6)-(4.9)). Hence, we derive the following unit cost functions for final goods:

$$c_Y^i = B_Y^i (w_H^i)^\alpha (w_L^i)^\beta \left(\int_0^n \tilde{p}_x^i(v)^\gamma dv \right)^{\frac{1-\alpha-\beta}{\gamma}}, \tag{6.5}$$

and

$$c_Z^i = B_Z^i (w_H^i)^\delta (w_L^i)^{1-\delta}. \tag{6.6}$$

Since intermediate goods are exclusively produced in the common market by using skilled, perfectly mobile labor, $c_x^i = a_x w_H^{A,B}$ with $w_H^{A,B}$ denoting the identical factor price for skilled workers in country A and B. The same argument for innovative activities yields $c_n^i = w_H^{A,B}/n$.

Due to the unit elasticity of demand, final-goods market clearing can be expressed by:

$$\sum_i p_Y^i Y^i = \sigma, \tag{6.7}$$

and

$$\sum_i p_Z^i Z^i = 1 - \sigma, \tag{6.8}$$

[4] Immobility of financial capital between country C and the integration bloc leaves our steady-state equilibrium results in place. It would, however, complicate the analysis of transitional dynamics considerably. With immobility of financial capital, instantaneous interest rates converge to the subjective rate of time preference, ρ, rather than being equal to ρ at every moment in time.

with p^i_m $(m = Z, Y)$ denoting the free-on-board prices in country i and Z^i (Y^i) representing aggregate output of traditional (industrial) final-goods producers in country i. With non-tariff barriers to trade, consumers have to pay a price for imports which exceeds free-on-board prices by a margin which just reflects barriers to trade: $p^{i,j}_m = \tilde{p}^{i,j}_m \bar{t}$ if $i \neq j$ $(i, j = A, B)$, whereby $\bar{t}$ denotes the level of non-tariff barriers to trade $(0 < \bar{t} < 1)$ vis-à-vis country C. From one unit of exports, $(1 - \bar{t})$-units are used up by barriers to trade. Demand for exports is lowered by the barriers to trade. But, producers have to compensate for the losses of resources in the course of trade by means of higher production: $Y^{i,j} = C_Y/\bar{t}$ if $i \neq j$. These two effects offset each other. Revenues for producers are independent of barriers to trade.

Let us now consider the endogenous specialization patterns. We start with the assumption of equal initial endowment with unskilled labor of the countries in the initial common market. Furthermore, we impose $\xi > 1$. Due to identical factor prices for the mobile factor, we find $p^i_Z < p^j_Z$ for $w^i_L > w^j_L$ $(i, j = A, B; i \neq j)$. Furthermore, $p^A_Y = p^B_Y$ holds if and only if:

$$\omega \equiv \frac{w^A_L}{w^B_L} = \left(\frac{\mu + k^{\epsilon-1}}{1 + \mu k^{\epsilon-1}}\right)^{\theta}. \tag{6.9}$$

We can establish:

Lemma 6.1.1 *Suppose country i has the larger number of locally produced intermediate goods ($\mu^i = n^i/n^j > 1$). Then factor and goods-market clearing requires $\omega^i = w^i_L/w^j_L > 1$ and $s^i_Z = 0$.*

Proof: Applying Shephard's Lemma to (6.6) and (6.5) with (6.7) and (6.8) we obtain for the national factor market clearing conditions for unskilled labor: $\bar{L}^i = \dfrac{\delta(1-\sigma)}{w^i_L} + \dfrac{\alpha\sigma s^i_Y}{w^i_L}$. Note that in the three-country setting with $s^C_Z > 0$, $s^B_Z < 1$. Suppose that $\omega^i = 1$. With $\mu^i > 1$, $p^i_Y < p^j_Y$. Therefore, $s^j_Y = 0$ and $s^i_Y = 1$. Simultaneous market clearing for unskilled labor in A and B requires $s^j_Z = \dfrac{\xi + 1 - s^C_Z}{2}$. By definition, $s^j_Z + s^C_Z \leq 1$, but this violates simultaneous factor-market clearing since $s^j_Z + s^C_Z = (\xi + 1 + +s^C_Z)/2 > 1$. With $\omega < 1$, $s^j_Z = s^j_Y = 0$. This does not constitute a factor-market equilibrium in country j. Hence, with $\mu^i > 1$, $\omega^i > 1$ has to hold. Q.e.d.

To be specific, we suppose that country A has an initial headstart ($\mu(0) > 1$). With $\mu > 1$, Z-production takes place in countries B and C. We can write the national factor market clearing conditions for unskilled labor as:

$$\bar{L}^A = \frac{\alpha\sigma s_Y^A}{w_L^A}, \tag{6.10}$$

$$\bar{L}^B = \frac{\alpha\sigma s_Y^B}{w_L^B} + \frac{\delta(1-\sigma)s_Z^B}{w_L^B}, \tag{6.11}$$

and

$$\bar{L}^C = \frac{\delta(1-\sigma)s_Z^C}{w_L^C}, \tag{6.12}$$

with $\bar{L}^i$ denoting country i's endowment with unskilled labor. Applying Shephard's Lemma to (6.5)), and taking the production function for intermediate goods as well as the R&D function into account, the market clearing conditions for skilled labor in the common market as well as in country C are:

$$H^{A,B} = \frac{(1-\delta)(1-\sigma)s_Z^B + \beta((1-\alpha-\beta)\gamma) + \beta)}{w_H^{A,B}} + g \tag{6.13}$$

and

$$H^C = \frac{(1-\delta)(1-\sigma)s_Z^C}{w_H^C}, \tag{6.14}$$

with $H^{A,B}$ and H^C denoting the endowment of the countries in the common market as well as of country C with skilled labor. The wage rate for skilled labor in country C is represented by w_H^C.

From (6.10) and (6.11) together with (6.9), we can derive the shares of the countries in Y-production for a given relative number of locally produced inputs in A and B:

$$s_Y^A = \frac{\Psi^\theta(\xi + s_Z^B)f}{\xi(f\Psi^\theta + 1)}, \tag{6.15}$$

$$s_Y^B = \frac{\xi - f\Psi^\theta s_Z^B}{\xi(f\Psi^\theta + 1)}, \tag{6.16}$$

with $f = \bar{L}^A/\bar{L}^B$. Equation (6.16) depicts an important trade-off. The larger the market share of country B in Z-production is, the smaller its share in worldwide Y-production. This, in turn, implies a smaller home market for intermediate-goods producers, making country B a less attractive location for innovators.

The decisive question with respect to the specialization patterns of the countries in the common market is: where does intermediate-goods production and innovation take place? Using the familiar no-arbitrage condition:

$$\frac{nG^i}{w_H} + \frac{\dot{P}^i}{P^i} = \rho \tag{6.17}$$

reveals that potential innovators decide on their location according to the profit differential

$$\text{sign}(G^A - G^B) = \text{sign}\left[s_Y^A \Psi^{-1} - s_Y^B\right]. \tag{6.18}$$

Plugging (6.15) and (6.16) into this equation, we arrive at:

$$\text{sign}(G^A - G^B) = \text{sign}(f\xi + fs_Z^B - \xi\Psi^\nu + fs_Z^B\Psi) \equiv M^*. \tag{6.19}$$

The smaller the market share of country B in Z-production, the more resources are available in B for Y-production. The larger the home market for intermediate-goods producers, the more attractive is country B as a location for potential innovators. The existence of country C ($s_Z^B < 1$) makes an interior solution more likely. The initial disadvantage of a smaller number of locally produced intermediate products which is translated into the production of Y-goods in the lagging country is less pronounced. Less resources are tied up in Z-production.
We establish

Proposition 6.1.1 *With $\xi > \dfrac{(1+k^{1-\epsilon})}{k^{(1-\epsilon)\nu} - 1}$, a stable interior solution exists. The country in the common market with the initial headstart ($\mu^i > 1$) specializes completely in the industrial sector, whereas the other country produces the traditional good as well.*

Proof: It is sufficient to consider only the case with $\mu(0) > 1$. The case with $\mu(0) < 1$ is symmetric. With $\mu = 1 + \varepsilon$ (ε being a very small number), $s_Z^A = 0$ (see Lemma (6.1.1). Hence, $M(\mu = 1 + \varepsilon) > 0$. $M^*(\infty) < 0$ if $\xi > \dfrac{(1+k^{1-\epsilon})s_Z^B}{k^{(1-\epsilon)\nu} - 1}$ (see (6.9) and (6.15)). Hence, the condition stated in the proposition is sufficient for $M^*(\infty) < 0$. The M^* function cuts the axis at least once from above. Applying the same stability analysis as in chapter 4 reveals the saddle path stability of the equilibrium and terminates our proof. Q.e.d.

In the following, we assume that an interior solution between A and B prevails. To complete the description of the three-country model for given barriers to trade and migration, we need to derive the market share of country B as a function of exogenous parameters. In addition, we need to deduce the steady-state innovation and growth rates. Then we can turn to the analysis of the enlargement process.

Country C, being completely specialized in Z-production, exports this good and imports the industrial final good. We disregard the possibility that country C imports both goods in exchange for asset earnings (net capital exports).[5] In order to allow for competitive exports of country C into the common market, unit costs of traditional-goods producers must be lower than in country B: $c_Z^B\bar{t} = c_Z^C$. Using unit cost function in the traditional-goods sector, we can rewrite this expression to:

$$\frac{w_L^C}{w_L^B} \equiv \omega_{C,B} = \bar{t}^{\frac{1}{\delta}} \left(\frac{w_H^{A,B}}{w_H^C} \right)^{\frac{(1-\delta)}{\delta}}. \tag{6.20}$$

Rewriting (6.18) for an interior equilibrium to $s_Y^A \Psi^{-1} = s_Y^B$ in the profit function of, say, firms in country A:

$$nG^A = (1-\alpha-\beta)(1-\gamma)\sigma \left[\frac{s_Y^A(\mu+1)}{\mu+k^{\epsilon-1}} + \frac{s_Y^B k^{\epsilon-1}(\mu+1)}{1+\mu k^{\epsilon-1}} \right] \tag{6.21}$$

we arrive at:

$$nG^A = (1-\alpha-\beta)(1-\gamma)\sigma = \Phi. \tag{6.22}$$

Note that in an interior long-run equilibrium, $G^A = G^B$. In the steady-state equilibrium, the intersectoral and international factor allocations are constant and all variables grow at constant rates. With (6.10)-(6.14) this implies that all factor prices are constant. Hence, we can write the no-arbitrage condition as:

$$\frac{nG}{w_H^{A,B}} - \rho = g. \tag{6.23}$$

Using (6.22), and (6.13) in (6.23) leads us to:

$$H^{A,B} = \frac{(1-\delta)(1-\sigma)s_Z^B + \sigma(1-\alpha)}{w_H^{A,B}} - \rho. \tag{6.24}$$

Consequently, we can express (6.20) as:

$$\begin{aligned} \omega_{C,B} &= \bar{t}^{\frac{1}{\delta}} \left[\frac{(1-\delta)(1-\sigma)s_Z^B + \sigma(1-\alpha)}{(1-\delta)(1-\sigma)} \frac{H^C}{H^{A,B}+\rho} \right]^{\frac{(1-\delta)}{\delta}} \\ &= \omega(s_Z^B, \bar{t}), \end{aligned} \tag{6.25}$$

$$\text{with} \qquad \frac{\partial \omega_{C,B}}{\partial s_Z^B} > 0, \quad \text{and} \quad \frac{\partial \omega_{C,B}}{\partial \bar{t}} > 0.$$

[5]For a general treatment of trade in assets in an a two-country endogenous growth framework, see Dinopolous et al. (1993).

Solving for the market clearing condition for unskilled labor in all three countries with respect to s_Z^B, we receive after some calculation:

$$s_Z^B = \frac{f\Psi^\theta + 1 - \xi\omega_{C,B}f^*}{f\Psi^\theta + 1 + \omega_{C,B}f^*}, \tag{6.26}$$

with $f^* = \bar{L}^C/\bar{L}^B$. Taking (6.25) and (6.26) together, we can express s_Z^B as a function of $\bar{t}$, f, f^*, and μ, with:

$$\frac{\partial s_Z^B}{\partial \bar{t}} < 0, \quad \frac{\partial s_Z^B}{\partial f^*} < 0, \quad \frac{\partial s_Z^B}{\partial f} > 0, \quad \text{and} \quad \frac{\partial s_Z^B}{\partial \mu} > 0.$$

The intuition of the first two partial derivatives is straightforward. Liberalization of trade between countries A and B on the one hand and country C on the other hand (i.e., an increase in $\bar{t}$) strengthens the competitive position of country C in the traditional-goods production. Its exports in the common market will be expanded. As a consequence of fiercer competition, country B loses market shares in Z-production. Unskilled labor is released in this sector and shifted into the other employment possibility, the production of industrial-final goods. A larger resource pool of unskilled labor in country C allows for a larger market share of this country in Z-production. Consequently, s_Z^B declines. A larger $\bar{L}^A$ implies a larger s_Y^A. In country B, unskilled labor is displaced from industrial final-goods production and shifted into the traditional-goods sector. The effect of a larger $\bar{L}^B$ on B's market share in traditional-goods production is also positive as a glance at (6.26) reveals. The expansion of B's resource base of unskilled labor allows for more Y, but also for more Z-production.

With the help of (6.24) and the no-arbitrage equation, we can derive the innovation rate in the three-country steady-state equilibrium with trade and migration barriers as:

$$g = \frac{H^{A,B}\Phi - \rho\bar{\Delta}}{\bar{\Delta} + \Phi}, \tag{6.27}$$

with $\bar{\Delta} = (1-\delta)(1-\sigma)s_Z^B + \beta\sigma + (1-\alpha-\beta)(1-\gamma)\sigma$.

The worldwide growth rate of real GDP is proportional to the innovation rate. The growth rate of real GDP is composed of the weighted output growth rates of final-goods production, with the weights being the expenditure shares of the respective goods. By noting that $\dot{Z} = 0$ and with constant intersectoral allocation we find for the growth rate of the world's real GDP:

$$g_R^W = ((1-\alpha-\beta)(1-\gamma)\sigma/\gamma)g. \tag{6.28}$$

Similar relationships can be found for the countries in the common market with an active R&D-sector. By similar reasoning for the world as a whole, we obtain the growth rate of real GDP for the country being completely specialized in the industrial sector: $g_R^A = ((1-\alpha-\beta)(1-\gamma)/\gamma)g$. In country B, GDP is equal to $p_Z^B Z^B + p_Y Y^B$. Hence, the growth rate of real GDP results from the output growth rates weighted with B's relative share in the two sectors: $g_R^B = ((1-\alpha-\beta)(1-\gamma)/\gamma)g(s_Y^B\sigma/(s_Y^B\sigma + s_Z^B(1-\sigma))$. It is once more important to note that all consumers benefit from the growth process equally, independent of their location.

Now we are equipped with a framework which allows for a detailed analysis of the impact of a gradual and stepwise enlargement process on countries' specialization and growth patterns.

6.1.2 Trade Liberalization

Enlargement of the common market takes place via a gradual relaxation of barriers to trade between the member states of the common market and the new member, country C. With a free trade agreement, barriers to trade vanish completely. Gradual relaxation of barriers to trade enables us to employ marginal analysis rather than comparing discrete levels. Since it turns out that the effects of trade liberalization are strictly monotone, we can draw straightforward conclusions for discrete integration steps from our marginal analysis (the establishment of a free trade agreement).

With respect to the change of specialization patterns in the initial common market and to relative wages associated with trade liberalization, we can establish:

Proposition 6.1.2 *i.) Enlargement via trade liberalization leads to less dispersed production patterns and wage convergence between the "old" countries in the integration bloc. ii.) The probability of an interior solution increases.*

Proof: Ad i.) Totally differentiating M^* we obtain:
$\dfrac{d\mu}{d\bar{t}} = -\dfrac{(\partial M^*/\partial s_Z^B)(\partial s_Z^B/\partial \bar{t})}{(M^*(\mu^*))'} < 0$. This is due to the fact that $(M^*(\mu^*))' < 0$, $\partial M^*/\partial s_Z^B > 0$ (see (6.19)), and $\partial s_Z^B/\partial \bar{t} < 0$ (see (6.26)). With (6.9) we hence find $(d\omega/d\bar{t}) < 0$. Ad ii.) A necessary condition for the existence of an interior solution is $M^*(\infty) < 0$, i.e. $\xi > \dfrac{s_Z^B(k^{1-\epsilon}+1)}{k^{(1-\epsilon)\nu}-1}$. Since s_Z^B decreases with trade liberalization (see (6.26) and (i.)), this condition is more likely to be met. Q.e.d.

In the course of trade liberalization between country C and the common market, country B's traditional-goods producers lose part of their competitive stance. Resources are shifted from the traditional-goods sector to the industrial final-goods sector. This provides a larger home market for intermediate-goods producers in country B. Country A faces fiercer competition from country B's industrial final-goods producers. In contrast, however, country A being already completely specialized, cannot side step. A's market share in Y-production drops. Country B becomes more attractive as a location for intermediate-goods producers and innovative activities relative to A (see (6.28)). Innovation takes place exclusively in country B until a new steady-state equilibrium is reached. In the new steady-state, a larger relative number of differentiated inputs is assembled in country B. Differences in production patterns between countries A and B diminish.

We observe wage convergence in the sense that the wage gap between the countries in the new long run equilibrium has decreased. Due to the larger relative number of locally produced inputs and given transport costs in the intermediate-goods sector, the productivity gap of unskilled labor between the two countries becomes smaller. Unskilled labor in country B has to compensate for a smaller relative number of imported goods which are higher priced than locally produced inputs. The relationship between specialization patterns and barriers to trade is monotone. Hence, with a free trade agreement, minimal dispersion of specialization patterns is achieved. The wage gap is minimized as well.

The decline in μ reinforces the direct reduction in B's market share: $\frac{ds_Z^B}{d\bar{t}} = \frac{\partial s_Z^B}{\partial \bar{t}} + \frac{\partial s_Z^B}{\partial \mu}\frac{d\mu}{d\bar{t}} < 0$. Taking the decline of s_Z^B into account in (6.27), we can establish:

Proposition 6.1.3 *Trade liberalization fosters world-wide growth.*

The intuition is straightforward. Integrating country C via trade liberalization enhances country C's competitive situation. Fiercer competition from country C partially drives out country B from traditional-goods production. Hence, skilled labor is released from this sector. The released skilled workers are employed in other areas of economic activity. More skilled workers are employed in the R&D sector. Steady-state innovation and growth rates increase.

The effect on real GDP growth is more pronounced in B than in A. This follows directly from the increase in s_Y^B, together with the decrease in s_Z^B

(see (6.16) and (6.26)). But consumers in all countries benefit from faster growth to the same extent by means of more rapidly decreasing prices of industrial-final goods. The terms of trade for faster growing countries decrease at a higher speed. Due to the dynamic inefficiency inherent in our dynamic framework, faster growth is equivalent to a positive dynamic welfare effect. This positive dynamic welfare effect which is experienced by all households, irrespective of their location, has to be contrasted with the static welfare effects. The latter are composed of direct price effects due to maintained barriers to trade and wage income effects. Rather than carrying out a complete welfare analysis, we establish:

Proposition 6.1.4 *Both factors of production in country C achieve a higher income level with trade liberalization. In contrast, skilled labor in the common market as well as unskilled labor in country A experience a reduction in wage levels. The effect on the wage income of unskilled labor in country B is ambiguous.*

Proof: The increase in w_H^C and w_L^C can be directly deduced from the increase in s_Z^C together with (6.12) and (6.14). Similar reasoning applies to $w_H^{A,B}$ and w_L^A by noting the decrease of s_Z^B and s_Z^A in (6.24) and (6.10). Whereas ω increases, the effect on the absolute wage level in country B for unskilled labor hinges on the relative shift of resources between the final-goods sectors. Q.e.d.

The improved export position of country C leads to higher remuneration of both factors of production in C via more demand for labor from the expanded Z-sector in C. In the initial common market, unskilled labor in country A bears the main adjustment burden. In contrast to country B which can partly avoid competition by climbing up the production ladder, country A's unskilled workers face indirect pressure from the integration measures via the reallocation of resources in B. Country A loses part of its productivity advantage. Unskilled labor in Germany and France is the largest potential opponent of the enlargement process rather than unskilled workers in Spain and Portugal. If the growth rate effect is sufficiently pronounced, it might, however, be possible that the dynamic welfare gain more than offsets the income losses.

In a nutshell, enlargement via trade liberalization fosters growth and leads to convergence of production patterns and wages in the initial common market. Especially with respect to a potential sequence of migration steps, it is crucial to ask these integration steps, lead to the same results.

6.1.3 Second Integration Step: Liberalizing Impediments to Migration

Before migration barriers vis-à-vis country C are relaxed, these barriers are prohibitive. We will now investigate the implications of a relaxation of these barriers to migration. We implicitly assume that natural migration barriers exist only for unskilled workers. They face significant natural migration barriers which make migration between the countries in the initial common market not worthwhile for them. If, however, wages are much lower in country C, an incentive exists for unskilled labor to emigrate from country C after the relaxation of artificial barriers to migration. We look at the implications of these migration streams.

Relaxation of Migration Barriers for Unskilled Labor

With migration of unskilled labor from country C to the common market, two possible scenarios arise. Either L^C workers migrate exclusively to the high-wage country A, or they are split equally between the two established countries in the integration bloc (e.g. by migration law). In both cases f^* decreases. In the first case (case I), the relationship between the unskilled labor in A to the one in B changes: f increases. In the second case (case II), f remains unchanged. Both scenarios lead to the same qualitative results. Hence, we discuss them together.

With immigration of unskilled labor in the integration bloc, the total endowment with unskilled labor of countries A and B increases. The larger resource base allows for a larger market share of country B in Z-production. With immigration taking place to country A only, s_Y^A increases. This releases unskilled workers from Y-production in B (s_Y^B decreases) which are shifted into Z-production. In the second case, the larger endowment of B is transmitted directly into an increase in s_Z^B. With the larger (smaller) s_Y^A (s_Y^B), the larger home market for intermediate-goods producers in A relative to the one in B attracts additional intermediate-goods producers. We can establish

Proposition 6.1.5 *Relaxation of barriers to migration for unskilled labor creates an inflow of unskilled labor in the common market, leading to more dispersed production patterns between countries A and B as well as to wage divergence.*

Totally differentiating M^* for case II yields: $\dfrac{d\mu}{df^*} = -\dfrac{f(1+\Psi)}{(M^*(\mu^*))'}\dfrac{\partial s_Z^B}{\partial f^*} < 0$

since $(M^*(\mu^*))' < 0$ and $\frac{\partial s_Z^B}{\partial f^*} < 0$ (see (6.26)). With migration, f^* decreases and μ increases. In case II, with an increasing f and $\frac{\partial s_Z^B}{\partial f} > 0$ as well as $\frac{\partial M^*}{\partial f}$, μ as well as ω increases as well. Q.e.d.

Hence, relaxation of barriers to migration for unskilled labor increases the wage gap and provides a larger potential for regional policy measures. Production patterns become more dispersed. In the new steady-state equilibrium, in addition to the larger relative number of intermediate products, a larger share of industrial final-goods is produced in the center country.

We observe a shift of resources (skilled labor) into the traditional-goods sector drawing skilled workers away from the dynamic sector via a higher wage rate. The increase in s_Z^B is reinforced by the increase in μ (see (6.26)). By taking (6.27) into account we can establish

Proposition 6.1.6 *Immigration of unskilled labor to countries A and B dampens the incentive to undertake investment in R&D. The steady-state innovation and growth rates decline. Production patterns in the integration bloc drift apart.*

The reduction of artificial barriers to migration between countries A and B on the one hand and country C on the other hand brings about a negative dynamic welfare effect. Integration via relaxation of barriers to migration for unskilled labor and trade liberalization are two very different integration measures. They yield opposite effects with respect to the effects on growth and specialization patterns. This can be seen as a rationale for the integration of technologically lagging countries by means of free trade agreements only. Rather than liberalizing migration barriers, it is preferable from the point of view of dynamic efficiency to establish a free trade zone with the third country. Furthermore, trade liberalization brings about convergence, an explicit policy target in an integration bloc. Sectoral shocks have less asymmetric impacts on the countries in the initial common market.

Let us now turn to an analysis of the relaxation of artificial barriers to migration for skilled labor.

Relaxation of Migration Barriers for Skilled Labor

With the elimination of artificial barriers to migration, skilled workers are completely mobile between all three countries. The common labor market for skilled labor is extended to country C. We can express the clearing condition for this market as:

$$H^{A,B} + H^C = \frac{\Delta}{w_H} + g. \qquad (6.29)$$

In this market, the common wage rate, w_H, prevails. With the no-arbitrage condition, (6.29) and $nG = \Phi$, we find for the steady-state innovation rate:

$$g^M = \frac{(H^{A,B} + H^C)\Phi - \rho\Delta}{\Phi + \Delta}. \qquad (6.30)$$

Comparing (6.27) and (6.30) shows that the impact of the relaxation of barriers to migration on innovation and growth is not clear-cut. Using (6.27) and (6.30) we derive the following condition for which relaxation of barriers to migration for skilled workers fosters growth and innovation:

$$1 > \Gamma, \qquad (6.31)$$

with

$$\Gamma = \left(\frac{(1-\delta)(1-\sigma)\bar{s}_Z^B + \sigma(1-\alpha)}{(1-\delta)(1-\sigma)(1-\bar{s}_Z^B)} \frac{H^C}{H^{A,B} + \rho} \right),$$

and $\bar{s}_Z^B$ denoting B's market share with factor immobility and free trade. Equation (6.31) simply reflects a condition for $w_H^{A,B} > w_H^C$ in the pre-liberalization situation. This can be deduced from a comparison of (6.14) with (6.24). With $w_H^{A,B}$ being larger than w_H^C, the relaxation of artificial barriers to migration induces immigration of skilled workers from C to A and B. The economic mechanism behind the growth rate effects becomes more obvious if we take a look at the factor input relationships in the pre-liberalization world. With free trade pricing conditions in the traditional-goods sector and cost-minimizing factor demand of traditional-goods producers it turns out that (6.31) is equivalent to $\frac{L_Z^B}{H_Z^B} > \frac{L_Z^C}{H_Z^C}$. With free migration and incomplete specialization, factor input relationships will be equalized between countries. Hence, migration of unskilled labor implies that, on average, less skilled labor is employed in the traditional-goods sector. Skilled labor will be released to the dynamic sector. Innovation and growth rates are larger in the new steady-state.

We can establish:

Proposition 6.1.7 *Suppose that traditional-goods producers in country B use skilled labor less intensively in the pre-liberalization situation than their counterparts in country C. Complete relaxation of artificial migration barriers for skilled workers in the course of the enlargement process enhances the* *incentive to undertake R&D. Innovation and growth rates are larger in the integrated equilibrium. In the reverse case, skilled labor moves into country C, leading to a smaller growth and innovation rate.*

With $w_H^{A,B} > w_H^C$, enlargement via free migration implies a reduction in $\omega_{C,B}$ which, in turn, implies a smaller market share of country B in traditional-goods production. With a similar argumentation as above, we obtain a larger μ. Hence, immigration of skilled labor into the initial integration bloc leads to a more pronounced center-periphery pattern between the two established countries. Needless to say that with $w_H^{A,B} < w_H^C$ in the pre-liberalization world, exactly the reverse effect on specialization patterns can be observed.

6.1.4 Brief Summary

This subsection has dealt with an important aspect of regional integration: the enlargement process taking place by integrating a technologically lagging country. Our analysis demonstrated that enlarging a common market not only affects the long-run growth path of all countries together, but also has significant implications for the relationship between the established countries. Integration alters the incentive to undertake investments, but also the location decisions of firms. Depending on the effects on centripetal and centrifugal forces, the relative periphery or the industrial core in the initial common market becomes more attractive in the course of the enlargement.

Our theoretical framework predicts very different implications of integration measures on the relationship between the established countries. Whereas trade liberalization leads to convergence between the established countries, just the opposite is true with respect to the liberalization of migration barriers for unskilled labor. Opposite effects also arise with respect to the implications for the overall growth patterns. Trade liberalization improves the conditions for R&D investment, leading to higher growth, while the migration of unskilled labor into the common market has a dampening effect on the incentives to invest in R&D. An important policy implication emerges. From the point of view of dynamic efficiency but also with respect to convergence between the established countries, trade liberalization is the superior integration step. This also provides a rationale for the often observed sequential integration policies. Trade liberalization is undertaken well before free factor flows are allowed for.

The analysis in this section also provides a second important insight.

Through reallocation of resources, fiercer competition from the newly integrated country is transmitted to the center country. The relative periphery in the common market can adjust to competitive pressures by climbing up the technology ladder. The center country cannot avoid the new competition. Its unskilled workers bear the main adjustment burden. They will be the ones potentially opposing the enlargement process most vehemently.

6.2 Integrating a Developed Country

The integration of a further country which is not able to pursue local innovation displays one extreme end of the spectrum of possible specialization patterns of the newly integrated country. In this section we look at the other extreme end of this spectrum. The candidate for integration is a technologically developed country such as Austria, Sweden, or Finland.

The basic procedure of the investigation in this section is similar to the one in the preceding section. First, we establish the specialization patterns of a common market consisting of two countries with a third country being the candidate for integration. Then, we gradually and stepwise integrate the third country. We focus once more on the impact of the enlargement process on specialization, production and growth patterns of the involved countries. Since the newly integrating country exhibits a positive rate of local innovation, its rate of innovation will be affected as well. We stick to our basic assumption excluding any regime switches in national specialization patterns. We focus on two basic integration steps: liberalization of trade and migration barriers.[6] As in section 6.1, we find that the different integration steps may have very different implications for specialization and growth patterns. But our analysis also reveals that decisive differences exist between the integration of a developed and a lagging country into an existing integration bloc.

The situation under investigation differs technically in one important aspect from the situation we analyzed in the preceding section. Since the factor which is employed in the R&D and intermediate-goods sector was perfectly mobile between the countries which were specialized in these activities, costs of intermediate-goods as well as R&D costs were equalized across countries. Location decisions of potential innovators were only governed by the interac-

[6] A larger variety of issues involved in the enlargement process in the EU (e.g. the impact of fiscal measures such as regional policies and the common agricultural policy) is discussed in a non-technical manner in a CEPR (1992) study.

tion of the competition and demand effect. Factor price differentials of the factor used intensively in innovative activities did not exist. In the present situation, where innovation takes place in the third country as well, matters are different. In the pre-liberalization situation, barriers to migration and trade exist. Hence, there is no reason why nominal and real factor prices should be equalized. Factor prices and, consequently, cost differentials prevail between the potential locations for innovators. The location decisions of innovators, in turn, influence relative costs in the different countries. This circular relationship complicates the analysis considerably.

Therefore, in order to keep the analysis in this section tractable, we develop a modified dynamic model of economic geography. In the terminology of Rivera-Batiz/Romer (1991a), this approach adopts a combination of the lab equipment and the knowledge-driven model. All three vertically linked sectors in the economy produce with a similar production function. Producer costs in the different countries are linked to each other via (restricted) international trade in a perfectly competitive final good.

In the next section, we develop the modified dynamic model of economic geography. Labor is the only factor of production. The production structure in all three vertically linked sectors (final-goods production, intermediate-goods production and innovation) is similar. Since intermediate-goods producing firms require the blueprints of the respective differentiated input which is developed in the R&D laboratory, market structures are remarkably different in the three sectors. In the final-goods sector, perfect competition prevails, whereas differentiated inputs are supplied by monopolists. Each intermediate good is produced by one firm only. We derive the unique steady-state equilibrium with a core-periphery pattern in the initial integration bloc. Innovative activities are undertaken in the core country in the integration bloc, as well as in the country which is a candidate for integration. Building on the three-country equilibrium with restricted trade and migration barriers, we address the consequences of the enlargement process.

6.2.1 A Regional "Lab Equipment Model"

Initially, $\bar{L}^i$ $(i = A, B, C)$ consumer-worker households reside in each country. Countries A and B together form the integration bloc. Country C is the candidate for integration. For given barriers to migration, households in all countries have no incentive to migrate and can, therefore, be regarded as immobile. Each household is endowed with one unit of labor which is supplied inelastically. Labor is the only basic factor of production. Households consume the only consumption good, Y.

Consumers in all three countries face the same intertemporal utility function with logarithmic static utility (see (5.1)). Hence, we obtain for the static and dynamic demand function:

$$\tilde{p}_Y^i C_Y^i = E^i, \tag{6.32}$$

and

$$\frac{\dot{E}^i}{E^i} = r^i - \rho. \tag{6.33}$$

With free mobility of capital and normalization of worldwide expenditures ($E = E^A + E^B + E^C$) to one, the instantaneous interest rates in all three countries are equal to the subjective rate of time preference ($r^A = r^B = r^C = \rho$).

Final-goods producers employ labor as well as differentiated inputs:

$$Y^i = \left(L_Y^i\right)^{1-\alpha} \left(\int_0^n \tilde{x}_Y^i(v)^\gamma dv\right)^{\frac{\alpha}{\gamma}}, \quad 0 > \gamma, \alpha > 1, \tag{6.34}$$

with L_Y^i denoting labor input in Y-production in country i. The quantity of input of each differentiated intermediate good is represented by $\tilde{x}_Y^i$.

Intermediate-goods producers face an identical production function:

$$x^i(v') = \left(L_x^i(v')\right)^{1-\alpha} \left(\int_0^n \tilde{x}_{x(v')}^i(v)^\gamma dv\right)^{\frac{\alpha}{\gamma}}, \quad 0 > \gamma, \alpha > 1. \tag{6.35}$$

The subscript x depicts the factors of production used in each variety of the intermediate-goods sector. Equations (6.35) and (6.34) allow for two alternative interpretations. Taking them literally implies that final-goods and intermediate-goods producers assemble their products under the same production function. This set-up can, however, also be interpreted similar to much of the growth literature (see e.g. Romer (1989) and Lucas (1988)). Rather than producing intermediate goods themselves, intermediate-goods producers purchase final goods and transform them one-to-one into intermediate goods. Additional resources are not required for this transformation process. Both interpretations lead to the same results in our present framework. Hence, the assumption of identical production functions is in line with much of the growth literature.

Unit costs of final-goods producers result from cost-minimizing behavior as

$$c_Y^i = B(w_L^i)^{1-\alpha} \left(\int_0^n \tilde{p}_x^i(v)^{1-\epsilon} dv\right)^{\frac{\alpha}{1-\epsilon}}, \tag{6.36}$$

with w_L^i and $\tilde{p}_x^i$ denoting the input prices for a producer in i for labor and intermediate goods. Identical production functions yield $c_x^i = c_Y^i$. This is especially intuitive with our interpretation of a costless one-to-one transformation of the final goods in differentiated inputs. Intermediate-goods production (or the ability to transform final goods) requires the respective blueprint of the technology. This blueprint is developed in the R&D laboratory.

We adopt an R&D function reminiscent of the lab equipment case discussed in chapter 3:

$$\dot{n}^i = A_n^i \left(L_n^i\right)^{1-\alpha} \left(\int_0^n \tilde{x}_n^i(v)^\gamma dv\right)^{\frac{\alpha}{\gamma}} n^\Phi, \quad A_n^i > 0, \tag{6.37}$$

with L_n^i and $\tilde{x}_n^i$ denoting the factor inputs used in R&D laboratories located in country i. This formulation of the R&D-function is a combination of the lab equipment with the knowledge-driven specification. Choosing a lab equipment specification along the lines of Romer (1990) and Rivera-Batiz/Romer (1991a) (see also the discussion in Barro/Sala-i-Martin (1992)) with $\dot{n}^i = A_n^i \left(L_n^i\right)^{1-\alpha} \left(\int_0^n \tilde{x}_x^i(v)^\alpha dv\right)$ has a decisive drawback for our purposes. With this formulation, which can be obtained from (6.37) by setting $\gamma = \alpha$, demand and competition effects offset each other at every moment in time. Our economic geography set-up collapses. Transport costs play no longer any role for the location decisions of innovators. In order to avoid this characteristic of the specific parameter constellation, we adopt the more general formulation in (6.37). To allow for a positive growth path of the economies under consideration, we introduce international knowledge spillovers.

To illustrate the growth characteristics of the formulation more clearly, we assume for a moment a closed economy. The basic pattern is the same with our three-country framework. Each brand of the intermediate goods is used to the same extent in the R&D sector as well as in the intermediate-goods sector. Using the fact that the total amount of intermediate goods is constant in (6.35), we can express (6.37) as:

$$\dot{n} = A_n L_n^{1-\alpha} L_x^\alpha n^{\frac{\alpha}{\gamma}\frac{1-\gamma}{1-\alpha}}.$$

With $\alpha = \gamma$, the specific lab equipment case, constant returns with respect to the accumulable factor (n) prevail in the accumulation equation. This is a necessary input in an endogenous growth model (see Sala-i-Martin (1990)). The inequality $\gamma > \alpha$ (which will turn out to be a necessary condition for a stable interior solution), however, implies decreasing returns to n in the accumulation equation. In order to compensate for falling returns we introduce knowledge spillovers ($n^{\mathcal{D}}$). With $\mathcal{D} = 1-\alpha(1-\gamma)/\gamma(1-\alpha)$, constant returns prevail in (6.37) at every moment in time.[7]

With (6.34)- (6.37); we find that in addition to cost-equalization in the final-goods and the intermediate-goods sector in each country, the following condition for R&D costs prevails:

$$c_n^i = c_Y^i n^{\mathcal{D}}. \tag{6.38}$$

Hence, by applying Shephard's Lemma to the unit cost functions, we obtain the demand function faced by intermediate-goods producers located in country i:

$$\tilde{x}(v)^i = \sum_j \left\{ \frac{\tilde{p}_x^{i,j}(v)^{-\epsilon}}{\int_0^n \tilde{p}_x^{i,j}(v')^{1-\epsilon} dv'} \alpha s^i p_Q Q \right\}, \tag{6.39}$$

with $p_Q Q = \sum_j p_Y^i Y^i + \sum_j n^i p_x^i x^i + \sum_j c_n^i \dot{n}^i (i = A, B, C)$, the nominal value of all industries' output demanding differentiated inputs. The market share of country i in overall nominal production is denoted by s^i.

As in the preceding chapters, we introduce natural transport costs in the intermediate-goods sector. It is costly to trade producer goods and services across national borders. These natural transport costs are denoted by the parameter k. Between the established countries in the integration bloc, all artificial barriers to trade and migration are removed. Before the enlargement process takes place, however, artificial barriers to trade and migration exist between countries in the integration bloc (A and B) on the one hand, and country C on the other hand. We denote these barriers to trade, which are of non-tariff nature with the parameter ζ $(0 < \zeta < 1)$ and model them – as in the preceding sections – similar to transport costs. In other words, artificial barriers to trade drive a wedge between revenues per unit of sales

[7] This is certainly a restrictive assumption. In a more general set-up, it suffices that constant returns prevail asymptotically. Writing the R&D function as $\dot{n} = L_n g(n)$ with $g' > 0$, it suffices that $h(n) = g(n)/n$ approaches a positive number in the long-run. The elasticity of $h(n)$ approaches 1 as n grows very large. The economy converges to a steady-state with a positive and constant growth rate (see Grossman/Helpman (1991, p.76f) for the discussion of such a trajectory for a simple but related growth framework). In our specific set-up, $h(n)/n$ equals one at every moment in time. It is straightforward to extend our set-up to the more general case without changing any of the qualitative results. Since this generalization adds nothing – besides further algebra – to the model, we chose to assume a linear R&D function from the outset.

for producers and the price consumers have to pay. In addition, non-tariff barriers to trade are accompanied by resource costs. Natural and artificial barriers to trade are modelled in an iceberg type manner.

Consumer prices, $\tilde{p}_x$, and revenues which producers receive per unit sold are related via $\tilde{p}_x^{i,j} = p_x^i$ if $i = j$, and $\tilde{p}_x^{i,j} = p_x^i / e$ if $i \neq j$. We denote transport costs of trade between country i and j as $k_{i,j} \in]0, 1[$. If intermediate goods are sold across national borders in the integration bloc, $e = k_{A,B}$. If they are exported to or from country C, $e = \tilde{k}_{A,C} := k_{A,C}\zeta$. The parameter $\tilde{k}_{A,C}$ denotes the natural and state-imposed impediments to trade together. A similar relation holds for demand and output: $x^{i,j} = \tilde{x}^{i,j}$ if $i = j$, and $x^{i,j} = \tilde{x}^{i,j}/e$ if $i \neq j$. Intermediate-goods producers maximize their profits:

$$G^i(v) = (p_x^i(v) - c_x^i(v))x^i(v).$$

Together with the demand function (6.39) and our iceberg type formulation of barriers to trade, we find the optimal price as a mark-up on costs:

$$p_x^i = \frac{c_x^i}{\gamma}. \tag{6.40}$$

Since production costs for inputs differ, prices may differ as well.

In the appendix, we argue that asset bubbles cannot arise in our framework. Hence, the value of firms is equal to the discounted stream of profits. The familiar no-arbitrage condition (4.18) results. The final-goods market clears if $\sum_i p_Y^i Y^i = \sum_i \tilde{p}_Y^i C_Y^i = E$. With respect to intermediate goods, matters are more complicated. Note that $p_Q Q$ on the RHS of (6.39) entails production values of intermediate goods producers as well. In order to obtain a net demand function, we have to eliminate intermediate-goods production from the RHS of (6.39). By doing so, we arrive at:

$$\sum_i n^i p_x^i x^i = \frac{\alpha}{1-\alpha}\left(1 + \sum_i c_n^i \dot{n}^i\right), \tag{6.41}$$

whereby we used the final-goods market clearing condition.

With Shephard's Lemma applied to (6.36), we obtain with (6.38) the national labor market clearing conditions:

$$\bar{L}^i = \frac{(1-\alpha)s^i p_Q Q}{w_L^i}. \tag{6.42}$$

6.2.2 The Steady-State Equilibrium

Now, we investigate the long-run evolution of the economies in the integration bloc as well as of the candidate for integration. We derive the three-country long-run equilibrium for given barriers to trade and migration, as well as the transitory dynamics on the path towards this equilibrium.

Country B represents the periphery in the integration bloc. Due to technological disadvantages in the R&D sector it is not profitable to undertake R&D in country B. Technically expressed, A_n^B is very small. Innovation might, however, take place in countries A and C, whereby country A depicts the core country in the initial integration bloc. Examples for the periphery in the EU integration bloc are Greece, Ireland, Spain, and Portugal. In these countries, broadly speaking, almost no private innovative activities are undertaken, as our discussion in chapter 2 revealed. The core countries in the EU integration bloc are Germany, France, the Netherlands, and the UK. The candidate for integration which is at the same technological level as the core country in the integration bloc could be, for example, Austria, Finland, Sweden, Switzerland etc.

We focus on situations with incomplete specialization in final-goods production. In country B, final-goods production has to take place at every moment in time anyway, since final-goods production represents the only source of employment in country B. Competitive production of final goods in both countries in the integration bloc requires that $c_Y^A = c_Y^B$. The pricing relationship of A and B vis-à-vis country C depends very much on the direction of trade. We can distinguish between two basic cases. In case I, country C is an importer of the final good. It imports final goods either in exchange for intermediate goods, or finances its imports with the receipts from foreign based assets. In the reverse case (case II), country C constitutes the exporter of the final-good. Which of the two regimes arises depends on the relative size of the countries as well as on the initial distribution of assets and locally produced intermediate goods across countries.

In case I, production costs have to be lower in the integration bloc in order to compensate for non-tariff barriers to trade which arise in the course of trade: $c_Y^A = c_Y^B = c_Y^C \zeta$. In case II, production has to be less costly in country C compared to A and B: $c_Y^A = c_Y^B = c_Y^C / \zeta$. The present analysis is considerably complicated since intra-industry trade of the core country in the integration bloc with the country outside the integration bloc takes place. These trade flows are burdened with artificial barriers to trade. All state-imposed impediments to trade are the same in all sectors. In order to simplify the notation in the analysis, we introduce the parameter ϑ which measures state-imposed trade barriers in the two trade regimes. In other words, in case I, $\vartheta = \zeta$ and $\vartheta = \zeta^{-1}$ in case II, with $c_Y^A/c_Y^C = \vartheta$. With the help of this definition we can discuss the two trade regimes jointly.

Using $c_x^i = c_Y^i$ with (6.36), we find the following relation which allows for competitive production:

$$\omega_{A,C} := \frac{w_L^A}{w_L^C} = \vartheta \left(\frac{\bar{\mu} + \tilde{k}_{A,C}^{\epsilon-1} \vartheta^{\epsilon-1}}{\bar{\mu} \vartheta^{1-\epsilon} \tilde{k}_{A,C}^{\epsilon-1} + 1} \right)^{\bar{\theta}}, \tag{6.43}$$

and

$$\omega_{C,B} := \frac{w_L^B}{w_L^C} = \vartheta k_{A,B}^{\frac{\alpha}{1-\alpha}} \left(\frac{\bar{\mu} \vartheta^{1-\epsilon} \tilde{k}_{A,C}^{\epsilon-1} + 1}{\bar{\mu} + \bar{k}^{\epsilon-1} \vartheta^{\epsilon-1}} \right)^{\bar{\theta}}, \tag{6.44}$$

with $\bar{k} = \tilde{k}_{B,C}/\tilde{k}_{A,B}$, $\bar{\mu} = n^A/n^C$, and $\bar{\theta} = \alpha(1-\gamma)/((1-\alpha)\gamma)$.

For given levels of integration, i.e. for constant natural as well as artificial barriers to trade and migration, relative wages in an innovating country become the larger, the larger the relative number of locally produced intermediate goods is. For example: $\text{sign}\partial\omega_{A,C}/\partial\mu = \text{sign}(1 - \tilde{k}_{A,C}^{2(\epsilon-1)}) > 0$.

With factor market clearing (see (6.42)), we obtain the equilibrium market shares in the countries: $s_Y^A/s_Y^B = \omega_{A,B}\bar{L}^A/\bar{L}^B$, $s_Y^A/s_Y^C = \omega_{A,C}\bar{L}^A/\bar{L}^C$, and $s_Y^C/s_Y^B = \omega_{C,B}\bar{L}^C/\bar{L}^B$.

It is noteworthy that the trade structure not only influences relative costs in the final-goods sector, but in the intermediate-goods sector as well. Hence, state-imposed barriers to trade drive a twofold wedge between production costs and the prices to be paid by consumers. On the one hand, state-imposed barriers to trade make it costly to shift differentiated goods across national borders. Since f.o.b. prices are independent of the location of sales, non-tariff barriers to trade lead to a premium on imported brands' prices compared to prices of locally produced goods. This is the conventional direct effect. In addition, an indirect effect can be observed. This indirect effect results from the intersectoral linkage of costs in every economy, combined with the competitive pricing conditions across countries. The two effects may operate in opposite directions. For example, in case I, the indirect effect leads to $c_Y^A = c_Y^C\zeta$, and hence, to $c_x^A = c_x^C\zeta$. The c.i.f. price of exported inputs from country C in country A is $c_x^A/(k_{A,C}\gamma)$, whereas the price of locally produced brands is c_x^A/γ. The two partial effects of state-imposed impediments to trade just cancel out. But due to natural transport costs in the intermediate-goods sector, input prices of imported varieties are always higher than the prices of locally produced ones. If intermediate goods are exported in the reverse direction, the two effects (direct and indirect) reinforce each other. The ratio of input prices of imported goods relative to locally produced ones is $(\zeta \tilde{k}_{A,C})^{-1} > 1$.

The trade structure has a decisive impact on the competitive position of intermediate-goods producers in country A and C, respectively. With country C being a net importer of final goods, intermediate goods are more costly to produce in C than in A. The reverse is true for country C exporting the final good. In addition to the cost difference in intermediate-goods production, the trade structure also implies cost differences in the R&D-sector.

Against this background, we investigate under which circumstances an interior solution with $0 < \bar{\mu}^* < \infty$ results. We investigate the two cases jointly. With final-goods production taking place at every moment in time in each country, $\hat{c}_n^A = \hat{c}_n^C$ has to hold at every moment in time. When trade liberalization measures are undertaken unexpectedly, this does not change this relation. Hence, the location decisions of firms are based on the profit rate differences in the potential locations (countries A and C).

With $G^A/c_n^A > (<) G^C/c_n^C$, it is more profitable to locate in country A (C). In an interior solution, $G^A/c_n^A = G^C/c_n^C$ has to hold.

By using the profit function together with (6.38)-(6.40), we can express the profit rate differential:

$$\begin{aligned}
\operatorname{sign}\left(\frac{G^A}{c_n^A} - \frac{G^C}{c_n^C}\right) &= \operatorname{sign}\left\{ s^A \left(\frac{\zeta^{-\epsilon} - k_{A,C}^{\epsilon-1}}{\bar{\mu}\zeta^{1-\epsilon} + k_{A,C}^{\epsilon-1}}\right) - s^C \left(\frac{1 - \zeta^{-\epsilon} k_{A,C}^{\epsilon-1}}{\bar{\mu} k_{A,C}^{\epsilon-1} \zeta^{1-\epsilon} + 1}\right) \right. \\
&\quad \left. + s^B \left(\frac{\zeta^{-\epsilon} - k_{A,C}^{\epsilon-1}}{\bar{\mu}\zeta^{1-\epsilon} + k_{A,C}^{\epsilon-1}}\right) \right\}. \qquad (6.45)
\end{aligned}$$

The terms on the RHS of (6.45) display the interaction of demand and competition effects. Furthermore, a cost advantage effect exists. Due to barriers to trade, a production cost differential arises. Innovators and intermediate-goods producers in the country exporting final goods have a cost-advantage compared to their competitors in the other country. In other words, it is more profitable to locate in the country with the larger s^i (larger local market), in the country with the smaller number of locally producing competitors (less price competition) and in the country which is an exporter of the final good (with a production cost advantage). Since these factors of influence on location decisions point partially in opposite directions, an interior solution becomes feasible. Note that intra-community trade between countries A and B is less burdened with impediments to trade. Hence, a larger local market in country B benefits production in country A. Using factor market clearing-conditions together with (6.43) and (6.44), we can express the condition for an interior solution as:

$$\begin{aligned}\tilde{M}(\tilde{k}_{A,C},\bar{k},f,\bar{f},\mu,\vartheta) &= 0 = \\ & f\left(\frac{\mu\tilde{k}_{A,C}^{\epsilon-1}\vartheta^{1-\epsilon}+1}{\mu+\tilde{k}_{A,C}^{\epsilon-1}\vartheta^{\epsilon-1}}\right)^{\eta}\left(\frac{1-\tilde{k}_{A,C}^{\epsilon-1}\vartheta^{\epsilon}}{1-\tilde{k}_{A,C}^{\epsilon-1}\vartheta^{-\epsilon}}\right)+ \\ &+\bar{f}k_{A,B}^{\frac{\alpha}{1-\alpha}}\left(\frac{\mu\tilde{k}_{A,C}^{\epsilon-1}\vartheta^{1-\epsilon}+1}{\mu+\bar{k}^{\epsilon-1}\vartheta^{\epsilon-1}}\right)^{\eta}\left(\frac{1-\bar{k}^{\epsilon-1}\vartheta^{\epsilon}}{1-\tilde{k}_{A,C}^{\epsilon-1}\vartheta^{-\epsilon}}\right)-1,\end{aligned} \tag{6.46}$$

with $\bar{f}=\bar{L}^B/\bar{L}^C$. By defining

$$P=\vartheta^{(1-\epsilon)\mathcal{D}}\left[f\left(\frac{1-\tilde{k}_{A,C}^{\epsilon-1}\vartheta^{\epsilon}}{1-\tilde{k}_{A,C}^{\epsilon-1}\vartheta^{-\epsilon}}\right)+\bar{f}k_{A,B}^{\frac{\alpha}{1-\alpha}}\left(\frac{1-\bar{k}^{\epsilon-1}\vartheta^{\epsilon}}{1-\tilde{k}_{A,C}^{\epsilon-1}\vartheta^{-\epsilon}}\right)\right],$$

we can establish

Proposition 6.2.1 *For* $\tilde{k}_{A,C}^{(1-\epsilon)\eta} > P > \tilde{k}_{A,C}^{(\epsilon-1)\eta}$, *a unique steady-state equilibrium with* $0<\mu^*<\infty$ *exists.*

Proof: See Appendix.
In the absence of artificial barriers to trade, the condition in Proposition 6.2.1 is reminiscent of the condition in Proposition 5.1.1.

Unfortunately, with $\tilde{k}_{A,C}\neq\bar{k}$, $\tilde{M}$ cannot be solved explicitly. For the general case, we have to express the steady-state growth and innovation rates as a function of the endogenous variable $\bar{\mu}$. By using the no-abitrage condition, (6.38), (6.42) and (6.46), we obtain the innovation rate in a country with an active innovative sector:

$$g=\frac{B(1-\gamma)\alpha G_1G_2}{1-\alpha}-\rho, \tag{6.47}$$

with $B=\gamma^{\frac{-\alpha}{1-\alpha}}$, $G_1=(\bar{\mu}+1)/(\bar{\mu}+\zeta^{-1})$, and

$$G_2=\bar{L}^A+\bar{L}^B k_{A,B}^{(\epsilon-1)\bar{\theta}}\left(\frac{\bar{\mu}+\vartheta^{\epsilon-1}\tilde{k}_{A,C}^{\epsilon-1}}{\bar{\mu}+1}\right)^{\theta}+\bar{L}^C\vartheta\left(\frac{\bar{\mu}\vartheta^{1-\epsilon}\tilde{k}_{A,C}^{\epsilon-1}+1}{\bar{\mu}+1}\right)^{\theta}.$$

All three countries experience the same rate of steady-state growth of real output: $\hat{Y}=g(1-\alpha-\beta)(1-\gamma)/\gamma$. This follows from the fact that all countries produce final goods. Even the country with no local innovative base has the same output growth rate as its counterparts. This growth path is brought about via the import of a growing number of differentiated inputs leading to permanent productivity increases in the final-goods sector in each country.

6.2.3 Trade Liberalization

On the basis of the three-country model outlined in the preceding section, we are now able to address the long-run implications of the enlargement process. We distinguish between the gradual removal of artificial barriers to trade and the relaxation of barriers to migration. With respect to trade liberalization, distinguishing between our two cases (I and II) proves to be important. Nevertheless, we find some general patterns arising in the course of enlargement via trade liberalization.
We establish:

Proposition 6.2.2 *i.) Trade liberalization leads to a shift of intermediate-goods production to the country which imports final goods. An interior solution with innovation taking place in the country importing final goods becomes more probable. ii.) With $\tilde{k}_{A,C} = \tilde{k}$, the market share of the country importing final goods in total production (s^i) increases. iii.) Given that the countries in the integration bloc are importing (exporting) the final good, for $\bar{k} > \tilde{k}_{AC}$ enlargement via trade liberalization leads to wage convergence (divergence) in the initial integration bloc.*

Proof: See Appendix.
The intuition behind this is the following. Trade liberalization leads to a decreasing cost advantage of intermediate-goods producers in the country exporting the final good. For example, in case I, the cost gap of intermediate-goods production between countries A and C narrows; the cost advantage in A has to be less pronounced in order to guarantee competitive pricing in the final-goods sector. This cost effect dominates the potential increase in relative price competition in the importing countries' intermediate-goods sector. For given $\bar{\mu}$, it is more profitable to locate in the country with lower relative costs compared to the initial equilibrium. In the transition period, innovation takes place in this country until a new $\bar{\mu}$ is established at which increased price competition in the final-goods importing country compensates for the reduction in the cost differential. Compared to the initial steady-state, a larger relative number of intermediate goods is produced in the final-goods

importing country. It may even lead to complete concentration of innovative activities in the final-goods importing country. If the complete concentration of innovation can be observed in the pre-liberalization equilibrium, trade liberalization may lead to the occurrence of an interior solution with innovation taking place in A as well as in C.

The larger relative number of locally produced intermediate goods and the reduction in the cost disadvantage for local intermediate-goods producers overcompensates the loss in the level of protection which the country importing final goods realizes. It becomes more profitable to produce in this country. The relative wage rate shifts in favor of this country (see 6.42).

If it is relatively less costly to import intermediate goods from country C than from country A (i.e. $\bar{k} > k_{A,C}$), a decrease in the relative number of locally produced goods in country C is equivalent to a relative productivity gain of country B compared to country A. To ensure competitive pricing in the final-goods sector, $\omega_{A,B} = w_L^A / w_L^B$ decreases. With *i.)*, this implies that, in case I with a decreasing $\bar{\mu}$, wage convergence can be observed. In case II with an increasing $\bar{\mu}$, wage divergence in the initial integration bloc takes place. Note that with $\bar{k} = k_{A,C}$, relative wage rates in the initial integration bloc are unaffected by trade liberalization. Relative cost differentials of inputs between country A and B are the same, independent of the location of intermediate goods production. Such a setting takes place if the three countries are located along a line with country A being in the center. Transporting intermediate goods from C to B via A (and vice versa) is as costly as shipping them directly to country B. The cost differential for final-goods producers in A and B is always equal to $k_{A,B}$, no matter whether the respective final good is produced in A or C. Hence, $\omega_{A,B} = k_{A,B}^{\frac{\alpha}{\alpha-1}}$.

What are the growth rate effects of trade liberalization? Looking at the steady-state equation for the innovation rate (6.47) reveals that various effects pointing in different directions are at work in order to produce an interior solution. With a corner solution, the growth rate effects are, however, clear-cut. Trade liberalization enhances growth. If innovation is completely concentrated in one country only, say country A (with $\bar{\mu} = \infty$ in case II), [8]

[8] With balanced trade, country C must export final goods in order to balance the trade deficit in intermediate products. We exclude the most unlikely case where one country (or bloc of countries) imports all intermediate goods as well as a certain portion of domestic final-goods consumption.

the steady-state innovation rate can be expressed by (see (6.47)):

$$g^A = g = \frac{B(1-\gamma)\alpha}{1-\alpha}\left[\bar{L}^A + \bar{L}^B\zeta^{(\epsilon-1)\theta} + \zeta^{(1+2(\epsilon-1)\theta)}k_{A,C}^{\epsilon-1}\bar{L}^C\right] - \rho. \quad (6.48)$$

With innovation being concentrated in country C only, the same results emerge. Trade liberalization speeds up steady-state growth.

In order to investigate the growth effects of trade liberalization for the interior solution case, we assume $\bar{k} = k_{A,C}$. This allows for an explicit solution of (6.46) with respect to $\bar{\mu}$. Inserting the result into (6.47) still leaves a number of opposing effects on the costs of innovation, as well as on the profits of firms producing intermediate goods. Determining the sign of the effect of trade liberalization on steady-state innovation and growth rates is still a tedious task. It is not possible to derive a sensible analytical solution. However, running a very large number of simulations revealed a u-shaped relationship between the level of artificial trade barriers and the innovation and growth rates. Starting from high barriers to trade, trade liberalization slows down the growth process. With initially low barriers to trade, further trade liberalization enhances the growth process. This relationship is depicted in Figure 6.1, in both cases for specific parameter values.

We establish:

Proposition 6.2.3 *With a corner solution, enlargement via trade liberalization leads unambiguously to faster growth. In the interior solution case, trade liberalization brings about a higher (lower) growth rate if it takes place against the background of low (high) initial barriers to trade.*

The reasons for the non-monotone relationship between the level of artificial barriers to trade and the innovation rate are two underlying opposite effects. On the one hand, a reduction in the barriers of trade means fiercer competition for an intermediate-goods producer in country i. Fiercer competition is brought about by increased relative competitiveness of intermediate goods producers in the other country or by an increase in the relative number of local competitors, creating a downward pressure on the profits of intermediate-goods producers. This is a standard Schumpeterian effect. More competition reduces expected profits of innovators and, therefore, slows down the innovation process. On the other hand, lower barriers to trade reduce costs directly (see (6.36)), implying lower R&D costs (see (6.38)) as well.

Whereas the first force decreases expected returns, the second one leads to higher profits in the R&D sector and to further entry into this sector. With high (low) barriers to trade, the first (second) effect dominates.

Figure 6.1: The growth effect of enlargement via trade liberalization with two innovating countries

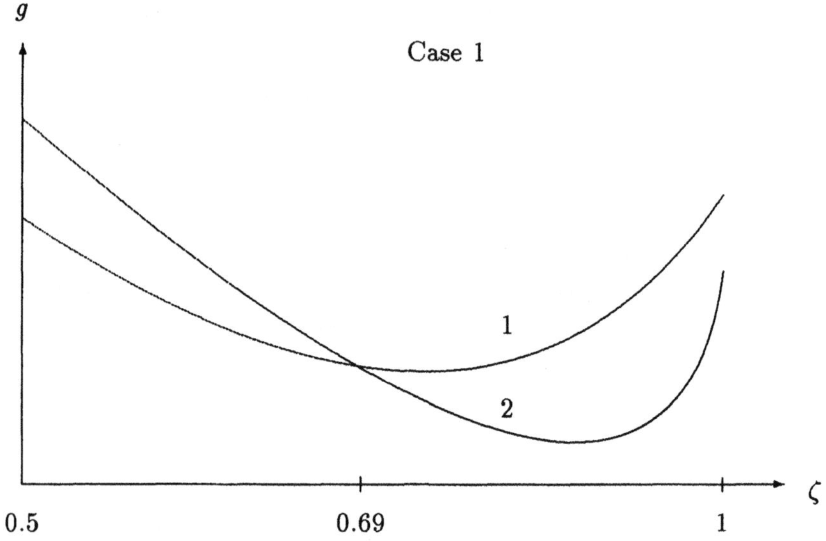

Line 1: $k_{A,C} = 0.7, \tilde{P} = 1, \epsilon = 6, \theta = 0.5$
Line 2: $k_{A,C} = 0.7, \tilde{P} = 0.5, \epsilon = 6, \theta = 0.5$

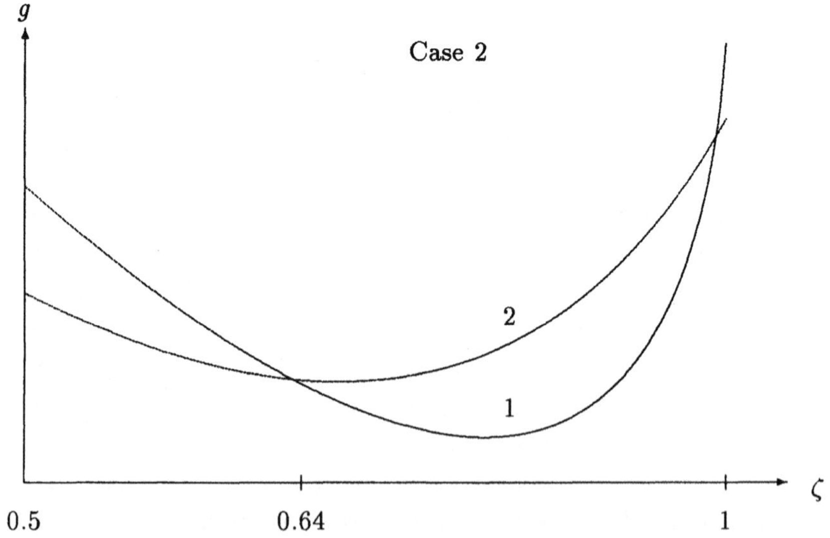

Line 1: $k_{A,C} = 0.7, \tilde{P} = 2, \epsilon = 10, \theta = 0.5$
Line 2: $k_{A,C} = 0.5, \tilde{P} = 5, \epsilon = 3, \theta = 0.5$

6.2.4 Complete Integration of Country C in the Common Market

In a second enlargement step, artificial barriers to migration are removed between the integration bloc and country C. A relaxation of artificial barriers to migration induces migration from or to country C. Since we assume non-equivalent natural migration costs (we suppose that individuals can be ranked according to their ties with their home country, i.e. by their natural migration costs), a removal of state-imposed migration barriers makes migration to the high-wage country profitable. Note that we assume that $\bar{L}^A$ and $\bar{L}^B$ denote the countries' populations after migration has occurred within the integration bloc. In other words, with $\omega_{A,C} > 1 (< 1)$ country C constitutes the emigration (immigration) country. It turns out, however, that both cases yield the same qualitative patterns. We analyze the consequences of migrations flows from or to country C at the margin. Since the effects are monotone, we can draw straightforward conclusions for the discrete case. All this is done against the background of a completed free trade zone between all three countries ($\zeta = 1$). It is important to note that a complete elimination of artificial barriers to trade implies price equalization in the final-goods sector. But in the presence of transport costs in the intermediate-goods sector, nominal as well as real wage differentials exist (see (6.43) and (6.44)).

By looking at the implications of enlargement via liberalization of factor flows on regional specialization patterns, we can state:

Proposition 6.2.4 *i.) A relaxation of barriers to migration vis-à-vis country C brings about a shift of intermediate-goods production to the immigration country. Complete concentration of innovative activities in this country becomes more probable. ii.) Migration increases the wage gap between the host and source country of migration. With A displaying the immigration country and $\bar{k} > k_{A,C}$, the wage gap between the established countries increases as well.*

Proof: See Appendix.

The mechanism with respect to the specialization patterns is straightforward. With immigration to country A, for example, A's labor force increases. This larger labor force can only be employed if A's share in total production increases. This, in turn, provides a larger local market for intermediate-goods producers in A. Investing in R&D in country A becomes more attractive. The larger relative number of intermediate goods in the new steady-state compensates for this enhanced local market in country A via fiercer price competition in A. The average price of inputs in A relative to that in C increases due to the larger number of locally produced intermediate goods in A. For sufficiently pronounced migration streams, complete concentration of innovation can be observed. This is the case if, for any finite $\bar{\mu}$, the competition effect cannot compensate for the larger local market in A. For each $\bar{\mu}$ innovation is more profitable in A than in C. A larger number of locally produced intermediate goods causes a larger productivity gap between A and C. Hence, relative wages shift in favor of country C. If natural migration costs do not increase too steeply for inhabitants of country C, a cumulative migration process might be possible. This results from the absence of any centrifugal force.

Migration leads to an increased wage gap which, in turn, causes people with even higher natural migration costs to migrate from C to A etc.. All effects are reversed if country C is the immigration country.

With $\bar{k} = k_{A,C}$, the relative wage rate between the "old' countries in the integration bloc is fixed and depends only on transport costs between A and B. If, however, $\bar{k} > k_{A,C}$, the location of intermediate-goods production matters for the relative wage rate between the two "old" countries in the integration bloc. The cost differential for final-goods producers in B as compared to their competitors in A is more pronounced if differentiated inputs are imported from A rather than from country C. Hence, an increase in $\bar{\mu}$ increases this cost differential. The relative wage rate $\omega_{A,B}$ increases due to the higher productivity of immobile labor in A relative to B. This is the case if country A is the host country of workers emigrating from country C.

The growth rate effect of migration is unambiguous. No matter in which direction migration takes place, concentration of the labor force in the high-wage country brings about a further concentration of production (see proposition 6.2.4). Hence, transport costs are saved. These resources can be used for other productive purposes. Resources are shifted to the innovative sector. Growth and innovation rates increase. This result occurs in the presence of an interior solution as well as with a corner solution.
We establish:

Proposition 6.2.5 *A complete integration of country C via a removal of state-imposed barriers to migration fosters growth, no matter whether an interior solution or a core-periphery patterns results.*

Proof: See Appendix.

6.2.5 Discussion

What are the main lessons of the analysis of this section, especially in comparison to the analysis of the integration of a less developed country into the common market? As a first general result, we found that the enlargement process when integrating a developed country leads unambigously to faster growth if we undertake the integration process against the background of sufficiently low initial barriers to trade. This contrasts substantially with our results in the case of integrating a lagging country in section 6.2, where especially the liberalization of migration barriers may lead to a reduction of growth rates. Given the suboptimality of the growth process, a reduction of the growth and innovation rate brings about a dynamic welfare loss for all participating countries. This can be regarded as one possible explanation as to why relatively well developed countries are very reluctant to open their borders via a complete relaxation of migration barriers. The formation of NAFTA is a prominent recent example. Whereas trade liberalization will be undertaken completely, there are no plans for a removal of barriers to migration. Since consumers in all countries benefit from the growth process via trade to the same extent, it is even in the interest of the lagging country to avoid measures which are growth reducing.

A second general result is that enlargement leads to the concentration of production. Especially with respect to the vulnerability of countries to asymmetric sectoral shocks, this is bad news for policy makers. The growth effects and the effects of integration measures on specialization patterns are independent of the underlying trade structure and our division into the two cases. The overall results of the model are much more general than the specific discussion of the model seems to indicate in the first place.

As a last point we would like to mention that in this section enlargement may lead to wage divergence between the established countries. Hence, the integration of a developed country can serve as an additional explanation for the non-occurence of income divergence in the EU in recent years.

Appendix

Proof of Proposition 6.2.1

An interior equilibrium exists if $\tilde{M}(\bar{\mu} = 0) > 0$ and $\tilde{M}(\bar{\mu} = \infty) < 0$. With (6.46) this yields the expression in *proposition 6.2.1* . Since $\tilde{M}(\bar{\mu})$ is strictly decreasing in $\bar{\mu}$ (sign $\partial\tilde{M}/\partial\bar{\mu}$ =-sign $\eta < 0$), a $\bar{\mu}^*$ exists for which $\tilde{M} = 0$. Since $\tilde{M}$ decreases monotonically with $\bar{\mu}$, $\bar{\mu}^*$ is the unique equilibrium.

We analyze the local stability of the steady state equilibrium for $\bar{\mu} < \bar{\mu}^*$. For $\bar{\mu} > \bar{\mu}^*$, the analysis is symmetric. With $\bar{\mu} < \bar{\mu}^*$, $\tilde{M} > 0$ and consequently $g^C = 0$, i.e. $\dot{\bar{\mu}} > 0$. At $\bar{\mu} = \bar{\mu}^*$, $g^c = g^A$ and, therefore, $\dot{\bar{\mu}} = 0$. We define the total value of innovative firms in A: $N^A = nP^A$. Hence, $\dot{N}^A/N^A = g + \dot{P}^A/P^A$. Using the no-arbitrage condition in A as well as (6.39)-(6.42) yields:

$$\frac{\dot{N}^A}{N^A} = \rho + g - \frac{(1-\gamma)\alpha p_Q Q \Gamma_1(\bar{\mu})\bar{\mu}}{\tilde{c}_n^A(\bar{\mu}+1)}, \tag{A.6.1}$$

with

$$\Gamma_1(\bar{\mu}) = \frac{s^A(\bar{\mu}+1)\vartheta^{-\epsilon}}{\bar{\mu}\vartheta^{1-\epsilon} + \tilde{k}_{A,C}^{\epsilon-1}} + \frac{s^B\vartheta^{-\epsilon}(\bar{\mu}+1)}{\bar{\mu}\vartheta^{1-\epsilon} + \bar{k}^{\epsilon-1}} + \frac{s^C(\bar{\mu}+1)\vartheta^{-\epsilon}\tilde{k}_{A,C}^{\epsilon-1}}{\bar{\mu}\vartheta^{1-\epsilon}\tilde{k}_{A,C}^{\epsilon-1}+1}$$

and

$$s^A = \left[k_{A,B}^{(\epsilon-1)\bar{\theta}}\left(\frac{\bar{\mu}+\bar{k}^{\epsilon-1}\vartheta^{\epsilon-1}}{\bar{\mu}+\tilde{k}_{A,C}^{\epsilon-1}\vartheta^{\epsilon-1}}\right)^{\bar{\theta}} \bar{f}/f + 1 + (\vartheta f)^{-1}\left(\frac{\bar{\mu}\vartheta^{1-\epsilon}\tilde{k}_{A,C}^{\epsilon-1}+1}{\bar{\mu}+\tilde{k}_{A,C}^{\epsilon-1}\vartheta^{\epsilon-1}}\right)^{\bar{\theta}}\right]^{-1}$$

$$s^B = \left[k_{A,B}^{(1-\epsilon)\bar{\theta}}\left(\frac{\bar{\mu}+\bar{k}^{\epsilon-1}\vartheta^{\epsilon-1}}{\bar{\mu}+\tilde{k}_{A,C}^{\epsilon-1}\vartheta^{\epsilon-1}}\right)^{-\bar{\theta}} f + 1 + (\vartheta \bar{f})^{-1} k_{A,B}^{(1-\epsilon)\bar{\theta}}\left(\frac{\bar{\mu}\vartheta^{1-\epsilon}\tilde{k}_{A,C}^{\epsilon-1}+1}{\bar{\mu}+\bar{k}^{\epsilon-1}\vartheta^{\epsilon-1}}\right)^{\bar{\theta}}\right]^{-1}$$

$$s^C = \left[\vartheta k_{A,B}^{(\epsilon-1)\bar{\theta}}\left(\frac{\bar{\mu}+\bar{k}^{\epsilon-1}\vartheta^{\epsilon-1}}{\bar{\mu}\tilde{k}_{A,C}^{\epsilon-1}\vartheta^{1-\epsilon}}\right)^{\bar{\theta}} \bar{f} + 1 + \vartheta f\left(\frac{\bar{\mu}\vartheta^{1-\epsilon}\tilde{k}_{A,C}^{\epsilon-1}+1}{\bar{\mu}+\tilde{k}_{A,C}^{\epsilon-1}\vartheta^{\epsilon-1}}\right)^{\bar{\theta}}\right]^{-1},$$

and $\tilde{c}_n^i = c_n^i n$. Using $p_Q Q = (1+\tilde{c}_n^A g)$ (note that $g^C = 0$) in A's factor market clearing condition to replace g in (A.6.1) and the factor market clearing conditions in (A.6.1), we can rewrite (A.6.1) to:

$$\frac{\dot{N}^A}{N^A} = \left[\frac{L^A}{\Gamma_2(\bar{\mu})} + \rho\right] N^A - \frac{(1-\gamma)\alpha\Gamma_1(\bar{\mu})\Gamma_2(\bar{\mu})\Gamma_3(\bar{\mu})\bar{\mu}}{(1-\alpha)(1+\bar{\mu})} - \frac{1}{\Gamma_3(\bar{\mu})}, \tag{A.6.2}$$

with

$$\Gamma_2(\bar{\mu}) = s^A\left(\frac{\bar{\mu}+1}{\bar{\mu}+(\tilde{k}_{A,C}\vartheta)^{\epsilon-1}}\right)^{\bar{\theta}}$$

and

$$\Gamma_3(\bar{\mu}) = (1/\bar{B})\left(\frac{\bar{\mu}+(\vartheta\tilde{k}_{A,C})^{\epsilon-1}}{\bar{\mu}+1}\right)^{\bar{\theta}}.$$

We analyze the equilibrium dynamics with the help of figure 6.2. Without loss of generality, we draw $\dot{N}^A$ as an upward sloping line in $N^A-\bar{\mu}$-space. The

Figure 6.2: The equilibrium dynamics

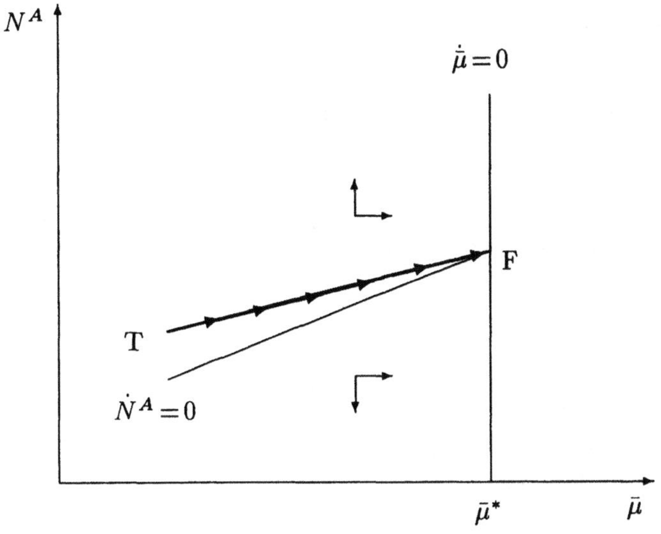

arrows indicate the movement of the economy from any point with $\bar{\mu} < \bar{\mu}^*$. The path TF is the unique trajectory which leads to the long-run equilibrium. Any other path leads either to an ever increasing N^A or to N^A approaching zero (and hence to $g^A = g^C = 0$), thereby either violating households' transversality condition or entailing unfulfilled expectations. Q.e.d.

Proof of Proposition 6.2.2:

ad i.) Case 1: With $\vartheta = \zeta$ we can rewrite $\tilde{M}(\bar{\mu}) = 0$ as:

$$f\left(\frac{\bar{\mu}(\tilde{k}_{A,C})^{\epsilon-1}+1}{\bar{\mu}+(\tilde{k}_{A,C})^{\epsilon-1}\zeta^{2(\epsilon-1)}}\right)^{\eta}\left(\frac{1-(\tilde{k}_{A,C})^{\epsilon-1}\zeta^{2\epsilon-1}}{1-(\tilde{k}_{A,C})^{\epsilon-1}\zeta^{-1}}\right)+$$

$$+k_{A,B}^{\frac{\alpha}{1-\alpha}}\bar{f}\left(\frac{\bar{\mu}(\tilde{k}_{A,C})^{\epsilon-1}+1}{\bar{\mu}+(\bar{k})^{\epsilon-1}\zeta^{2(\epsilon-1)}}\right)^{\eta}\left(\frac{1-(\bar{k})^{\epsilon-1}\zeta^{2\epsilon-1}}{1-(\tilde{k}_{A,C})^{\epsilon-1}\zeta^{-1}}\right)-1=0.$$

We can immediately infer $\partial\tilde{M}/\partial\zeta < 0$, i.e. $\frac{d\bar{\mu}}{d\zeta} = -\frac{\partial\tilde{M}/\partial\zeta}{\partial\tilde{M}/\partial\bar{\mu}} < 0$.

Rewriting P for $\vartheta = \zeta$ yields:

$$P(\vartheta=\zeta)=\zeta^{(1-\epsilon)\eta}\left(\frac{f(1-\tilde{k}_{A,C}^{\epsilon-1}\zeta^{2\epsilon-1}}{1-\tilde{k}_{A,C}^{\epsilon-1}\zeta^{-1}}+k_{A,B}^{\frac{\alpha}{1-\alpha}}\frac{\bar{f}(1-\bar{k}^{\epsilon-1}\zeta^{2\epsilon-1}}{1-\bar{k}^{\epsilon-1}\zeta^{-1}}\right)=\zeta^{(1-\epsilon)\eta}P^*.$$

Our condition for an interior solution becomes: $\zeta^{2(1-\epsilon)\eta}P^* > 1 > \tilde{k}_{A,C}P^*$.

The LHS as well as the RHS of this inequality decrease with trade liberalization. In other words, starting from a corner solution with innovation taking place in country A, $g^C > 0$ and a corner solution in C (when starting from an interior solution) become more likely.

ad ii.): With $\bar{k} = \tilde{k}_{A,C}$, it is feasible to rewrite the condition for an interior solution as:

$$\left(\frac{s^A + s^B}{s^C}\right)^{\frac{\bar{\theta}-1}{\bar{\theta}}} = \left(\frac{1 - \vartheta^{-\epsilon}\tilde{k}_{A,C}^{\epsilon-1}}{(\vartheta^{-\epsilon} - \tilde{k}_{A,C}^{\epsilon-1}\vartheta^{\epsilon-1})\vartheta^{\bar{\theta}}(1 + k_{A,B}^{\frac{\alpha}{1-\alpha}})}\right). \tag{A.6.3}$$

With $\vartheta = \zeta$, the RHS is:

$$\frac{1 - k_{A,C}^{\epsilon-1}\zeta^{-1}}{\zeta^{-(1-\bar{\theta})} - k_{A,C}\zeta^{2\epsilon-1-\bar{\theta}}}.$$

Since $\bar{\theta} < 1$, this expression is increasing in ζ. For the equality in (A.6.3) to hold, $(s^A + s^B)/s^C$ has to decrease.

ad iii.)

$$\frac{d\omega_{A,B}}{d\zeta} = \frac{\partial\omega_{A,B}}{\partial\zeta} + \frac{\partial\omega_{A,B}}{\partial\bar{\mu}}\frac{d\bar{\mu}}{d\zeta} \leq 0,$$

since sign $\left(\frac{\partial\omega_{A,B}}{\partial\zeta}\right)$=sign $(\tilde{k}_{A,C} - \bar{k}) \leq 0$, sign $\frac{\partial\omega_{A,B}}{\partial\bar{\mu}}$=sign $(\tilde{k}_{A,C} - \bar{k}) \leq 0$ and $\frac{d\bar{\mu}}{d\zeta} < 0$ (see proposition 6.2.1). Q.e.d.

Case II: Proceeding in the same manner as above yields the reverse results.

Proof of Proposition 6.2.4:

ad i.)

For $\zeta = 1$ we can write $\tilde{M}(\bar{\mu})$ as:

$$f\left(\frac{\bar{\mu}(\tilde{k}_{A,C})^{\epsilon-1} + 1}{\bar{\mu} + (\tilde{k}_{A,C})^{\epsilon-1}}\right)^{\eta} + k_{A,B}^{\frac{\alpha}{1-\alpha}}\bar{f}\left(\frac{\bar{\mu}(\tilde{k}_{A,C})^{\epsilon-1} + 1}{\bar{\mu} + \bar{k}^{\epsilon-1}}\right)^{\eta} - 1 = 0.$$

Case I: Migration from C to A increases f as well as $\bar{f}$. From the above expression we find $\partial\tilde{M}/\partial f > 0$ and $\partial\tilde{M}/\partial\bar{f} > 0$. Consequently, $-dL^C = dL^A$:

$$\frac{d\bar{\mu}}{dL^C} > 0.$$

Rewriting the condition for the existence of an interior solution for $\zeta = 1$ yields:

$$(k_{A,C})^{(1-\epsilon)\eta} > \tilde{P} > (k_{A,C})^{(\epsilon-1)\eta},$$

with $\tilde{P} = (f + \bar{f} k_{A,B}^{\frac{\alpha}{1-\alpha}})$ increasing with migration from C to A. Hence, $g^A > 0$ as well as $g^C = 0$ becomes more likely.

Case II: Migration from A to C or from B to C reduces f and $\bar{f}$. Hence, the reverse result follows. Q.e.d.

ad ii.)
By taking $\partial\omega_{A,B}/\partial\bar{\mu} \geq 0$ together with *Proposition 6.2.4*, we find that $\omega_{A,B}$ increases (decreases) in case I (II) or stays constant if $\bar{k} = \tilde{k}_{A,C}$.
The same argument applies to $\omega_{B,C}$. Using $\partial\omega_{B,C}/\partial\bar{\mu} > 0$ and *Proposition 6.2.4*, we find the increase (decrease) in $\omega_{B,C}$ in case I (II).

Proof of Proposition 6.2.5:

First, we look at the interior solution case.
With $\zeta = 1$, $G_1 = 1$ follows. Deriving:

$$\bar{\mu} = \frac{\tilde{P}^{1/\eta} - (k_{A,C})^{\epsilon-1}}{1 - (k_{A,C})^{\epsilon-1}\tilde{P}^{1/\eta}}$$

with $\tilde{P}$ derived from $\tilde{M}(\bar{\mu}) = 0$ and inserting this into G_2 yields:

$$G_2(\zeta = 1) = L^A + L^B k_{A,B}^{(\epsilon-1)\bar{\theta}} \left(\frac{\tilde{P}(1 + k_{A,C}^{\epsilon-1})}{\tilde{P}+1}\right)^{\bar{\theta}} + L^C \left(\frac{1 + k_{A,C}^{\epsilon-1}}{\tilde{P}+1}\right)^{\bar{\theta}}. \quad \text{(A.6.4)}$$

Hence, we can deduce for $-dL^C = dL^A$:

$$\text{sign}\frac{dG_2}{dL^C} = \text{sign}(1 - \tilde{P}^{\bar{\theta}}).$$

Noting that $\bar{\mu} > 1 (\bar{\mu} < 1)$, it follows that $\omega_{A,C} > 1$ $(\omega_{A,C} < 1)$ for $\tilde{P} > 1$ $(\tilde{P} < 1)$. Migration from C to A (A to C) will take place only if $\tilde{P} > 1$ $(\tilde{P} < 1)$. In both cases, G_2 and, consequently, g (see (6.48) increase.

For migration to occur from B to C (in the case $\tilde{P} < 1$), the result is even more pronounced: $dG_2/dL^C = -k_{A,B}^{(\epsilon-1)\bar{\theta}}\tilde{P}^{\bar{\theta}} + 1 > 0$ $(dL^C = -dL^B)$.
Q.e.d.

Secondly, we investigate the corner solution scenario. Say country A displays the innovative center ($\bar{\mu} = \infty$). Then:

$$G_2 = L^A + L^B k_{A,B}^{(\epsilon-1)\bar{\theta}} + L^C k_{A,C}^{(\epsilon-1)\bar{\theta}}.$$

All other terms in the steady-state innovation equation are independent of migration. Since $dL^A = -dL^C$, migration from C to A increases G_2 and, consequently, $g^A = g$. If country C represents the innovative center, the same growth effect results. Q.e.d.

6.3 Leapfrogging through Integration

6.3.1 The Issue

In the preceding sections of this chapter, we assumed the general specialization patterns as well as the relative income positions of countries to be given. Integration changed the distance between the countries, but in no case led to a complete reversal of specialization patterns and income positions. In the following, we will put this assumption under scrutiny and investigate possible scenarios under which specialization patterns among countries switch due to the enlargement process.

Recently, Brezis et al. (1993) addressed the possibility that the poorer country leapfrogs the richer country, leading to a change in technological leadership. They show that, in the presence of local technological spillovers a lagging country might be able to leapfrog its rival country as a result of exogenous technological change. The lagging country will adopt the new technology which has a larger potential, but a lower initial productivity. Over time the lagging country will catch-up and finally leapfrog the initial leader. A related argument has been put forward in Englmann/Walz (1995) in a regional context. Leapfrogging is the result of exogenous technological change. The idea that leading firms or nations are less willing to adopt new technologies, opening the possibility for the follower to catch up has been used by Nelson/Winter (1982) at the firm level. In the industrial organization literature, a number of authors have dealt with the possibility of leapfrogging in technological races at the firm level (see e.g. Fudenberg et al. (1983), Grossman/Shapiro (1987), Gruber (1992), and Harris/Vickers (1987)).

We provide a different source of the leapfrogging process. Rather than introducing a new technology, we allow for a complete removal of artificial barriers to trade and migration which the poorer country faces. In other words, we argue that leapfrogging might occur through integration. Integration reveals the poorer country's (i.e. the candidate for integration) comparative advantage, which was hidden behind barriers to migration and trade. We show that it is feasible that the newly integrated country leapfrogs the peripheral country in the initial integration bloc. Specialization patterns switch among these two countries.

To illustrate our basic idea more clearly, suppose that the Czech Republic is integrated in the EU, which consists of – broadly speaking – an economic center (Germany, France) and an economic periphery (Greece, Portugal, Spain, Ireland). Due to the closeness to the larger market, the Czech Republic has an advantage as a location for advanced production sectors as compared to the EU periphery. This advantage was overcompensated by the disadvantage of impediments to migration and trade in the pre-integration setting, most notably in earlier years through the existence of the Iron Curtain, and in more recent years through the existence of non-tariff impediments to trade as well as restrictions to factor flows. Relaxing these impediments in the course of regional integration might enable the Czech Republic to overcome its initial disadvantage and the absence of a local technological base. Due to the closeness of the larger market (Germany), it becomes more attractive for intermediate-goods producers to locate in the Czech Republic rather than in the EU-periphery. The relative specialization patterns of the EU periphery and the Czech Republic switch. The same is true for the relative income patterns.

The potential threat of new competition from the Eastern European countries has been often stressed by the more peripheral countries in the EU. Especially after the fall of the Berlin Wall and the removal of the Iron Curtain, they faced the threat that Middle European countries may become more attractive to international investors. One most visible example is the decision of Volkswagen to expand worldwide capacity by investing in Skoda in the Czech Republic rather than in Seat in Spain. We argue that the enlargement of the common market might reinforce this threat.

A related argument was recently put forward by Motta et al. (1995) who show that trade can lead to a switch in leadership. Their argument is, however, settled at the firm level in a partial equilibrium, game theoretical framework rather than at the country level with a general equilibrium setting.

6.3.2 Endogenous Specialization Patterns

We adopt the same framework as in section 6.1. Countries A and B form together the initial integration bloc. Before integration takes place, innovators locate in A as well as in B. An interior solution results. Our basic argument applies even more forcefully to situations in which a corner solution prevails in the initial integration bloc. Country C lacks a local technological base. Innovation as well as intermediate-goods production does not occur in the candidate for integration (C) in the pre-integration setting. In contrast to 6.1, this is, however, not caused by technological inferiority in the production of the industrial final good, but is attributed to a bad starting position of country C with respect to the initial number of intermediate goods.

Given the lack of local innovation, country C has to import the entire set of intermediate products which are burdened with natural impediments to trade (transport costs) as well as state-imposed, non-tariff barriers to trade. This leaves C's Y-sector with a substantial cost disadvantage. Given a sufficiently large cost disadvantage due to the lack of a local technological base compared to C's factor endowment, Y-production proves unprofitable in country C. To demonstrate this more clearly, suppose country C imports the industrial final good in exchange for exports of the traditional final good. All other settings prove even more disadvantageous for the production of the industrial final good in country C. Note that the overall goods-market clearing condition requires that the traditional final good be produced in two countries (see section 6.1). Furthermore, production of industrial final goods must take place in A as well as in B in order to provide a local market for intermediate-goods producers in the respective country.

For the case in which traditional-goods production occurs in B as well as in C (whereby C is the exporting country), production costs of traditional final goods have to be lower in C than in B:

$$\bar{t}c_Z^B = c_Z^C, \tag{6.49}$$

with $\bar{t}$ $(0 < \bar{t} < 1)$ denoting the non-tariff barriers to trade.

Furthermore, a similar condition has to hold in the industrial final-goods sector. Here, with C being the importer of this good, its production costs can be higher than those of producers in the integration bloc. Imports of industrial products into C coexist with domestic production if:

$$c_Y^A = c_Y^B = \bar{t}c_Y^C. \tag{6.50}$$

If, however, c_Y^C exceed the production costs of importers from A and B by more than t^{-1}, Y-production is not profitable anymore in country C. Given that the countries in the integration bloc are much better endowed with skilled labor than country C and that this factor is used more intensively in industrial compared to traditional final-goods production, this latter situation emerges; Y-production is not profitable in country C in the pre-integration setting. We assume that this holds and start the integration process from such a setting.

With integration, matters change substantially. We compare the pre-integration situation with the situation after the complete entry of country C in the common market. All migration and (artificial) trade barriers are removed at once. This implies $\bar{t} = 1$ and $w_H^{A,B} = w_H^C = w_H$. Note that in the presence of complete trade liberalization, the direction of final-goods trade becomes irrelevant with respect to pricing conditions. For $c_Z^B = c_Z^C$, we simply obtain (see (6.6)):

$$\frac{w^C}{w^B} := \omega_{C,B} = 1. \tag{6.51}$$

With free trade, we can rewrite the competitive pricing condition in the industrial final-goods sector ($c_Y^B = c_Y^C$) together with (6.5) as to:[9]

$$\omega_{C,B} = \left(\frac{\mu k_{A,C}^{\epsilon-1} + k_{B,C}^{\epsilon-1}}{\mu k_{A,B}^{\epsilon-1} + 1} \right)^{\theta}, \tag{6.52}$$

whereby $k_{i,j}$ denotes transport costs which arise in the course of intermediate-goods trade from country i to j ($i, j = A, B, C, i \neq j$) and $\mu = n^A/n^B$ represents the relative number of intermediate-goods production in A compared to the one in B.

The decisive question is whether, for a given μ in the pre-integration steady-state, the RHS of (6.52) is larger than one, implying with simultaneous Z-production in B and C, $p_Y^C < p_Y^B$. If the RHS is larger than one, specialization patterns will switch. After integration, country C has a cost advantage in Y-production for $\omega_{C,B} = 1$. The relative wage rate will never increase above one since unskilled workers in country B will always find an employment opportunity in Z-production. To understand the intuition behind the switch in specialization patterns more clearly, let us have a closer look at the condition for which the RHS of (6.52) becomes larger than one. For a given μ in the pre-integration steady-state, we obtain for this condition:

$$\Lambda := \mu k_{A,B}^{\epsilon-1} + 1 - \mu k_{A,C}^{\epsilon-1} - k_{B,C}^{\epsilon-1} < 0. \tag{6.53}$$

[9]For $n^C > 0$, (6.52) can be expressed as: $\omega_{C,B} = \left(\frac{n^A k_{A,C}^{\epsilon-1} + n^B k_{B,C}^{\epsilon-1} + n^C}{n^A k_{A,B}^{\epsilon-1} + n^B + n^C k_{B,C}^{\epsilon-1}} \right)^{\theta}$. Since $\partial \omega_{C,B}/\partial n^C > 0$, an expansion of n^C reinforces our argument.

Since A is the industrial leader, $\mu > 1$. Transport costs are larger from country A to B than from A to C (note that with $\mu > 1$ $k_{A,B} < k_{A,C}$ is a necessary condition for $\Lambda < 0$). This is the case if country C is, in economic terms, closer to the center country than country B. The eastern European countries (Poland, Hungary, Czech Republic) are, compared to Portugal and Greece, an example for such a setting. For example, with just-in-time production processes, it is cheaper to trade intermediate goods between Germany and the Czech Republic than between Germany and Greece. The more pronounced the concentration of intermediate-goods production in the pre-integration steady-state is (i.e. the larger μ), the more likely is that $\Lambda < 0$ holds. The advantage of country B due to its local technological base is relatively less pronounced. Table 6.1 presents some numerical examples for which a switch in specialization patterns takes place after the enlargement of the common market. For $\mu = \infty$ (i.e. with a corner solution prevailing), $k_{A,B} < k_{A,C}$ is a sufficient condition for $\Lambda < 0$.
We can establish

Proposition 6.3.1 *With $\Lambda < 0$ after the enlargement process has been undertaken, a switch in specialization patterns takes place. Production of industrial final goods is shifted from country B to country C.*

Table 6.1 reveals that even for $k_{A,C} \geq k_{A,B} = k_{B,C}$ a switch in specialization patterns is feasible as long as the relative number of locally produced intermediate goods in country B is small.[10] $k_{A,C} \geq k_{A,B} = k_{B,C}$ displays the notion that country A is the geographic center. A, B, and C are located along a line with A being at the center. However, if it is sufficiently costly to ship goods from A to B compared to trading between A and C and μ is sufficiently large, average costs of differentiated inputs are higher in B than in C. The same argument applies for $\mu = 1$ if $k_{A,C}$ is sufficiently large compared to $k_{A,B}$. Average costs of imports (one half from A and one half from B) in C are lower than importing half the set of available inputs from A to B at high costs and producing the other fifty per cent domestically.

What happens if specialization patterns switch? With $\Lambda < 0$, it is not feasible to produce the traditional final good and the industrial final good in country B at the same time. The employment opportunity in Z-production prevents wages for unskilled labor in B from falling below those in C. With

[10] Unfortunately, there is little consensus in the empirical literature with regard to the value of the elasticity of substitution ϵ (see Baier/Bergstrand (1998), Chari et al. (1996) and Feenstra (1994)).

Table 6.1: Numerical examples for $\Lambda < 0$

μ	$k_{A,B}$	$k_{A,C}$	$k_{B,C}$	ϵ
1	0.8	0.95	0.9	2
3	0.7	0.95	0.7	2
5	0.8	0.95	0.76	4
5	0.5	0.7	0.35	3
∞	0.9	0.91	0.909	5

identical costs for skilled and unskilled labor in both countries (B and C) and lower average costs of inputs in C than in B, Y-production in B is no longer feasible. Y-production in B vanishes completely. This leaves potential intermediate-goods producers in B with no domestic market. The profit differential which is decisive for location decisions of potential innovators can be expressed by:

$$\text{sign}(G^A - G^B) = \text{sign}\left[s_Y^A \Psi^{-1} - s_Y^B\right]. \tag{6.54}$$

With $s_Y^B = 0$, $G^A > G^B$ for all μ. Innovation ceases completely in country B.

In order to derive the new three-country long-run equilibrium after integration has taken place, we suppose that $\bar{L}^B = \bar{L}^C$ holds. The effect of asymmetric endowments with unskilled labor in the two countries can be derived from section 6.1 by altering f^*. The basic results of this section remain, however, unchanged.

With $\bar{L}^B = \bar{L}^C$, B and C's specialization patterns are exactly reversed compared to the situation in section 6.1. In the new steady-state, country C has the specialization patterns of country B and vice versa. Note, however, that the relative wages for unskilled labor are unaffected by the switch in production patterns. Independent of specialization patterns, they are $\omega_{B,C} = 1$. Hence, since unskilled labor benefits from the growth process in the economy as a whole, independent of the location of the dynamic sectors, they experience the same welfare level in cases with and without a switch in specialization patterns. This important fact leads to:

Proposition 6.3.2 *Governments maximizing welfare of the residents do not have any reason to intervene in order to avoid the switch in specialization* *patterns. Residents in countries A and B are equally well off, indpendent of the occurence of a switch in specialization patterns.*

It is interesting to look at the transitional dynamics. We can distinguish between two cases. In the first case, the effects of complete integration of the factor market for skilled labor dominates the trade related effects with respect to specialization patterns, and we end up in a corner solution with $\bar{\mu} := n^A/n^C = \infty$ with n^i denoting the number of locally differentiated goods produced in country i. In the other case, we find an interior solution.

Let us first look at the case with an emerging interior solution in the common market consisting of all three countries. We denote $\bar{\mu}^*$ as the equilibrium number of intermediate goods produced in A compared to the respective number in C. In the steady-state equilibrium, country A is specialized completely in the industrial sector, producing the industrial final good, intermediate goods and locating active innovators. In contrast, country B represents the periphery being specialized completely in Z-production. Country C is engaged in all sectors of the economy. We start with $n^C = 0$ and, consequently, with $\bar{\mu} = \infty$ at the time the enlargement is undertaken. Hence, in the transition towards the interior solution steady-state, the innovation rate is higher in country C than in A. Since $\dot{\bar{\mu}}/\bar{\mu} = (g^A - g^C)$, $g^C > g^A$ necessitates that $\bar{\mu}$ decreases over time and approaches its steady-state value $\bar{\mu}^*$. Our discussion in section 4 and 6.1 revealed that for $\bar{\mu} \in [0, \mu^*[$, $G^C > G^A$ implying with identical costs of innovation due to mobility of skilled labour that innovation takes place exclusively in C during the transition.

Matters are different if a corner solution prevails in the new steady-state. If in the old pre-integration steady-state a corner solution prevailed, a transitional period does not exist after the enlargement step. Final-goods production is shifted immediately and innovation takes place in the center country A only. If the new steady-state is approached from an interior steady-state, innovation takes place only in country A. Relative wage rates increase in favor of unskilled workers in country A.

To sum up, we have shown that the enlargement of a common market may enable the newly integrated country to leapfrog its rival which initially produced the industrial final good. Specialization patterns among countries B and C switch. In the steady-state with an interior solution, localized growth processes cease in the "old" lagging country and may take place in the country entering the integration bloc. At the same time, however, we showed that there is no reason to worry about this situation from the perspective of policy makers in country B as long as incomplete specialization patterns prevail. Income levels are the same in country B and C. Furthermore, all consumers benefit to the same extent from the growth process via trade. Hence, households in country B and C are equally well off. There are no losers or winners due to the leapfrogging process.

6.4 Summary

Enlargement of the common market by integrating a further country alters the specialization and growth patterns of the new entrant and the integration bloc as a whole. But, it may also change the relationship between the "old" countries in the integration bloc decisively. This is one of the main messages of our analysis in this chapter. Especially, with regard to the integration of a lagging country, we derive an interesting result. The burden of adjustment of fiercer competition caused by the integration of the lagging country is imposed on the center country in the integration bloc rather than the periphery. The latter, competing directly with the new entrant, can side-step this competition by shifting resources into the technologically advanced sector. The center country, in contrast, is already completely specialized and is, therefore, not able to avoid additional competition. Enlargement via trade liberalization leads to convergence of steady-state wage rates between the established countries of the integration bloc. This is, however, not a general pattern. Other integration steps (e.g. liberalization of migration barriers for unskilled labor) have just the opposite effect. These conflicting effects can be considered as an explanation for our hypothesis of a non-significant relation between integration and convergence.

A second major finding of this chapter is that the effects of different steps of integration differ distinctly with respect to the integration of a lagging country compared to the enlargement via integration of a developed country. This is especially true with respect to the liberalization of migration barriers. Whereas the relaxation of barriers to migration unambiguously leads to a positive dynamic welfare effect with the integration of an advanced country, a relaxation of barriers to migration for unskilled labor vis-à-vis a lagging country slows down growth and brings about a negative dynamic welfare effect. This suggests that complete integration of a lagging country should be less likely than complete integration of an advanced country. Casual empiricism confirms this hypothesis (e.g. integration of Turkey in EU, Mexico in NAFTA).

Furthermore, we argued that integration can induce a complete reversal of specialization and growth patterns. The new entrant may become second in the hierarchy of the three countries with respect to their relative degree of specialization in the technological sector while the initial second becomes last. The new entrant, being initially specialized in the traditional-goods sector, hosts industrial final-goods production as well as intermediate-goods producers and active innovators. The switch in specialization patterns and the relocation of innovative activities and local growth processes, however, does not have any effects on the well-being of the residents of the respective countries. Thereby, an important pattern of our entire analysis is repeated. Households gain from the growth process via trade in goods (which incorporate new technical knowledge) independent of the location of innovative processes. A larger technological base, however, may lead to higher levels of income via higher productivity of the immobile factor in the production which uses differentiated goods. This is the consequence of higher prices for imported inputs due to transport costs. As long as countries compete in the traditional-goods sector, this productivity gap does not matter at all. Income levels are independent of the location of the innovation process. In this situation, no reason exists for governments to compete for mobile investment in R&D. Countries do not have to worry about the switch in specialization patterns from a welfare point of view.

Chapter 7

General Summary

Starting with an assessment of empirical observations of the evolution of regional income and specialization patterns, we analyzed a wide array of integration steps and measures, building on a basic model of endogenous regional growth. Our main objective was to overcome the two major shortcomings of the existing literature on regional integration: the negligence of growth rate effects and the concentration on the assumptions of conventional trade theory. The discussion of the existing literature in chapter 3 highlights these shortcomings. The brief literature overview also stresses the important distinction between international and regional integration. Nevertheless, our analysis makes use of many insights of the static literature on regional integration. Therefore, the present study represents a complement rather than a substitute of the existing literature on regional integration.

Against the background of the objective of our study, it is important to note three empirical observations for the European case in section 2. First, we find substantial disparities in per capita income across European regions and even more pronounced disparities in local R&D. Secondly, we show that the evolution of per capita income among European regions follows a declining pattern of convergence in the post World-War II period. Initial strong convergence was followed by non-convergence among European countries and regions since the early 1970's. We could observe neither β- nor σ-convergence for the post-1970 period. Our analysis casts doubts on a positive relationship between regional integration and income convergence. Thirdly, we argue on the basis of the growth-accounting literature that technological change which is highly localized is the major driving force behind growth processes in developed economies. All of these observations are used as stylized facts in our theoretical analysis.

In chapter 4, we put forward a theoretical framework which constituted the basis for our analysis of the long run effects of regional integration. Incorporating aspects of regional economics and economic geography (transport costs, factor mobility) in a model of endogenous growth for open economies gave us a general framework with which the long run implications of regional integration can be addressed. In this basic model, location and migration decisions of private households (and hence, specialization and trade patterns of countries) as well as the innovation and growth rates are endogenously determined. This dynamic general equilibrium model, while depicting a large variety of possible scenarios, lends itself - due to its simplicity – to an analysis of the long run implications of a wide array of integration steps and measures.

The most prominent features of this modeling framework are, on the one hand, the multiplicity of equilibria and on the other hand, the possibility of asymmetric interior solutions with innovation taking place in two countries. Despite their equal innovation rates, the two countries have substantially different production patterns and income levels.

The decisive questions throughout our entire discussion in chapters 5 and 6 are: in what manner do integration measures alter location and migration decisions of agents and, consequently, the specialization and trade patterns of countries? What are the main channels through which investment decisions are affected and how does this translate into changes of regional and overall growth?

Our first analysis of a deepening of the integration process reveals that integration among two countries being separated by sufficiently low initial barriers to trade always leads to faster growth, but in many cases also to a further concentration of production. Countries become more vulnerable against sectoral shocks. The positive growth rate effect which is caused by a reallocation of resources is equivalent to a dynamic welfare gain for consumers.

Taking the discriminatory character of regional integration into account, we derive conditions under which the results of static analysis carry over to a dynamic setting. Integration with a trade creation effect, besides the positive static welfare effect, also has a positive dynamic welfare effect, as long as the integration bloc is relatively specialized in the dynamic sector. Similarly, with a trade diversion effect, a negative dynamic welfare effect of integration emerged. Hence, the dynamic analysis of the discriminatory effect of regional integration which takes place only among a subset of countries reinforces the results of traditional static analysis. Our analysis, by incorporating dynamic effects, goes one step beyond static analyses.

Our basic dynamic general equilibrium framework also enabled us to look at the effects of a harmonization of policies, as well as regional policy measures undertaken in an economic union. Two main policy implications shall be stressed here. First and most importantly, we show that, with respect to regional policy, a potential trade off between the regional policy objective (i.e. the reduction of regional income disparities) and dynamic efficiency exists. Even if regional policy suceeds in reducing the income gap between regions (in per capita terms), this might draw resources away from the dynamic sector, leading consequently to slower growth. Achieving the regional policy objective has to be paid for with a dynamic welfare loss. Some regional policy measures even indirectly strengthens the agglomerative advantage of the center country and induce more pronounced regional disparities. The lesson for regional policy makers is that one should not only look at the most immediate and direct effects. Rather it proves essential to analyze the effect of a policy on agglomerative advantages and disadvantages, as well as the incentive for investment in order to be able to carry out a successful policy with the least economic costs.

Secondly, we show that harmonization of policies in an economic union may worsen the relative position of the lagging country and lead to more pronounced differences in specialization patterns. Harmonization of policies has negative effects on interregional allocation in the economic union.

Besides focusing on long run implications of regional integration, the analysis of the enlargement process displays a novel feature of our study. We addressed the overall effects of the enlargement process as well as the effects on each country separately. The latter results indicate the differing positions of each country towards the enlargement process. Distinguishing between different integration steps yields important policy advice. It allowed us to find an answer to the questions concerning the sequencing of the enlargement process: is it sensible to integrate economies only partially in an integration bloc or does full integration always lead to the best international (dynamic) allocation?

It proved essential to distinguish between the integration of a lagging country and an advanced economy in an existing integration bloc. The two scenarios lead in some respects to sharply diverging, even opposite effects. We showed that an integration of an advanced country in an integration bloc from which it is initially separated by barriers to trade which are not too high leads unambiguously to faster growth. This type of enlargement process brought about a positive dynamic welfare effect benefiting consumers in all countries. As with the integration of an advanced country, the integration of a lagging country altered the growth rate in the three-country equilibrium via a reallocation of resources. But with the integration of a lagging country, it might very well be that resources are drawn away from the dynamic sector leading to a reduced growth rate. In this case, integrating the lagging country only partially might be sensible.

Our analysis of the integration of the lagging country revealed a number of additional interesting results. We showed that the enlargement process may lead to a reduction of the income gap between the established countries. The initial periphery in the integration bloc is pushed, through new competition by the entrant, into climbing up the "technological ladder". Its relative local technological base expands and the income gap with respect to the technological leader diminishes.

Endogenizing general specialization patterns revealed that a switch in general specialization patterns is feasible. We stressed a new source for the possibility of leapfrogging. Rather than emerging from the introduction of a new technology, leapfrogging occurs through integration. Equally important, however, is that it turns out that such a switch in specialization patterns leaves the welfare of households in the respective countries completely unaffected. Hence, there is no reason for governments to try to avoid such a change of production patterns induced by the enlargement process.

At the beginning of this study, we stressed the fact that our analysis has to be selective. Many aspects of regional integration were not addressed. Two important theoretical extensions of our framework shall be mentioned here. Both involve important policy areas related to the integration process. First, incorporating the possibility of unemployment in the present growth framework would allow for an investigation of the effects of regional integration on countries' employment and unemployment levels. Against the background of high unemployment levels in Western market economies, this is an important issue. Aghion and Howitt (1994) have made a first start in integrating the possibility of (search) unemployment in a growth framework.

A second important extension involves the relation between financial integration and regional growth. Here, too, quite a number of attempts have already been made for a closed economy framework (see e.g., Bencivenga/Smith (1991), Bencivenga et al. (1996) and the overview of Levine/Zervos (1996)). Important regional issues such as the effect of financial deregulation on financial centers could be combined with the effects on the growth process. Both areas (and many more) are fruitful avenues for future research.

Even more important, however, is an empirical assessment of the relation between growth and regional integration. Baldwin (1989) and Henrekson et al. (1997) have made important steps in this direction. Both studies find potentially economically and statistically significant growth effects of regional integration. But, especially the latter paper points to the problems associated with the empirical investigation of the link between growth and regional integration. Therefore, further empirical research is without doubt needed.

List of Main Symbols

c_n	:	R&D-costs
c_Y	:	unit costs of industrial final-goods producers
c_Z	:	unit costs of traditional final-goods producers
C_Y	:	consumption of industrial final good
C_Z	:	consumption of traditional final good
E	:	aggregate total nominal consumption expenditures
E^i	:	aggregate nominal consumption expenditures in country i
f	:	endowment of country A relative to B with the immobile factor
$\bar{f}$	:	endowment of country A relative to C with the immobile factor
g	:	innovation rate
G	:	(static) profits of intermediate-goods producers
H	:	endowment with mobile factor
K	:	stock of physical capital
k	:	transport costs
$\bar{L}^i$	:	endowment of country i with the immobile factor
n	:	total number of differentiated inputs
n^i	:	number of differentiated inputs produced in country i
P	:	value of innovating firm
p_x	:	price of intermediate goods
p_Y	:	price of industrial final goods
p_Z	:	price of traditional final goods
r	:	risk free market rate of interest
r^K	:	rental rate of physical capital

s_Y^i	:	market share of country i in Y-production
s_Z^i	:	market share of country i in Z-production
t	:	time index
U	:	utility function
w_L	:	wage rate of unskilled labor
w_H	:	wage rate of skilled labor
W	:	stock of knowledge
x	:	production of an intermediate-goods producer
Y	:	output in industrial final-goods production
Z	:	output in traditional final-goods production
ϵ	:	elasticity of demand for intermediate goods
μ	:	relative number of known intermediate goods in country A relative to those in the other innovating country
ξ	:	parameter of demand for immobile factor in industrial final-goods relative to traditional final-goods sector.
ρ	:	rate of time preference
ϱ	:	parameter of R&D overlap
σ	:	weight parameter in static utility function
ω	:	relative wage rate for unskilled labor

References

Aghion, P. and P. Howitt (1992), "A Model of Growth through Creative Destruction", *Econometrica* 60, 323-351.

Aghion, P. and P. Howitt (1994) "Growth and Unemployment", *Review of Economic Studies* 61, 477 - 494.

Allais, M. (1960), *L'Europe Unie, Route de la Prosperitie"*, Paris.

Anderson, J.E. and D. Marcouiller (1998), "Trade, Location, and Security", *Paper presented at the Arne Ryde Foundation symposium on New Issues in Trade and Location*, Lund, Sweden.

Armstrong, H.W. (1995), "Convergence among Regions of the European Union, 1950-1990", *Papers in Regional Science* 74, 143-152.

Aschauer, D. (1989), "Is Public Expenditure Productive?", *Journal of Monetary Economics* 24, 177-200.

Audretsch, D. B. and M. P. Feldman (1993), "The Geography of Innovation and Production", in: CEPR (ed.): *The Location of Economic Activity: New Theory and Evidence.*

Baier, S.L. and J.H. Bergstrand (1998), "The Growth and Regionalization of International Trade", *Paper presented at the Arne Ryde Foundation symposium on New Issues in Trade and Location*, Lund, Sweden.

Baldwin, R.E. (1989), "The Growth Effects of 1992", *Economic Policy*, 247-281.

Baldwin, R.E., H. Braconnier, and R. Forslid (1998), "MNCs, Growth and Location Externalities", *Paper presented at the Arne Ryde Foundation symposium on New Issues in Trade and Location*, Lund, Sweden.

Balassa, B. (1961), *"The Theory of Economic Integration"*, Irwin, Homewood, Illinois.

Barro, R. (1974), "Are Government Bonds Net Wealth?", *Journal of Political Economy*, 82, 1095-1117.

Barro, R. (1990), "Government Spending in a Simple Model of Endogenous Growth", *Journal of Political Economy* 98, S103-S125.

Barro, R. (1991), "Economic Growth in a Cross Section of Countries", *Quarterly Journal of Economics* 106, 407-433.

Barro, R. and X. Sala-i-Martin (1991), "Convergence across States and Regions", *Brookings Papers on Economic Activity* 1, 107-182.

Barro, R. and X. Sala-i-Martin (1992), "Convergence", *Journal of Political Economy* 100, 223-251.

Barro, R. and X. Sala-i-Martin (1995), *"Economic Growth"*, McGraw-Hill.

Barro, R., G. Mankiw, and X. Sala-i-Martin (1995), "Capital Mobility in Neoclassical Models of Growth"; *NBER Working Paper*, No. 4206.

Baumol, W.J. (1986), "Productivity Growth, Convergence, and Welfare: What the Long-Run Data Show", *American Economic Review* 76, 1072-1085.

Ben-David, D. (1994), "Income Disparities Among Countries and the Effects of Free Trade", in: L.L. Pasinetti and R.M. Solow (eds.), *Economic Growth and the Structure of Long-Run Development*, London: MacMillan, 45-63.

Ben-David, D. (1995), "Convergence Clubs and Diverging Economies", *Foerder Institute Working Paper*, No. 40-95.

Bencivenga, V.D. and B.D. Smith (1991), "Financial Intermediation and Endogenous Growth", *Review of Economic Studies* 24, 195-218.

Bencivenga, V. R., B.D. Smith und R.M. Starr (1996), "Equity Markets, Transaction Costs, and Capital Accumulation: An Illustration, *World Bank Economic Review* 10(2).

Benassy, J.P. (1998), "Is There Always Too Little Research in Endogenous Growth Models with Expanding Product Variety", *European Economic Review* 42, 61-69.

Berliner Morgenpost (1998), *"EU nimmt Kurs auf weltweit groessten Wirtschaftsmarkt"*, 1.4.1998.

Bernard, A. and S.N. Durlauf (1991), "Interpreting Tests of the Convergence Hypothesis", *Working Paper, Stanford University.*

Black, D. and J.V. Henderson (1999), "A Theory of Urban Growth", *Journal of Political Economy*, (forthcoming).

Blanchard, O. and S. Fischer (1989), *"Lecture Notes on Macroeconomics"*, MIT Press: Cambridge (Ma.).

Borts, G.H. and J.L. Stein (1964), *"Economic Growth in a Free Market"*, Columbia University Press, New York.

Boskin, M.J. and L.J. Lau (1990), "Post-War Economic Growth of the Group-of-Five Countries: A New Analysis", *Technical Paper No. 217, Stanford, CA.*

Boskin, M.J. and L.J. Lau (1993), "Capital, Technology, and Economic Growth," in: Rosenberg, N., Landau, R., and Mowery D.C. (eds.), *Technology and the Wealth of Nations*, Stanford University Press, 17-55.

Brezis, E.S, P. Krugman, and D. Tsiddon (1993), "Leapfrogging in International Competition: A Theory of Cycles in National Technological Leadership", *American Economic Review* 83, 1211-1219.

Busch, B., K. Lichtblau, and C. Schnabel (1998), "Kohaesionspolitik, Konvergenz und Arbeitslosigkeit in der Europaeischen Union", *Jahrbuch fuer Wirtschaftswissenschaften* 49, 1-25.

Cabellero, R. and A.B. Jaffee (1993) "Standing on the Giant's Shoulder: An Assessment of Knowledge Spillovers and Creative Destruction in a Model of Economic Growth," *NBER Macroeconomics Annual* 8, 15-73.

Capellin, R. and W. Molle (1988), "The Co-ordination Problem in Theory and Policy", in: Molle, W. and R. Cappellin (eds.), *Regional Impact of Community Policies in Europe*, Avebury Publisher: Aldershot.

Cass, D. (1965), "Optimum Growth in an Aggregate Model of Capital Accumulation", *Review of Economic Studies* 32, 233-240.

CEPR (1992), *"Is Bigger Better? The Economics of EC Enlargement,"* CEPR Annual Report 1992, London.

Chari, V.V., P.J. Kehoe, and E.R. McGrattan (1996), "Sticky Price Models of the Business Cycle: Can the Contract Multiplier Solve the Persistence Problem?, *Federal Reserve Bank of Minneapolis Research Department Staff Report No. 217*, Dec. 1996

Coe, D.T. and E. Helpman (1995), "International R&D Spillovers", *European Economic Review* 39(5), 859-881.

Coe, D.T., E. Helpman, and A. W. Hoffmaister (1997), "North-South R&D Spillovers", *The Economic Journal* 107. 134-149.

Collins, (1994), "EC Social Policy", in: El-Agraa (1994).

Commission of the European Communities (1987), *"Third Periodic Report on the Socio-Economic Situtation and Development of the Regions in the Community,"* Luxembourg.

Commission of the European Communities (1988a), *"Research on the 'Costs of Non-Europe', Basic Findings, Volume 1"*, Luxembourg.

Commission of the European Commununities (1988b), Europe 1992, *European Economy* 35.

Commission of the European Communities (1991), *"Fourth Periodic Report on the Socio-Economic Situtation and Development of the Regions in the Community,"* Luxembourg.

Commission of the European Communities (1994), *"Fifth Periodic Report on the Socio-Economic Situtation and Development of the Regions in the Community,"* Luxembourg.

DeLong, J.B. (1988), Productivity Growth, Convergence, and Welfare: Comment", *American Economic Review* 78, 1138-1154.

Devereux, M.J. and B.J. Lapham (1994), "On the Stability of Economic Integration and Endogenous Growth", *Quarterly Journal of Economics* 109, 297-305.

Dinopolous, E., J.F. Oehmke, and P.S. Segerstrom (1993), "High-Technology-Industry Trade and Investment: The Role of Factor Endowment", *Journal of International Economics* 34, 49-71.

Durlauf, S.N. and P.A. Johnson (1992), "Local Convergence across National Economies", *NBER Working Paper* No. 3996.

El-Agraa, A. (1994) *"The Economics of the European Community"*, 4th ed., Harvester Wheatersheaf, New York.

Elizondo, R.L. and P. Krugman (1995), "Trade Policy and Third World Metropolis", *Journal of Development Economics* 49, 137-1150.

Englmann, F.C. and U. Walz (1995), "Industrial Centers and Regional Growth in the Presence of Local Inputs", *Journal of Regional Science* 35, 3-27.

Ethier, W. (1982), "National and International Returns to Scale in the Modern Theory of International Trade", *American Economic Review* 72, 389-405.

Ethier, W. and H. Horn, (1984), "A New Look at Economic Integration", in: H. Kierzkowski (eds.), *Monopolistic Competition and International Trade*, New York: Oxford University Press.

Feenstra, R. (1990) "Trade and Uneven Growth", NBER Working Paper No. 3276.

Feenstra, R. (1994), "New Product Varieties and the Measurement of International Prices", *American Economic Review* 84/1, 157-177.

Financial Times, (1994), *"All-Americas Free Trade Zone 'by 2005' "* Financial Times, 9.12.94, p.6.

Friedman, M. (1992), "Do Old Fallacies Ever Die?" *Journal of Economic Literature* 30, 2129-2132.

Fudenberg, D., R. Gilbert, J. Stiglitz, and J. Tirole (1983), "Preemption, Leapfrogging, and Competition in Patent Races," *European Economic Review* 22, 3-31.

Fujita, M. (1988), "A Monopolistic Competition Model of Spatial Agglomeration: Differentiated Product Approach", *Regional Science and Urban Economics* 18, 87-124.

Fujita, M. (1990), "Spatial Interactions and Agglomeration in Urban Economics", in: Chatterji, M. and R.E. Kuenne (eds.): *New Frontiers in Regional Economics*, Macmillan: London.

Fujita, M. (1993), "Monopolistic Competition and Urban Systems", *European Economic Review* 37, 308-315.

Fujita, M. and J.F. Thisse (1996), "Economics of Agglomeration", *Journal of the Japanese and International Economies* 10, 339-378.

Gasiorek, M., A. Smith and A. Venables (1992), "1992: Trade and Welfare – A General Equilibrium Model", *Paper presented at the CEPR Conference "Trade Flows and Trade Policy after 1992"*, January 1992.

Glaeser, E., H.D. Kallal, J. A. Scheinkman, and A. Schleifer (1992), "Growth in Cities", *Journal of Political Economy* 100/6, 1126-1152.

Grahl, J. and J. Sims (1993), "Endogenous Growth in the European Regions", in: CEPR (ed.): *The Location of Economic Activity: New Theory and Evidence.*

Griliches, Z. (1973), "Research Expenditures and Growth Accounting", in: B.R. Williams (ed.), *Science and Technology in Economic Growth*, London: Macmillan.

Grossman, G. and E. Helpman, (1990) "Comparative Advantage and Long-Run Growth", *American Economic Review* 80, 796-815.

Grossman, G. and E. Helpman (1991a), "Quality Ladders and Growth", *Review of Economic Studies* 58, 43-61.

Grossman, G. and E. Helpman (1991b), *"Innovation and Growth in the Global Economy"*, MIT Press, Cambridge (Mass.).

Grossman, G. and E. Helpman (1991c), "Trade, Knowledge Spillovers and Growth", *European Economic Review* 35, 517-526.

Grossman, G. and E. Helpman (1994), "Endogenous Innovation in the Theory of Growth", *Journal of Economic Perspective* 8, 23-44.

Grossman, G. and C. Shapiro (1987), "Dynamic R&D Competition", *Economic Journal* 97, 372-387.

Gruber, H. (1992), "Persistence of Leadership in Product Innovation", *Journal of Industrial Economics* 40, 359-375.

Hall, S., D. Robertson, M. Wickens (1992), "Measuring Convergence of the EC Economies", *The Manchester School* 55, Supplement, 99-111.

Hansen, N. (1990), "Do Producer Services Induce Regional Economic Development", *Journal of Regional Science* 30/4, 465-470.

Harhoff, D. (1995), "Firm Foundation and Regional Spillovers", *University of Mannheim, mimeo.*

Harris, C. and J. Vickers (1987), "Racing with Uncertainty", *Review of Economic Studies* 54, 1-22.

Harris, R.G. (1996), "Evidence and Debate on Economic Integration and Economic Growth", in: Howitt, P. (ed.), *The Implications of Knowledge-Based Growth for Micro-Economic Policies*, Industry Canada Research Series, Calgary: University of Calgary Press, 119-155.

Henrekson, M., J. Torstensson, and R. Torstensson (1997), "Growth Effects of European Integration", *European Economic Review* 41, 1537-1557.

Jaffe, A.B., M. Trajtenberg, and R. Henderson (1993), "Geographic Localization of Knowledge Spillovers as Evidenced by Patent Citations," *Quarterly Journal of Economics* 108/3,, 577-598.

Helpman, E., and P. Krugman (1985), *"Market Structure and Foreign Trade"*, MIT Press, Cambridge (Mass.).

Hilpert, U. (1992), "FAST, Archipelago Europe – Islands of Innovation" *Prospective Dossier No. 1: Science, Technology, and Social and Economic Cohesion in the Community.*

Horstman, I., and J.R. Markusen (1989), "Firm-Specific Assets and the Gain from Direct Foreign Investment", *Economica* 56, 41-48.

Jensen-Butler, C. (1993), "Development Strategies in the Southern European Periphery: Comparison with the Northern Periphery," in: Lundqvist, L., and L.O. Persson (eds.), *Visions and Strategies in European Integration*, Berlin, New York: Springer, 225-244.

Krugman, P. (1991a), *"Geography and Trade"*, MIT Press, Cambridge (Mass).

Krugman, P. (1991b), "History versus Expectations", *Quarterly Journal of Economics* 106, 651-667.

Krugman, P. (1991c), "Increasing returns and economic geography", *Journal of Political Economy* 99, 483-499.

Krugman, P. (1992), "A Dynamic Spatial Model", *NBER Working Paper*, No. 4219.

Krugman, P. and A.J. Venables (1990) "Integration and the Competitiveness of Peripheral Industry", in: C. Bliss and J. Braga de Macedo (eds.), *Unity with Diversity in the European Community*, Cambridge University Press, Cambridge.

Krugman, P. and A.J. Venables (1995), "Globalization and the Inequality of Nations", *Quartely Journal of Economics* 110, 857-880.

Krugman, P. and A.J. Venables (1996), "Integration, Specialization, and Adjustment", *European Economic Review* 40, 959-967.

Lach, S. and M. Schankerman (1989), "Dynamics of R&D and Investment in the Scientific Sector", *Journal of Political Economy* 97, 880-904.

Levine, R. and S. Zervos (1996), Stock Market Development and Long-Run Growth, *World Bank Economic Review* 10(2), 323-339.

Lichtenberg, F. (1992), "R&D Investment and International Productivity Differences", *NBER Working Paper*, No. 4161.

Lipsey, R.G. (1960), "The Theory of Customs Unions: A General Survey", *Economic Journal* 70, 496-513.

Lorenz, H.-W. (1989), *"Nonlinear Dynamic Economics and Chaotic Motion"*, Springer: Berlin, New York.

Lucas, R. (1987), *"Models of Business Cycles"*, Basil Blackwell: Oxford.

Lucas, R. (1988) "On the Mechanics of Economic Development", *Journal of Monetary Economics* 22, 3-42.

Lucas, R. (1989), "Why Doesn't Capital Flow From Rich to Poor Countries?", *American Economc Review, Papers and Proceedings* 80, 92-96.

Lloyd, P.-J. (1982), "A 3 Theory of Customs Unions", *Journal of International Economics* 12, 41-62.

Malecki, J. and P. Varaija (1986), "Innovation and Growth in Regional Structural Change", in: P. Nijkamp (ed.): *Handbook of Regional and Urban Economics*, vol. I, Elsevier Publisher: North Holland, 629-645.

Mankiw, N., D. Romer, and D. Weil (1992), "A Contribution to the Empirics of Economic Growth", *Quarterly Journal of Economics*437.

Marshall A. (1920) *"Principles of Economics"*, London: Macmillan.

Matsuyama, J. (1995), "Complementarities and Cumulative Processes in Models of Monopolistic Competition", *Journal of Economic Literature* 33, 701-729.

Molle, W. (1980), *"Regional Disparity and Economic Development in the European Community"*. Farnborough, England: Saxon House.

Motta, M., J.-J. Thisse, and A. Cabrales (1995), "On the Persistence of Leadership or Leapfrogging in International Trade", *CEPR Working Paper* No. 1106.

Myrdal, G. (1957), *"Economic Theory and Underdeveloped Regions"*, London: Duckworth.

Nelson, R.E. and S.G. Winter (1982), *"An Evolutionary Theory of Economic Change"*, Cambridge, Ma.: Harvard University Press.

Neven, D. and C. Gouyette (1994), "Regional Convergence in the European Community", *CEPR Discussion Paper Series*, No. 914.

Nogues, J.J., A. Olechowski, and A.L. Winters (1985), *"The Extent of Non-Tariff Barriers to Industrial Countries' Imports"*, Washington D.C.: World Bank.

Ohly, C. (1993), "What have we learned about the economic effects of EC integration?", *Economic Papers*, 103, 9/93.

Palivos, T. and Wang P. (1996), "Spatial agglomeration and endogenous growth", *Regional Science and Urban Economics* 26, 645-669.

Perroux, F. (1955), "Note sur la notion de pole de croissance", *Economic Appliquée* 7, 307-320.

Premer, M. and U. Walz (1994), "Regional Divergent Growth, Nontraded Goods and Factor Mobility", *Regional Science and Urban Economics* 24, 707-722.

Puga, D. and A.J. Venables (1996), "The Spread of Industry: Spatial Agglomeration in Economic Development", *Journal of the Japanese and International Economies* 10, 440-464.

Puga, D. and A.J. Venables (1997), "Prefential Trading Arrangements and Industrial Location", *Journal of International Economics* 43, 347-368.

Quah, D. (1993), "Galton's Fallacy and Tests of the Convergence Hypothesis", in: Anderson, T.M, and K.O. Moebne (eds.), *Endogenous Growth*, 37-53.

Quah, D. (1996), "Regional Convergence Clusters Across Europe", *European Economic Review* 40, 951-958.

Razin, A. and E. Sadka (1992), "International Migration and International Trade", *NBER Working Paper,* No.4230.

Rebelo, S. (1991), "Long Run Policy Analysis and Long Run Growth", *Journal of Political Economy* 99, 500-521.

Richardson, H.W. (1973), *"Regional Growth Theory"*, London: Basingstoke.

Riezman, R. (1984), "Customs Unions and the Core", *Working Paper No. 84-32, University of Iowa.*

Rivera-Batiz, F. (1988), "Increasing Returns, Monopolistic Competition, and Agglomeration Economies in Consumption and Production," *Regional Science and Urban Economics*, 18, 125-153.

Rivera-Batiz, L. and P. Romer (1991a), "Economic Integration and Endogenous Growth", *Quarterly Journal of Economics* 106, 531-556.

Rivera-Batiz, L. and P. Romer (1991b), "International Trade with Endogenous Technological Change", *European Economic Review* 35, 971-1001.

Rivera-Batiz, L. and P. Romer (1994), "Economic Integration and Endogenous Growth: An Addendum", *Quarterly Journal of Economics* 109, 307-308.

Rivera-Batiz, L. and D. Xie (1992) "GATT, Trade, and Growth", *American Economic Review* 82, 422-427.

Rivera-Batiz, L. and D. Xie (1993) "Integration among Unequals", *Regional Science and Urban Economics* 23, 337-354.

Romer, P. (1986) "Increasing Returns and Long-Run Growth", *Journal of Political Economy* 94, 1002-1037.

Romer, P. M. (1989), "Capital Accumulation in the Theory of Long-Run Growth", Barro, R. (ed.), *Modern Business Cycle Theory*, Harvard University Press.

Romer, P. (1990) "Endogenous Technological Change", *Journal of Political Economy* 98, S71-S102.

Romer, P. (1993), Idea Gaps and Object gaps in Economic Development, *Journal of Monetary Econonmics* 32, 543-573.

Romer, P. (1994), "New Goods, Old Theory, and the Welfare Costs of Trade Restrictions", *Journal of Development Economics*, 43, 5-38.

Saint-Paul, G. (1994), "Trade Patterns and Pollution", *Delta Working Paper*, No. 94-02.

Sala-i-Martin, X. (1990), "Lectures Notes on Economic Growth (II): Five Prototype Models of Endogenous Growth", *NBER Working Paper Series*, No. 3564.

Sala-i-Martin, X. (1996), "Regional Cohesion: Evidence and theories of regional growth and convergence", *European Economic Review* 40/6, 1325-1352.

Schulz, N. (1995), "Agglomeration als Gleichgewichtsergebnis in neueren Beitraegen der Standorttheorie", in: Gahlen, B., H. Hesse, and H.-J. Ramser (eds.): Tuebingen: Mohr Siebeck.

Scitovsky, T. (1956), "Economies of Scale, Competition and European Integration", *American Economic Review* 46, 71-91.

Siebert, H. (1969), *"Regional Growth. Theory and Policy"*, Scranton: International Textbook Company.

Solow, R. (1956), "A Contribution to the Theory of Economic Growth", *Quarterly Journal of Economics* 70, 65-94.

Solow, R. (1994) "Perspectives on Growth Theory", *Journal of Economic Perspectives* 8, 45-54.

Smith, A. and A. Venables (1988) "Completing the Internal Market in the European Community: Some Industry Simulations", *European Economic Review* 32, 1501-1525.

Stahl, K. (1983), "A Note on the Microeconomics of Migration", *Journal of Urban Economics* 14, 318-326.

Stahl, K. (1987), "Theories of Urban Business Location", in: Mills, E.S. (ed.): *Handbook of Regional and Urban Economics*, Amsterdam: North Holland, 759-820.

Starrett, D. (1978), "Market allocation of location choice in a model with free mobility", *Journal of Economic Theory* 17, 21-37.

Tirole, J. (1988), *"Theory of Industrial Organization"*, MIT Press, Cambridge (Mass.).

Venables, A. (1987), "Custom Unions and Tariff Reform with Imperfect Competition", *European Economic Review*, 31, 103-110.

Viner, J. (1950), *"The Customs Unions Issue"*, Carnegie Endowment for International Peace, New York.

von Hagen, J. and G. Hammond (1993), "Industrial Location. An Empirical Test for Marshallian Localization Economies"; in: CEPR (ed.): *The Location of Economic Activity: New Theory and Evidence.*

White, H. (1980), "A Heteroskedasticity-Consistent Covariance Matrix Estimator and a Direct Test for Heteroskedasticity," *Econometrica* 48, 817-838.

Walz, U. (1995a), "Endogenous Innovation and Imitation in an Equilibrium Growth Model", *European Journal of Political Economy* 11, 709-723.

Walz, U. (1995b), "Trade Liberalization, Factor Mobility, and Regional Growth", *Journal of Institutional and Theoretical Economics* 505-525.

Walz, U. (1996a), "The Long Run Implications of Regional Policy in an Economic Union", *Annals of Regional Science* 30, 165-183.

Walz, U. (1996b), "Growth (Rate) Effects of Migration", *Zeitschrift fuer Wirtschafts- und Sozialwissenschaft* 115, 199-221.

Walz, U. (1996c), "Transport Costs, Intermediate Goods, and Localized Growth", *Regional Science and Urban Economics* 26, 671-695.

Walz, U. (1997a), "Dynamic Effects of Economic Integration", *Open Economies Review* 8, 309-326.

Walz, U. (1997b), "Regional Integration and Growth in the Presence of an Outside World", *Review of International Economics* 5:4, 492-508.

Walz, U. (1997c), "Innovation, Foreign Direct Investment, and Growth", *Economica* 63-79.

Walz, U. (1998), "Does an Enlargement of a Common Market Stimulate Growth and Convergence?", *Journal of International Economics* 45, 197-321.

Walz, U. and D. Wellisch (1996), "Strategic Public Provision of Local Inputs with Endogenous Locational Decisions of Oligopolistic Firms", *International Tax and Public Finance* 3, 173-187.

Waniek, R. W. (1992), *"Die Regionalpolitik der Europaeischen Gemeinschaft"*, Bochum.

Wellisch, D. and U. Walz (1998), "Why Do Rich Countries Prefer Free Trade over Free Migration? The Role of the Modern Welfare State", *European Economic Review*, 42/10.

Wooton, I. (1988), "Towards a Common Market: Factor Mobility in a Common Union", *Canadian Journal of Economics*, 21.

Young, A. (1991), "Learning By Doing and the Dynamic Effects of International Trade" *Quarterly Journal of Economics*, 106, 369-405.

Index

Contributions to Economics

Hagen Bobzin
Indivisibilities
1998. ISBN 3-7908-1123-8

Helmut Wagner (Ed.)
Current Issues in Monetary Economics
1998. ISBN 3-7908-1127-0

Peter Michaelis/Frank Stähler (Eds.)
Recent Policy Issues in Environmental and Resource Economics
1998. ISBN 3-7908-1137-8

Jessica de Wolff
The Political Economy of Fiscal Decisions
1998. ISBN 3-7908-1130-0

Georg Bol/Gholamreza Nakhaeizadeh/
Karl-Heinz Vollmer (Eds.)
Risk Measurements, Econometrics and Neural Networks
1998. ISBN 3-7908-1152-1

Joachim Winter
Investment and Exit Decisions at the Plant Level
1998. ISBN 3-7908-1154-8

Bernd Meyer
Intertemporal Asset Pricing
1999. ISBN 3-7908-1159-9

GPSR Compliance

The European Union's (EU) General Product Safety Regulation (GPSR) is a set of rules that requires consumer products to be safe and our obligations to ensure this.

If you have any concerns about our products, you can contact us on ProductSafety@springernature.com

In case Publisher is established outside the EU, the EU authorized representative is:

Springer Nature Customer Service Center GmbH
Europaplatz 3
69115 Heidelberg, Germany

Batch number: 10725973

Printed by Printforce, the Netherlands